Liberal Causes in Rhyme

Timothy Callahan

DIAMOND MEDIA PRESS CO.
1-304-273-6157
https://www.diamondmediapressco.com/

Copyright © 2021

By Timothy J. Callah

All rights reserved.

ISBN Paperback: 978-195130286-3

They want to expel the Arabs and surround the Old City.
Thousands of would be Jewish "settlers" are giddy.
They want layers of Jews throughout East Jerusalem,
Achieved by Zionist ethnic cleansing enthusiasm.
That city was to be the capital of a Palestinian state.
Israel thinks enough "settlers" will make that too late.
The evictions violate international law.
Israel stuffs other people's land into its maw.
5/10/21
Inspired by "As Court Decision Nears, Battle Over Evictions
Spikes in East Jerusalem" by Patrick Kingsley NYT International 5-8-21

The standoffs across Jerusalem reflect,
The urge to get the Jewish boot off our necks.
We only want a homeland on our own land.
Backed against the wall, we make our stand.
The violence began when police entered the mosque.
They fired rubber bullets; Palestinians threw rocks.
Police dared enter Aqsa during Ramadan.
Israelis want us dead or gone.
5/11/21
Inspired by "Violence Erupts Between Israelis and Palestinians
After Raid" by Patrick Kingsley and Isabel Kershner
NYT Front Page 5-11-21

Nitwityahoo miscalculated that our resistance would wane.
Israelis try to eradicate us in vain.
More than the families of Sheikh Jarrah is at stake.
Our Palestinian homeland we will not forsake.
Our collective fate lies in the future of Sheikh Jarrah.
Victory there will not be our last hurrah.
We will overcome expulsions and occupation,
And come together despite dislocations.
5/13/21
*"Inspired by "Palestinians Under Siege"
by Rula Salameh NYT Opinion 5-12-21*

Nitwityahoo cultivates a more intolerant fascism,
An authoritarian type of racist nationalism.
Racist Jewish mobs beat Arabs in the streets.
The mobs are represented in Knesset seats.
Israel entrenches its undemocratic control.
Where that building stood now sits a hole.
U.S. aid must not enable human rights abuses.
The Israel lobby gives all the rat's excuses.
5/15/21
*Inspired by "We Need a New Mideast Approach"
by Bernie Sanders NYT Opinion 5-15-21*

Israel's "liberal democracy" is a farce.
Its dirty leaders need a wash.
Thanks to Zionist social engineering,
The end of Palestine is nearing.
Jewish racism and religious fanaticism
Have forced a Palestinian cataclysm.
5/23/17
*PG 406th Posting 5/28/17
timothyjcallahan.blogspot.com*

Israelis changed the history and the place names.
Palestine was no longer the same.
Jews planted trees over bulldozed homes.
The new forests covered Palestinian bones.
Israelis say the land was empty when they came.
But that claim is a lying shame.
4/19/17
*Inspired by *The Ethnic Cleansing of Palestine* by Ilan Pappe
*PG 401st Posting 4/23/17
timothyjcallahan.blogspot.com

Sunday, May 9, 2021
Poetry Group Six Hundred Thirteenth Posting 5/9/21

Rather than continue with Hoover-style complacency,
Biden invests in America faithfully.
His proposals echo Roosevelt's initiatives.
A new deal for the people is what it is.
His plan will cut child poverty in half.
Three and four year olds will play and laugh.
The money for children is the best investment.
Those who oppose it are offensive.
5/2/21
*Inspired by "F.D.R. Transformed the U.S.; Biden Could, Too"
by Nicholas Kristof NYT Sunday Review 5-2-21*

Abbas had to cancel elections, take note.
Israel won't let East Jerusalem vote.
Yet Oslo requires Israel to allow,
Elections there right now.
Jerusalem will not be forsaken,
Despite Israel's supposed taking.
See democracy's degeneration,
Under cruel military occupation.
5/3/21
*Inspired by "Palestinian Vote Postponed,
Prolonging Tension" by Patrick Kingsley
NYT International 4-30-21*

America is not the same country it was.
Neither is it the country it purports to be.
Too many Blacks are killed by the fuzz.
America is still a racist country.
Now systems do the work that once required,
Masses of racists overtly inspired.
There's tension between aspiration and current condition,
But denying racism is the Republicans' mission.
5/4/21
*"Inspired by "America Is Still Racist"
by Charles M. Blow NYT Opinion 5-3-21*

The "peace process" was designed by Israeli architects
(Their U.S. subcontractors saying what the heck)
To impede Palestinian emancipation,
And deny them a sovereign nation.
Israel covets the land they've still got.
Palestinians refuse to accept their lot.
5/5/21
*Inspired by Brokers of Deceit — How the U.S. Has
Undermined Peace in the Middle East by Rashid Khalidi*

In 1948, the Israelis took a heavy toll.
So we question the Zionist project as a whole.
Why couldn't the Jews share the land
And show respect for their fellow man?
5/15/17
*PG 405th Posting 5/21/17
timothyjcallahan.blogspot.com

The child was made anxious,
By the hard language,
Which was loud and scary.
The child was always wary.
When he was a little baby,
Mother stuck him in closets daily.
She would open the door once more,
And put him inside on the floor.
4/26/17
*PG 403rd Posting 5/7/17
timothyjcallahan.blogspot.com

Sunday, May 2, 2021
Poetry Group Six Hundred Twelfth Posting 5/2/21

An extremist Jewish supremacy group
(Such supremacists are at the problem's root)
Marched in the hundreds near Jerusalem's old city,
Chanting "Death to Arabs" with hate and no pity.
The mayor had asked the police to ban the march,
But was told that was impossible, which seems a farce.
Violence ensued and police were caught in the middle.
Why they couldn't prevent the melee is no riddle.
4/25/21
*Inspired by "Clashes Erupt Between Israelis and
Palestinians Near Jerusalem's Old City"
by Isabel Kershner NYT International 4-24-21

Bringing Hamas into talks was Mitchell's ambition,
But Hamas had to meet some preconditions:
Renounce violence and accept Israel's right to exist,
But with AmerIsrael there's always a twist.
Israel was not made to renounce violence.
The only precondition for Israel was silence.
Israel did not recognize Palestine's right to exist.
Can you blame the Palestinians for being pissed?
4/26/21
*Inspired by Brokers of Deceit – How the U.S. Has
Undermined Peace in the Middle East by Rashid Khalidi*

Biden and the liberals are coming for your burgers.
Democrats urge red meat purges.
They are all woke feminist vegetarians,
Without the values of Real Americans.
Buy a deep freezer and start hoarding meat.
Your favorite grocery store will soon be depleted.
It is time to dine and own the libs.
They will not take our steaks and ribs.
4/27/21
*"Inspired by "Republicans Manufacture Some Red Meat"
By Paul Krugman NYT Opinion 4-27-21*

Israel privileges one race at the expense of another.
America has long since provided the cover.
Israel, behold, is an apartheid state,
Defined by greed, brutality, and racist hate.
Palestinians are forcibly removed from their land.
In this injustice, the U.S. lends a hand.
America supports Israeli apartheid.
From history America cannot hide.
5/1/21
*Inspired by "Rights Group Accuses Israel of Conducting
Apartheid State" by Patrick Kingsley NYT International 4-28-21

Negotiations with Israel are fruitless.
Israel's promises are useless.
Their intentions are clear:
Palestinians out of here.
Israel never bargains in good faith.
The maps have changed.
How long must Palestinians wait
For a Palestinian state?
7/26/17
*PG 415th Posting 7/30/17
timothyjcallahan.blogspot.com

After the June war, Israelis were not timid.
They expanded Jerusalem's city limits.
Over twenty Palestinian villages were absorbed.
Israeli soldiers kicked in the doors.
6/26/17
*PG 411th Posting 7/2/17
timothyjcallahan.blogspot.com

They turned ethnically mixed areas
Into a pure ethnic space.
They put the indigenous behind barriers
And deny them a state.
The longer Israel denies Palestinians a deal,
The longer terrorists have a cause with wide appeal.
6/20/17
*PG 410th Posting 6/25/17
timothyjcallahan.blogspot.com

Sunday, April 25, 2021
Poetry Group Six Hundred Eleventh Posting 4/25/21

Professor Goldreich teaches young scientists.
He was picked for one of the Israel prizes.
But the education minister refused to grant it.
With the professor's views, he is not enchanted.
Goldreich has signed letters and petitions,
Calling for the occupation's elimination.
Likud pushes the left toward illegitimacy.
Israel is gripped by land greed, pitiably.
4/17/21
*Inspired by "Prize Awarded Annually in Israel
Lands in Court in 'a Repetitive Ritual'" by Isabel Kershner
NYT International 4-15-21

Before throwing her out the window, he beat her down.
Was she already dead before hitting the ground?
The anti-Semite killed the Jewish mother of three,
But because this was France, he pays no penalty.
He won't even be tried, because at the time of the crime,
On marijuana he was high.
Future racist killers now know:
Before killing Jews, get stoned.
4/18/21
*Inspired by "Pot Use Made Anti-Semitic Killer Unfit
to Stand Trial, a French Court Rules" by Roger Cohen
NYT International 4-18-21*

The Camp David/Madrid/Oslo framework had run its course.
But Obama didn't see that we needed a divorce.
For decades, the "peace process" upheld the status quo,
More Jewish "settlements" and Palestinian woe.
Obama accepted the stifling conventional wisdom,
Instead of inventing a new peace effort system.
Despite his critics, Obama was no radical.
The Israelis soon found him palatable.
4/19/21
*Inspired by Brokers of Deceit – How the U.S. Has
Undermined Peace in the Middle East by Rashid Khalidi*

Obama made Mitchell Presidential special envoy,
To deal with the Palestinian-Israeli conflict.
Mitchell had brought peace to Northern Ireland,
By getting the IRA to renounce violence.
He wanted to do the same thing with Hamas,
And bring it into the negotiating process.
But Congress thoroughly condemned his approach.
Both sides of the aisle were opposed.
Leading members of Congress sided with Israel,
Against the administration made miserable.
4/20/21
*Inspired by _Brokers of Deceit – How the U.S. Has
Undermined Peace in the Middle East_ by Rashid Khalidi

Sharing the land was not viable.
The Palestinians were undesirable.
So the expulsion had to occur.
Was it humane? No, sir.
Israeli soldiers intruded.
Palestinians were moved.
Boys and men were shot,
On Israel's history a blot.
7/7/17
*PG 412th Posting 7/9/17
timothyjcallahan.blogspot.com

The path a bullet takes
Determines the damage it makes.
But so does the bullet type.
Don't believe the bullet hype.
Expanding bullets explode
Reducing organs to liquid mode.
The fragments pulverize the bone
And make wounds that cannot be sewn.
6/17/17
*Inspired by "The Damage a Bullet Can do" by Leana S. Wen
NYT OP ED 6/17/17
*PG 409th Posting 6/18/17
timothyjcallahan.blogspot.com

Sunday, April 18, 2021
Poetry Group Six Hundred Tenth Posting 4/18/21

A precondition for well-being and equality,
Abortion is supported by a majority of the polity.
Republicans want a constitutional amendment
To criminalize abortion and end it.
Forcing women to give birth against their will,
Will be the subject of a future Republican bill.
Police-state surveillance will be required,
Strict compliance highly desired.
4/10/21
*Inspired by "The Authoritarian Plan for an Abortion
Ban" by Michelle Goldberg NYT Opinion 4-6-21

Children consulting parents consulting doctors is the sequence,
But Republicans ban gender-affirming medical treatments.
They override parents' considered decisions,
Regarding their own beloved trans children.
Republicans hurt trans youth for political gain.
Vulnerable, marginalized people they disdain.
Remember how Republicans fought gay marriage,
Gay people they still disparage.
4/12/21
*Inspired by "Republicans Find a Cruel New Culture War"
by Frank Bruni NYT Sunday Review 4-11-21*

Bibi bombed an Iranian nuclear facility.
(Mossad blew out the plant's electricity.)
He had this done just when Biden was able,
To bring the Iranians back to the table.
The crisis will help Bibi attract coalition partners.
Likud's opposition looks on broken hearted.
But America did not criticize Israel,
For making its situation more miserable.
4/13/21
*Inspired by "Israel's Role in Iran Blast Casts a Shadow
on U.S. Nuclear Talks" by Patrick Kingsley, David E. Sanger
and Farnaz Fassihi NYT Front Page 4-13-21*

Biden restored hundreds of millions in aid
To Palestinians, which Trump forbade.
Biden rehabilitates U.S. relations
With Palestinians, with patience.
The Israeli Ambassador was against it.
He said helping Palestinians is anti-Semitic.
Republicans said it is not in U.S. interests
To help a people so afflicted.
4/14/21
*Inspired by "Palestinians to Receive Aid Cut Off Under Trump"
by Pranshu Verma and Rick Gladstone NYT International 4-8-21

That summer Israel killed Gazan civilians.
Thousands died including hundreds of children.
Israeli soldiers fired heavy shells
That made thousands of homes hells.
They had no empathy with the people they were killing.
The artillery men are always willing.
7/20/17
*PG 414th Posting 7/23/17
timothyjcallahan.blogspot.com

Menstruating women are impure.
They bring bad luck for sure.
So they are kept in rough sheds.
That's what their religion says.
Some of them die of snakebite.
Illiteracy contributes to their plight.
Teenage girls do not object.
They are part of the sect.
7/10/17
*PG 413th Posting 7/16/17
timothyjcallahan.blogspot.com

We have mass shooting after mass shooting.
For the gun lobby, Republicans are rooting.
They think the answer to the problem is more guns.
They are the dangerous ones.
7/10/17
*PG 413th Posting 7/16/17
timothyjcallahan.blogspot.com

Sunday, April 11, 2021
Poetry Group Six Hundred Ninth Posting 4/11/21

The long struggle to block access to the ballot,
Has relied on legal schemes invalid.
The Supreme Court gutted the Voting Rights Act.
Democrats fight for those protections back.
The new Georgia elections law is Jim Crow 2.0.
Suppressed Black voters is where the state wants to go.
Support federal voting rights legislation,
To avoid democracy's devastation.
4/2/21
*Inspired by "The New Jim Crow In Georgia"
by Jason Morgan Ward NYT Op-Ed 4-11-21*

Georgia has cut by more than half,
The time in which voters can ask,
For an absentee ballot.
Republicans are callous,
Because 65 percent,
Of the ballots re-sent,
Were for Joseph R. Biden.
Trump is now in hiding.
Republicans don't like that outcome.
Now they'll be fewer voters for Democrat votes to come from.
4/3/21
*Inspired by "What Georgia's Voting Law Really Does"
by Nick Corasaniti and Reid J. Epstein
NYT National 4-3-21*

There are more guns than people in America.
That's what gives us our Wild West character.
More Americans have died from guns since 1975,
Than in all the wars America survived.
The U.S. has 4 percent of the world's population,
But 40 percent of guns in circulation.
Assault rifles are the weapons of choice,
When you want to kill people, not just make noise.
4/4/21
*Inspired by "How Do We Stop the Parade of Gun Deaths?"
by Nicholas Kristof NYT Sunday Review 4/4/21*

"Ghost guns" avoid serial numbers and regulation.
Eighty percent of a gun isn't one says the legislation.
They are easily finished and some non-guns come in kits.
They are untraceable, so the cops are outwitted.
White nationalists build secret arsenals
With ghost guns so farcical.
4/5/21
*Inspired by "How Do We Stop the Parade of Gun Deaths?"
by Nicholas Kristof NYT Sunday Review 4/4/21*

The vaccine is the Mark of the Beast!
By Satan, you will be seized.
With the Holy Bible, do not be a quibbler,
Christ is the ultimate deliverer.
Every batch contains aborted fetuses.
Take the shot and you are not Jesus's.
4/5/21
*Inspired by "White Evangelical Resistance Is Obstacle
in Vaccination Effort" by Elizabeth Dias and
Ruth Graham NYT Front Page 4-5-21*

The trial of Nitwityahoo has finally begun.
He is referred to as "Defendant No. 1".
Charged with bribery, fraud, and breach of trust,
He is now and was P.M. at the time of the bust.
He attacks the legitimacy of the judicial system,
But a majority of Israelis can't resist him.
They are drawn to the Arab blood on his hands,
And his beneficence with Arab lands.
4/6/21
*Inspired by "A Crisis Brews in Israel as 'Defendant No. 1'
Seeks to Cobble Together a Government"
by Isabel Kershner NYT International 4-6-21*

Let's all go around the table.
Stroke my ego as well as you are able.
Let me go first, for I am blessed:
You, sir, are the very best.
I have something to say too:
No one could be as great as you.
I am honored to be in this room,
Even though I sense doom.
6/13/17
*PG 409th Posting 6/18/17
timothyjcallahan.blogspot.com

Sunday, April 4, 2021
Poetry Group Six Hundred Eighth Posting 4/4/21

Religious nationalist colonists are fanatical.
Their racism, brutality, and greed unfathomable.
How their "settlements" are paid for you might be wondering:
Generous tax-free private American funding.
Americans can finance the commission of war crimes,
And get a full deduction at filing time.
3/27/21
*Inspired by Brokers of Deceit – How the U.S. Has
Undermined Peace in the Middle East by Rashid Khalidi

Women's rights should inform U.S. policy, foreign and domestic.
A good idea, and Biden's approach on Iran will test it.
Sanctions and Covid-19 wrecked the economy.
Women lost ground on their quest for autonomy.
Trump-imposed sanctions are counterproductive.
In dropping them, Biden should not feel reluctant.
Justifications for sanctions are unpersuasive.
The pressure on women is pervasive.
3/28/21
*Inspired by "Sanctions Hurt Iran's Women"
by Azadeh Moaveni and Sussan Tahmasebi
NYT Sunday Review 3-28-21*

The myth of Israeli peril is no mystery.
It derives from ignorance of history.
In 1948, Israel won handily in the end,
And won subsequent wars again and again.
In the '56 Suez War, Israel was on the winning track.
It took Sinai, but Ike made them give it back.
The '67 war of conquest was no contest.
To say Israel was endangered is nonsense.
Israel won the 1969-70 War of Attrition,
And ended up in a more dominant position.
Even in the closely fought war of 1973,
Israel won yet another victory.
In its 1982 Lebanon invasion,
Defeat never entered the equation.
Israel slaughtered Gazans in 2014.
Killing civilians had become routine.
The familiar trope of beleaguered Israel
Has made the Palestinians miserable.
3/30/21
*Inspired by Brokers of Deceit – How the U.S. Has
Undermined Peace in the Middle East by Rashid Khalidi*

The Republican Party is a race war monger,
That lost control of the forces it conjured.
After a lost election and an insurrection,
The party prays only for Trump's resurrection.
It still wants cuts in taxes, spending, and regulation.
But now add white supremacy dedication.
3/30/21
*Inspired by "Why Can't Republicans Be Populists?"
by Paul Krugman NYT Opinion 3-30-21*

Republicans drive our democratic decline.
To them, subverting elections is fine.
They use Trump's failed attempt to overturn the election,
As a guide to how to change the people's selection.
They build the infrastructure to subvert future contests.
Authoritarianism is what they always wanted.
White minority rule by the far right.
For that Republicans underhandedly fight.
3/31/21
*Inspired by "The GOP's Turn Against Democracy"
by Jamelle Bouie NYT Opinion 3-31-21*

The long struggle to block access to the ballot,
Has relied on legal schemes invalid.
The Supreme Court gutted the Voting Rights Act.
Democrats fight for those protections back.
The new Georgia elections law is Jim Crow 2.0.
Suppressed Black voters is where the state wants to go.
Support federal voting rights legislation,
To avoid democracy's devastation.
4/2/21
*Inspired by "The New Jim Crow In Georgia"
by Jason Morgan Ward NYT Op-Ed 4-1-21*

When a man is wounded on the ground,
Don't pump in another round.
Let the medics take him.
Doctors won't forsake him.
Use only necessary force.
From inhumanity divorce.
8/2/17
*PG 416th Posting 8/6/17
timothyjcallahan.blogspot.com

Sunday, March 28, 2021
Poetry Group Six Hundred Seventh Posting 3/28/21

Progressive Christians don't want tax cuts for the rich.
They want to slash poverty for kids.
For too long, conservatives held center stage.
It was Christian to put children in cages.
Woe unto you that are rich.
Getting into heaven will be a bitch.
Let progressive Christians set the character,
Of Christianity in America.
3/21/21
*Inspired by "Progressive Christians Arise! Hallelujah!"
by Nicholas Kristof NYT Sunday Review 3-21-21

Raise tax rates on the rich, which are too low,
But start by collecting what the rich already owe.
Their unreported income is the largest reason,
That unpaid taxes amount to hundreds of billions.
The government must enforce federal law.
Crack down on this epidemic of tax fraud.
Upgrade the I.R.S.'s outdated computer systems.
Hire more auditors to go the distance.
3/22/21
*Inspired by "How to Collect Unpaid Taxes"
NYT Editorial Sunday Review 3-21-21*

Strewn with the debris of successive demolitions,
Humsa is the target of ethnic cleaning missions.
Last time, the army took the hamlet's water tanks.
The IDF inflict Palestinian angst.
Israel is blind to unauthorized Jewish construction.
Jews get what they want; Palestinians get nothing.
This is a stark illustration of discrimination.
Israel wants Palestinian elimination.
3/22/21
*Inspired by "Sheepherding Village is Collateral Damage
in Fight for West Bank" by Patrick Kingsley and
Adam Rasgon NYT International 3-21-21*

After all the Arabs are shot once,
(Isn't that a clever pun?)
We look forward to shooting them a second time!
I'm talking about vaccines not war crimes.
But isn't it fun to pun?
I wish we were shooting them with guns.
3/24/21
*See the Jewish Link's article from the
"Purim Satire" edition 2-25-21*

The Emiratis know the honeymoon is over.
Bibi wanted their support, and they said, no sir.
He promised them F-35 fighter jets,
But Biden hasn't approved that yet.
What will the agenda of the new government be?
Emiratis will have to wait and see.
3/24/21
*Inspired by "Strained Arab Ties Sour a Pitch to Israeli Voter"
by Isabel Kershner NYT International 3-23-21

Myself only is what I care about.
Presidential precedents I flout.
There were bad people on both sides.
Only on one side, a woman died.
There were fine people amongst
The white supremacist bunch.
And all of them voted for me.
They like what they hear and see.
8/21/17
*PG 419th Posting 8/27/17
timothyjcallahan.blogspot.com

We purge names from voter rolls.
Polling places are moved or closed.
Voter ID cards are hard to get.
Minorities are no longer a threat.
Even if some get through,
And cast a vote or two,
They will not really count.
Gerrymandering voids them out.
8/6/17
*PG 417th Posting 8/13/17
timothyjcallahan.blogspot.com

Poetry Group Six Hundred Sixth Posting 3/21/2

George W. Bush enhanced the alignment,
Of Israel with the U.S. closer behind it.
The "settlements" were referenced by something friendlier:
"Existing major Israeli population centers",
Which Israel would annex one day.
Palestinians would have nothing to say.
This was the biggest break for Israel the Weasel,
Since Reagan stopped calling "settlements" illegal.
3/15/21
*Inspired by <u>Brokers of Deceit – How the U.S. Has
Undermined Peace in the Middle East</u> by Rashid Khalidi*

"Settlements" are ever expanding entities.
Religious Zionists say they were meant to be.
Decades of Israeli strategic planners,
Who were also Palestinian state banners,
Tried to make Palestine an impossibility.
This is long-term Israeli villainy.
But "settlements" will not stand in the way
Of Palestinian sovereignty.
3/15/21
*Inspired by <u>Brokers of Deceit – How the U.S. Has
Undermined Peace in the Middle East</u> by Rashid Khalidi*

Most Israelis oppose ceasing "settlement" construction.
Appeasing them is their government's prime function.
America responds with the solicitude of saints
To Israeli domestic political constraints.
Take into account the P.M.'s domestic problems,
Or you will feel the heat of the Israel lobby.
Care not about Palestinian leaders' problems,
Or you will feel the wrath of the Israel lobby.
3/16/21
*Inspired by <u>Brokers of Deceit – How the U.S. Has
Undermined Peace in the Middle East</u> by Rashid Khalidi*

On seven twenty-five the poor try,
But some end up committing suicide.
Financial struggles cause significant stress.
Sometimes poor people can't pay the rent.
Low-wage workers are deprived.
Raise the minimum wage to save lives,
And provide a better safety net,
Than any welfare system yet.
3/17/21
*Inspired by "When You Can't Pay Your Rent"
by Jason Cherkis NYT Op-Ed 3-11-21*

The Israeli shelling was not ceasing.
We saw people flying into pieces.
Israelis don't follow international rules.
They bombed hospitals and UN schools.
They killed people who tried to escape.
They kept up a steady kill rate.
Black Friday was like nothing we had seen.
At no point did America intervene.
9/6/17
*Inspired by The 51 Day War by Max Blumenthal
*PG 421st Posting 9/10/17
timothyjcallahan.blogspot.com

Most of those killed had nothing to do with the fight.
Nonetheless the bombers kept them in sight.
Israel made the Palestinians suffer.
The U.S. provided cover.
6/31/17
*PG 420th Posting 9/3/17
timothyjcallahan.blogspot.com

America is strapped to Israel's hip.
A six-shooter with an excellent grip.
America is Israel's shield,
Against any UN deals.
Uncle Sam is Israel's Dutch Uncle.
Every year he gives a bundle:
Israel's slave
Is the home of the brave.
8/22/17
*PG 419th Posting 8/27/17
timothyjcallahan.blogspot.com

Sunday, March 14, 2021
Poetry Group Six Hundred Fifth Posting 3/14/21

Congressional fiscal hawks are passive,
Regarding Israel aid so massive.
Israel's demands America appeases.
Israel spends the billions as it pleases.
It is exempt from the "buy American" provision,
Which to other foreign aid is a given.
All of Israel's money is given up front cordially.
Other recipients get installments quarterly.
3/8/21
*Inspired by <u>Brokers of Deceit – How the U.S. Has
Undermined Peace in the Middle East</u> by Rashid Khalidi*

No matter how kind a president is toward Israel,
Any perceived slippage and the lobby gets hysterical.
The histrionics bludgeon offending politicians,
Who are told to get back in line and listen.
Obama was condemned for taking the positions of Reagan.
Republicans are hypocritically blatant.
They all turn their backs on their idol.
Servility to Israel is more vital
3/8/21
*Inspired by <u>Brokers of Deceit – How the U.S. Has
Undermined Peace in the Middle East</u> by Rashid Khalidi*

U.S. presidents insisted on a "settlement" freeze.
No more of Palestine was Israel to seize.
They said the '67 borders with modification,
Should outline Palestine for codification.
But Israel rejects American demands,
And stubbornly refuses to share the land.
If that's not greed, what is it?
If they're not greedy, then give it.
3/8/21
*Inspired by <u>Brokers of Deceit – How the U.S. Has
Undermined Peace in the Middle East</u> by Rashid Khalidi*

The goodness of liberal Zionism is undeniable.
The two-state solution is still viable.
The left seeks a socially democratic Israel,
Where justice for Palestinians is critical.
Right now religious Zionists predominate.
Palestinians they abominate.
Keep faith with liberal Israelis.
Right now democracy there is flailing.
3/10/21
*Inspired by "The Feminist Trying to Save Liberal Zionism"
by Michelle Goldberg NYT Opinion 3-6-21*

Anti-Zionism is not anti-Semitism.
Ronald Lauder is anti-Westernism.
Palestinians he never mentions
Nor Occupation tensions.
Hatred of Israel is not irrational.
Zionism is international.
It's bad for our country,
Which is Israel's donkey.
9/20/17
**Inspired by WJC ad in NYT 9/20/17*
**PG 423rd Posting 9/24/17*
timothyjcallahan.blogspot.com

The soldiers tied a man to a tree
And shot him in the knees.
When an ambulance came,
To the driver they did the same.
They gave another man a flashlight,
And said turn it on 10 paces into night.
When the man complied,
The soldiers fired.
9/3/17
**PG 421rd Posting 9/10/17*
timothyjcallahan.blogspot.com

Sunday, March 7, 2021
Poetry Group Six Hundred Fourth Posting 3/7/21

Republican lawmakers want you to assume
That a bill's not bipartisan unless they approve.
But refocus bipartisanship away from Congress
And on Republican voters who applaud the bill's progress.
Yes, 60 percent of Republicans support Biden's plan.
That's bipartisanship the public understands.
This definition is far more expansive.
Republican lawmakers seek only personal advantage.
2/28/21
Inspired by "McConnell Doesn't Get to Define 'Bipartisan'"
by Michelle Cottle NYT Opinion 2-27-21

Israel should be vaccinating the Palestinians,
In parallel with its own citizens.
The Fourth Geneva Convention requires
The occupied to be cared for by the occupier.
Even the Oslo Accords, though never very effective,
Call for Israeli cooperation in epidemics.
Rest assured the "settlers" have been vaccinated.
The hundreds of thousands of them are elated.
2/28/21
Inspired by "Short of Doses, Palestinians set
Lockdown In West Bank" by Isabel Kershner
NYT Tension with Israel 2-28-21

Trumpism is replacing conservatism.
Policy is nothing compared to ferventism.
Emotion animates the G.O.P.
Issue debate is seldom seen.
Trump's appeal is more affect than agenda.
His followers' feelings are tender.
This is the party Trump remade.
Trumpism will not soon fade.
3/2/21
*Inspired by "Post-Policy G.O.P.: Animated by
Emotions, Not Issues" by Jonathan Martin NYT National 3-2-21*

Israel ended its brutal "Cast Lead" assault,
When the Bush administration came to a halt.
This offensive left fourteen hundred Gazans dead.
Those Israelis cast a lot of lead.
Obama never censured them for the atrocities.
Israel paid no penalty for any of these.
America and Israel are such close cohorts,
That Obama rejected the U.N. Human Rights report.
3/3/21
*Inspired by Brokers of Deceit – How the U.S. Has
Undermined Peace in the Middle East by Rashid Khalidi*

Their plan is a giveaway to the rich.
Convincing the base is a cinch.
By giving the rich money they don't need,
Republicans follow their party's creed:
Enrich the rich above all else.
Only the rich deserve government help.
Republicans want racial purity,
And an end to Social Security.
10/25/17
*PG 428th Posting 10/29/17
timothyjcallahan.blogspot.com*

Israelis are bad, but they don't care,
As long as they don't have to share.
Dollars flow from an eternal spring.
Zionism too America brings.
We enable the ethnic cleansing,
Which Americans are not sensing
Because Palestinians are banned from TV.
Americans are not allowed to see.
10/15/17
*PG 426th Posting 10/15/17
timothyjcallahan.blogspot.com

We will inflict damage to such an extent,
That Palestinians will know what we meant.
So much punishment will we mete out
They will know what we're all about.
We want Palestinians dead or gone.
To achieve this we drop bombs.
And keep them from U.S. TV.
Americans will never see.
9/26/17
*PG 424th Posting 10/1/17
timothyjcallahan.blogspot.com

Sunday, February 28, 2021
Poetry Group Six Hundred Third Posting 2/28/21

Israel will buy thousands of vaccines for Syria.
The outlook for the Palestinians is drearier.
Israel has supplied only a few thousand needles,
To the millions of occupied people.
But the fourth Geneva convention,
Which Israelis don't like to mention,
Requires the occupier to cooperate,
With local officials to coordinate,
The maintenance of public health in the population
Under cruel military occupation.
Israel ducks its legal responsibility.
Thousands of Palestinians will die consequently.
2/22/21
*Inspired by "Israel Secretly Agrees To Buy Vaccines
For Syria As Part of Prisoner Swap" by Patrick Kingsley,
Ronen Bergman, and Andrew E. Kramer
NYT Front Page 2-21-21*

Jews strove to transform Arab land to Jewish purity.
They justified their crimes with a claim of insecurity.
But in truth the cruelty of the occupation
Derives from scorn towards a conquered population,
Whom the victors delight to trample upon.
Jews don't fear them though they want them gone.
2/23/21
*Inspired by Brokers of Deceit – How the U.S. Has
Undermined Peace in the Middle East by Rashid Khalidi*

Want thousands of vaccines of high potency?
Then succumb to our vaccine diplomacy.
Promise to move your embassy to Jerusalem.
Show in other ways your Israel enthusiasm.
Hungary, Honduras, and Guatemala:
You've got lots of shots coming at ya.
To the Palestinians, we say no.
They've nothing to offer in a quid pro quo.
2/24/21
*Inspired by "Israel Vaccines Go to Far-Off Allies
Before Palestinians" by Patrick Kingsley
NYT Shot Diplomacy 2-24-21*

Texans didn't think regulators were necessary.
Since the deep freeze, that opinion varies.
Power companies who managed to stay on line
Raised prices and profits at the same time.
Don't complain about your sky high electric bill.
Marvel at the market's divine free will.
The idea is to create and preserve wealth.
A lower priority is the people's health.
2/24/21
*Inspired by "Et Tu, Ted? Why Deregulation Failed"
By Paul Krugman NYT Opinion 2-23-21*

They bombed civilians with intensity,
And without military necessity.
Journalists were constantly targeted,
To silence their baleful harkening.
The West cared little about these reporters,
And the targeted destruction of their quarters.
Israel killed people on a large scale.
It's easy to follow the killing trail.
10/24/17
*Inspired by The 51 Day War by Max Blumenthal
*PG 428th Posting 10/29/17
timothyjcallahan.blogspot.com

Israel silenced the media outlets.
Journalists couldn't do a thing about it.
Israel impeded the flow of facts.
Journalists and their offices were attacked.
American media was rare over there.
The folks back home didn't know or care.
And that's the way Israel wants it to be.
American Jews heartily agree.
10/26/17
*Inspired by The 51 Day War by Max Blumenthal
*PG 428th Posting 10/29/17
timothyjcallahan.blogspot.com

Sunday, February 21, 2021
Poetry Group Six Hundred Second Posting 2/21/21

Self-described prophets proliferate.
The natural and supernatural they equate.
Millions hang on their predictions,
Not knowing they are fiction.
Prophets prophesied that Trump would win.
Now those prophets are accused of sin.
They embarrassed the Holy Spirit,
And will never again get near it.
2/12/21
*Inspired by "Christian Prophecy Movement Is Hit
Hard by Trump's Defeat" by Ruth Graham
NYT Front Page 2-12-21*

The climax that he was always building toward,
Was the Jan 6 horde that roared.
Trump blessed mob violence at campaign rallies
Five dead was the insurrection's final tally.
Years of eroding trust in democracy
Led to Capitol Hill anarchy.
Republicans promoted his lethal falsehood,
That the election was fraudulent.
They acquitted him of the charge,
Though the evidence is large.
2/14/21
*Inspired by "Trump's Republicans, on Their Knees"
by Frank Bruni NYT Sunday Review 2-14-21*

Trump dismantled relations with the Palestinian side,
And let Israel's "settlement" project slide.
He ratified Israel's exclusive claim,
To the divided city of Jerusalem.
Biden expressed his desire for the two-state solution,
So Bibi said he'd build twelve hundred housing units,
In East Jerusalem for Jewish "settlers" only.
Nitwityahoo's calls for peace are phony.
2/15/21
*Inspired by "Want Israeli-Palestinian Peace?"
by Bernard Avishai and Sam Bahour
NYT Op-Ed 2-13-21*

Improve the financial condition of struggling parents.
Programs that help children are the fairest.
Having access to safety net programs in childhood,
Leads to better economic productivity in adulthood.
Inadequate nutrition, housing, and healthcare,
Makes climbing out of poverty rare.
The case for expanded child benefits is compelling,
A country that cares for children is telling.
2/17/21
*Inspired by "The Plot to Help America's Children"
by Paul Krugman NYT Opinion 2-16-21*

Texas should expand Medicaid under the ACA.
Some 1.4 million more would be insured today.
It would save thousands of poor people's lives,
But Texas is run by the Republican side.
You can count on the government not to do public good.
It tries to keep its funds from Planned Parenthood.
Essential health services, not abortion care,
Account for 96% of the work done there.
2/18/21
*Inspired by "Abortion Attacks Hurt the Poor"
by Samuel Dickman NYT OP-ED 2/17/21*

Four million Israelis have received at least one dose.
The number in the territories isn't even close.
In fact, few Palestinians have gotten a shot.
On Israel's record, here is another blot.
The disparity has provoked fierce debate:
Should we help these Arabs or leave them to their fate?
Vaccinating them would be in Israel's interest too,
Even if to ethics we are not true.
2/19/21
*Inspired by "Israel's Push to Vaccinate Raises
Host of Legal, Moral and Ethical Questions"
by Isabel Kershner NYT International 2-19-21*

It is fine that Jews want to unite.
But why unite behind Israel's far right?
Those parties are not concerned
With America's interests in the world.
The West requires a Palestine
To give the Muslim world a sign,
That we love justice just like they do.
Palestine will make that true.
10/20/17
*PG 427*th* Posting 10/22/17*
timothyjcallahan.blogspot.com

Sunday, February 14, 2021
Poetry Group Six Hundred First Posting 2/14/21

Charges of anti-Semitism are used
To silence criticism of Israeli abuse,
Of Palestinians on their own land
On which they deserve a homeland.
By definition, Israel is a racist endeavor.
It's against Trump's law to say that however:
Any Jewish state criticism
Is by Trump's definition anti-Semitism.
2/6/21
Inspired by "Campus Speech In the Era Of Zoom"
by John Leland NYT Metropolitan 1-24-21

Do the mentally ill
Truly have free will?
How many actions are driven
By the illness they were given?
I think the theory is doubtable,
That God holds them fully accountable.
2/6/21

After over a half century of immunity,
Israel lost its war crimes impunity.
The International Criminal Court determined
That it certainly has jurisdiction
Over the Palestinian territories occupied
By Israel, where so many civilians died.
The "settlements" themselves are war crimes.
Israel will be held accountable and it's about time.
2/7/21
*Inspired by "International Court Says It Has
Jurisdiction to Examine Israeli War Acts"
by Isabel Kershner NYT International 2-6-21*

Canary Mission is an anonymously run website
That hypes student activists for life.
Young Americans are profiled,
For protesting Israel so vile.
Their chances for good jobs are reduced,
Because they stood with Palestinians so abused.
Zionists say any criticism of Israel
Is anti-Semitic, not liberal.
2/8/21
*Inspired by "Campus Speech In the Era Of Zoom"
by John Leland NYT Metropolitan 1-24-21*

Israel's bloody incrimination
Knows no statute of limitation,
And will not go unpunished.
The I.C.C. will run it.
Israel is guilty of course,
Of disproportionate use of force.
Israel kills Palestinians.
It aims for civilians.
2/9/21
*Inspired by "International Court Says It Has
Jurisdiction to Examine Israeli War Acts"
by Isabel Kershner NYT International 2-6-21

It was all donation solicitation.
I don't deserve disqualification.
How the hell was I supposed to know,
That to the Capitol they would go?
Maybe I might have made a suggestion.
Did I know they would follow it without question?
Why are these events even being considered?
Everyone knows I will be acquitted.
2/10/21

A mother and child were among the dead.
When the shell broke through, they lay in bed.
In a flash their bodies broke into pieces.
That doesn't mean the bombardment ceases.
In fact, their house was hit again
By the same crew of artillery men,
Who never know the people they are killing,
Not caring if they're women and children.
10/23/17
*PG 428th Posting 10/29/17
timothyjcallahan.blogspot.com

Sunday, February 7, 2021
Poetry Group Six Hundredth Posting 2/7/21

Obama was the first president bearing Muslim names.
They plainly show his innate blame.
"Barack" is derived from the Arabic word for blessing.
By his name, his anti-Zionism he's confessing.
Hussein was Muhammad's grandson.
Obama was called Islam's blessed one.
His father was Muslim and Black.
All of this did not hold Obama back.
1/30/21
*Inspired by <u>Brokers of Deceit – How the U.S. Has
Undermined Peace in the Middle East</u> by Rashid Khalidi*

Representative Marjorie Taylor Greene
Is anti-Semitic and mean.
She says Jews used lasers on satellites,
The California wild fires to ignite.
She's a gun nut and according to her,
The Sandy Hook massacre never occurred.
Other conspiracy theories you will hear.
Ex-President Trump has her ear.
1/31/21

AmerIsrael's right-wings have long been cynical,
Pushing the familiar trope of victim Israel.
But did you know Obama persisted in this theme?
He couldn't say enough good things it seemed.
He was quick to long-windedly defend
The Jewish state, its means and ends.
"Imminent destruction" gave Israel a free pass
To kill, steal, subjugate and harass.
President Obama made his own job harder,
By making out that Israel was the martyr.
2/1/21
*Inspired by Brokers of Deceit – How the U.S. Has
Undermined Peace in the Middle East by Rashid Khalidi

Despite his pro-Israel rhetoric and stuff,
Republicans said Obama didn't do enough.
They attacked him for taking conventional positions,
Like there needs to be fair land division.
They said Obama was throwing Israel under the bus,
And that there should be no daylight between us.
Republicans support a foreign government over their own.
That far Obama never wanted to go.
2/2/21
*Inspired by <u>Brokers of Deceit – How the U.S. Has
Undermined Peace in the Middle East</u> by Rashid Khalidi

One can't fake not having psychosis.
That is a very visible diagnosis.
Mania is difficult to hide.
I don't know any manics who've tried.
Depression cannot be consciously masked.
Minimizing all symptoms is an impossible task.
Mental illness is stigmatizing.
It can't be concealed by lying.
12/13/17
*Inspired by A First-Rate Madness by Nassir Ghaemi
*PG 435th Posting 12/17/17
timothyjcallahan.blogspot.com

Israel starved Palestinians under the siege,
Who were aggrieved but not believed.
Israel allowed the minimum calorie intake needed.
Many Palestinian children were anemic,
And were not allowed crayons, clothing and shoes.
There was plenty of everything for the Jews.
Gazans live in a prison by the sea.
Israel won't let them be.
12/4/17
*PG 434th Posting 12/10/17
timothyjcallahan.blogspot.com

The Palestinians committed self-genocide,
When they did not sufficiently hide
From the tank shells we were sending,
Which they knew were life ending.
11/24/17
*PG 432nd Posting 11/26/17
timothyjcallahan.blogspot.com

Sunday, January 31, 2021
Poetry Group Five Hundred Ninety-Ninth Posting 1/31/21

Biden sees the goodness in practically everyone,
Even in those who don't think he squarely won.
Biden will help them improve their lives,
As duty and civility he revives.
Some Trump followers will become disillusioned.
They'll come to accept Trump losing.
They'll realize we are better off without him,
And that what he did to the Capitol was sin.
1/23/21
*Inspired by "To Succeed, the President Will Need
'Hope and History' to Rhyme" by Timothy Egan*

Biden's agenda will live or die in the Senate.
With the filibuster, the odds are against it.
It takes 60 percent to get anything done.
Republican votes for the legislation will be none.
The true progress of democracy depends
On the filibuster's end.
1/24/21
Inspired by "Democrats, Here's How to Lose in 2022"
by Ezra Klein NYT Sunday Review 1-24-21

Zionist zealots castigated U.S. presidents,
For perceived Zionist support hesitance.
Eisenhower, Nixon, Carter, and the elder Bush,
All needed sometimes an Israel lobby push.
But no one was so viciously reviled,
As Obama, whose transgressions were mild.
He voiced his concern for Palestinian rights,
But did not long stay in the fight.
1/25/21
*Inspired by Brokers of Deceit – How the U.S. Has
Undermined Peace in the Middle East by Rashid Khalidi*

Presidents try to push past the cocoon of platitudes,
So reassuring to those with Zionist attitudes.
Israeli domination is the status quo.
Presidents who try to change it are told no.
Decades of inertia kept policy on the same track
Leading toward failure and never looking back.
Whatever Israel demanded, it got,
Whether this facilitated peace or not.
1/26/21
*Inspired by Brokers of Deceit – How the U.S. Has
Undermined Peace in the Middle East by Rashid Khalidi*

Aid to families with children is a really good idea.
Democrats want to do that here this year.
They want to improve millions of Americans' lives,
While investing in the future at the same time.
Their legislation could cut child poverty in half.
Calling that communism is a gaffe.
After all, what could arouse more socialism dread,
Than feeding children and keeping a roof over their heads?
1/27/21
*Inspired by "Helping Kids Is a Very Good Idea"
by Paul Krugman NYT Opinion 1-26-21*

Trump spoke of Palestinians pejoratively.
Biden will work with the Palestinian Authority.
He will restore U.S. financial aid.
For two years Trump hasn't paid.
Religious Zionism is a selfish delusion.
Biden believes in the two-state solution.
He wants no more Israeli "settlement" activity,
And less U.S.-Israel servility.
1/27/21
*Inspired by "Biden to Restore Ties with Palestinians,
Reversing Trump's Policy"
by Michael Crowley NYT International 1-27-21

It's dangerous to keep a gun in the home.
A higher risk of suicide is well known.
Guns are far more lethal than other means,
Especially when no one intervenes.
Half of all suicides are by firearms,
Which cause grotesque harm:
The NRA warns keep it loaded.
That's how gun owners are goaded.
12/27/17
*Inspired by "The Gun Lobby v. Suicide Prevention"
by Erin Dunkerly, NYT, OP-ED 12/27/17
*PG 437th Posting 12/31/17
timothyjcallahan.blogspot.com

"Settlers" have democratic, legal, human, and civil rights.
The indigenous have nothing in the Zionist blight.
Though counted in the millions, they are voiceless.
Denied self-determination, they are choiceless.
No President who tried since 1967,
Could stop the "settlements" even after 9/11.
1/16/21
*Inspired by <u>Brokers of Deceit – How the U.S. Has
Undermined Peace in the Middle East</u> by Rashid Khalidi*

You'll never take back our country with weakness.
Go to the capitol and render legislators speechless.
And so President Trump committed sedition.
His violent MAGA mob surely did listen.
Now he stands impeached a second time.
He brought to the swamp his own special slime.
Hopefully, the Senate will convict him,
And our country never-again his victim.
1/17/21
*Inspired by "The Inevitable" by Michelle Goldberg
NYT Sunday Review 1-17-21*

Trump thought his capitol putsch his cause would help,
But he has no vision that is greater than himself.
In the end his pre-fascism fell short of fascism.
He is addicted not to idealism but to cashism.
His concerns never went further than a mirror.
He sees himself in his thousands of cheerers.
No worldview explains his truly big lie.
Imminent loss of power was the reason why.
1/18/21
*Inspired by "The American Abyss" by Timothy Snyder
NYT Magazine 1-17-21

Israel keeps gobbling up the pie
That the two sides are supposed to divide.
Freezing "settlement" expansion remains out of range.
Several presidents tried hard in vain.
We do so much for Israel that's unjust.
Couldn't it once do something for us?
How long will we concede to Israeli greed?
Our servility impedes world peace.
1/20/21
*Inspired by *Brokers of Deceit — How the U.S. Has
Undermined Peace in the Middle East* by Rashid Khalidi

Israel is a murderer who kills slowly.
Its murder of Palestine is holy.
The Palestinians aren't quite dead yet.
As to when, you may place your bet.
All they wanted was a fifth of what they had
But Holy Jehovah says they get no land.
1/22/16
PG 334th Posting 1/10/16
timothyjcallahan.blogspot.com

The wave comes in with a roar and goes out with a hiss.
A charging lion becomes retreating serpents.
The pitcher winds up before delivering the pitch.
The catcher casually throws the ball back.
9/8/09
PG *334th Posting 1/10/16*
timothyjcallahan.blogspot.com

Repetition teaches you.
Then the spirit reaches you,
And you become a host
Of the Co-Equal Holy Ghost.
8/30/09
PG 334th Posting 1/10/16
timothyjcallahan.blogspot.com
Poems 6 and 7
Poet Against Israel by Timothy J. Callahan

Sunday, January 17, 2021
Poetry Group Five Hundred Ninety-Seventh Posting 1/17/21

After a decade of deliberation,
Iran approved a bill of criminalization,
For those convicted of sexual misconduct,
And honor killings so fucked up.
A special female police unit will protect women.
Victims of violence will feel less timid.
Tell Trumpists that Iran is not the Taliban.
We should make peace if we still can.
1/10/21
*Inspired by "Iran Moves Bill to Outlaw Sexual Violence
and Harassment of Women" by Farnaz Fassihi
NYT International 1-7-21*

Reverend Barber believes in "fusion coalition".
All races against poverty is his tradition.
Most who marched in Moral Monday protests were white.
Anyone who wants dignity for the poor was invited.
Black in America I cannot be,
But I feel deep empathy.
1/11/21
*Inspired by "Why We Need a Second Great Migration"
by Charles M. Blow NYT Sunday Review 1-10-21*

The G.O.P. wants tax cuts for the rich.
But it needs more than plutocracy to win.
So it courts whites with thinly disguised racist appeals,
And pushes conspiracy theories unreal.
All the Trumpists' rage is based on lies.
What atrocity will Republicans next devise?
They destroy the country they want to lead.
Democracy is not part of their Christian creed.
1/12/21
*Inspired by "This Putsch Was Decades
in the Making" by Paul Krugman
NYT OP-ED 1-12-21*

I am Ambassador David Friedman.
I stand with the Zionist greedmen,
Who are no longer thieves of stolen land.
Palestinians are not Israelis' fellow man.
I cast aside any notion of evenhandedness.
Palestinians must learn whose land this is.
Nitwityahoo got Jerusalem and the Golan Heights.
Israel did nothing to ease the Palestinians' plight.
I ran their emissaries out of Washington,
And cut financial aid to none.
1/13/2021
*Inspired by "The Trump Appointee who 'Changed
the Narrative' in Israel" by David M. Halbinger
NYT National 1-10-21*

I know what the dog feels like chasing the car:
"Who the fucking hell do you think you are?"
Then the chain of reason snaps me back.
I did not even know I began the attack.
10/10/09
*PG 337th Posting 1/31/16
timothyjcallahan.blogspot.com

The neighborhoods with the lowest rent
Shouldn't expect help from the government.
In fact, they should expect lead
In the water that they get.
1/25/16
*PG 337th Posting 1/31/16
timothyjcallahan.blogspot.com

The working poor are poor despite working.
The middle classes look on smirking.
The rich don't know about this
In their mansions of bliss.
9/12/09
* PG 335th Posting 1/17/16
timothyjcallahan.blogspot.com
Poems 5, 6, and 7 originally from
Poet Against Israel by Timothy J. Callahan

Sunday, January 10, 2021
Poetry Group Five Hundred Ninety-Sixth Posting 1/10/21

So much the Republicans did not think strange.
Trump undercut efforts to address climate change.
Scores of environmental rules he reversed
Global warming has only gotten worse.
He replaced competent people with loyalist liars,
Who think nothing of unmatched floods and fires.
Biden will banish holdover Trump appointees,
Who to federal agencies are like a disease.
1/2/21
*Inspired by "Trump Tried, but Failed, to Derail
Climate Report That Steers Future Policies" by
Christopher Flavelle NYT National 1-2-21*

The Abraham Accords are a catastrophic betrayal,
But to Palestinian aspirations, not fatal.
Once the Arabs have embassies in Tel Aviv,
Israel will not want them to leave.
They will have more leverage with Israel
To make the Palestinians less miserable.
Don't forget the whole world minus the U.S.
Wishes Palestinians the very best.
1/3/21
*Inspired by "Final Achievement for Mideast Envoy: Leaving
With Respect of All Sides" by David M. Halbfinger
NYT International 1-3-21*

In the fall of 1991 and the spring of '92,
President Bush dared try something new.
He held up $10 billion in loan guarantees,
For proof they would not go toward building in the territories.
Bush boldly and openly singled out the Israel lobby
As the peace process's biggest problem.
But his efforts to curb "settlements" came to naught.
He lost interest when reelection he sought.
1/4/21
*Inspired by <u>BROKERS OF DECEIT – How the U.S. Has
Undermined Peace in the Middle East</u> by Rashid Khalidi*

I just want to find 11,780 votes.
Brad, don't tell me I won't.
You are committing a criminal offense,
Because you know how this election really went.
There's nothing wrong with saying you've recalculated.
As a Republican, you stand self-emasculated.
I won by hundreds of thousands, and that's a fact.
You only have to find me a fraction of that.
1/4/21
*Inspired by "On Tape, Trump Pushes Georgia
to 'Find' Votes" by Michael D. Shear and Stephanie Saul
NYT Front Page 1-4-21*

I won in a landslide; there's nothing to decide.
March on the Capitol and defy!
You are special, and I love you.
The U.S. government is not above you.
I told you January 6th would be wild.
Our worst enemies are the meek and mild.
Break down doors and send the occupants scattering.
Congress will elect me after a proper battering.
1/9/21

I did all the praying and grace saying,
But the Prosperity Gospel is not paying.
Life is so beautiful; life is so hard.
You don't always get what you want from God.
2/15/16
PG *340ᵗʰ Posting 2/21/16*
timothyjcallahan.blogspot.com

Don't look down when you're climbing a tree.
Wait till you sit on the branch where you'll be.
Unless you're holding on in a safe spot,
If someone tells you to look down, do not.
10/23/09
Poem 7 from Poet Against Israel by Timothy J. Callahan
PG *339ᵗʰ Posting 2/14/16*
timothyjcallahan.blogspot.com

Sunday, January 3, 2021
Poetry Group Five Hundred Ninety-Fifth Posting 1/3/21

In the Madrid-Washington talks of 1991-93,
Palestinians were to negotiate with their adversary.
But AmerIsrael imposed a transition period,
During which Israel remained silent on issues serious.
The interim period was extended for years.
Final status talks never came near.
All the while Israel kept up its "settlement" building,
And more of its other people's land tilling.
Palestinian disillusionment meant,
The second intifada would be a six year event.
12/26/20

Inspired by Brokers of Deceit – How the U.S. Has
Undermined Peace in the Middle East by Rashid Khalidi

Is normalcy forever obsolete?
Republicans believe Biden is a cheat.
They consume entirely different "facts",
And replace science with religious tracts.
Texas brought a seditious lawsuit,
Which the U.S. Supreme Court gave the boot,
But not before 146 Republicans signed on.
Congress members supported a con.
But remember, 70 of them didn't.
They did democracy's bidding,
And they are a source of hope.
Them I invoke.
12/27/20
*Inspired by "Is Normalcy Obsolete?" by Frank Bruni
NYT Sunday Review 12-27-20*

Trump's executive order is as strong as Samson is:
No criticism of Israel on college campuses.
Professors are fired, denied tenure, or threatened with suits.
About Palestinian suffering, they can't tell the truth.
Legislators too are cowed into silence,
When it comes to Israeli racist violence.
State censorship is but one of the right's tools
Used to protect greedy Zionist ghouls.
12/28/20
*Inspired by "The Post-Trump Future of Literature"
by Viet Thanh Nguyen NYT Sunday Review 12-27-20*

The second intifada was a direct result
Of disillusionment and insult
Of the Palestinian population,
During nine years of "peace process" occupation.
Statehood was indefinitely deferred.
The pursuit of sovereignty was interned.
Israeli "settlements" were expanded.
America was never even-handed.
Palestinians saw they had been led into a trap.
They attacked Israel the rat.
12/30/20
*Inspired by <u>BROKERS OF DECEIT – How the U.S. Has
Undermined Peace in the Middle East</u> by Rashid Khalidi*

U.S. policy derives from Israeli political discourse.
Whatever you Israelis say, we endorse.
Support the Israeli consensus on any given issue.
What you Israelis want, we wish you.
Even if Israel wants to act out of malice,
Don't upset its internal political balance.
Republicans want no daylight between us.
America sucks Israel's penis.
12/31/20
*Inspired by BROKERS OF DECEIT – How the U.S. Has
Undermined Peace in the Middle East by Rashid Khalidi*

Disregard for the concerns of the poor
Made the government ignore them more.
Indifference caused the crisis and prolonged it.
They saw the black community and wronged it.
To save money for people of wealth,
They sacrificed the poor people's health.
The Flint disaster is not yet solved.
Governor Rick Snyder is not absolved.
He's not sure if race played a part.
He should look into his own cold heart.
3/25/16
PG 345th Posting 3/27/16
timothyjcallahan.blogspot.com

I have a sundial
Outside my domicile,
Which I look at while
In futile denial.
10/3/09
Poem 7 from Poet Against Israel by Timothy J. Callahan
PG 341st Posting 2/28/16
timothyjcallahan.blogspot.com

Cuba, Venezuela, and China were behind a plot,
To install rigged voting machines (or not).
Powell was too insane even for the Trump campaign,
But right-wing media treated her in a friendly vein,
And when Tucker dared question her credibility,
He faced a backlash of inevitability.
Fox News called Biden president elect,
And faced an onslaught of Trump's invective.
Fox News is losing audience to Newsmax,
An alternative usually further from the facts.
12/19/20
*Inspired by "For Many in the Right-Wing Media,
the Election May Never Be Over"
by Jeremy W. Peters NYT National 12/16/20*

Reagan called for an immediate "settlement" freeze,
But in the end Begin was appeased.
Reagan opposed Israeli sovereignty over the West Bank,
But Begin made sure the Reagan Plan sank.
He forced both Carter and Reagan to back down,
With the help of his supporters in Washington town.
Likud has always perpetuated the occupation,
And denied Palestinians self-determination.
12/20/20
*Inspired by BROKERS OF DECEIT – How the U.S. Has
Undermined Peace in the Middle East by Rashid Khalidi*

Formidable figurehead of a personality cult,
Trump could have been a hero, but chose to be a dolt.
With conspiracy theorists he consults.
Martial law may be the result.
Trump shares his grievance with his rabid base,
Without evidence they call it a fraud case.
Most Republicans are very hesitant
To call Biden the next president.
Trump is the troller in chief,
A spreader of grief.
12/21/10
*Inspired by "Trump in Grip of Grudges"
by Alexander Burns and Jonathan Martin
NYT News Analysis 12-21-20

One false premise was that Israel would make concessions,
Once its security was beyond contention.
So after 1991 and Iraq's crushing defeat,
From its harsh positions, Israel was expected to retreat.
One American administration after another,
Gave Israel billions plus diplomatic cover.
Each got Israeli rigidity in return.
How many times must America get burned?
12/22/20
*Inspired by BROKERS OF DECEIT – How the U.S. Has
Undermined Peace in the Middle East by Rashid Khalidi

Lady Liberty finally had to wince,
Listening to the AIPAC conference.
Presidential candidates swore to be slaves,
And if necessary knaves,
To enable Israeli greed,
And fulfill the apocalypse creed.
Only Sanders knows that Nitwityahoo
Is not one to pledge fealty to.
3/22/16
PG 345th Posting 3/27/16
timothyjcallahan.blogspot.com

Jesus is my hero but not my god.
He never existed outside his bod.
Still he had a lot of wise things to say,
And encouragement to get through the day.
He showed the moneychangers who was boss.
Didn't punk out when came time for the cross.
4/20/09
PG 344th Posting 3/20/16
timothyjcallahan.blogspot.com

Agamemnon,
Put your jacket on.
This war is almost ten years old.
Let's not lose it to the common cold.
6/23/09
PG 342nd Posting 3/6/16
timothyjcallahan.blogspot.com
Poems 6 and 7 from <u>Poet Against Israel</u>
by Timothy J. Callahan

Republicans rely on voter suppression.
Tossing out votes is a logical extension.
Party leaders are guided by fear of Trump.
They say love of country is for chumps.
Where does the anti-democracy party go from here?
It will assault elections in future years.
Republicans desire white minority rule,
So for them democracy is not cool.
12/14/20
Inspired by "Republicans Who Embraced Nihilism"
NYT Editorial 12-12-20

Trump would bend reality to his criminal desires,
But among the courts, there are no buyers.
Republicans tried to scrap the results of elections,
And discredit the people's selections.
Had these schemers succeeded,
Police action would've been needed.
They would've plunged the country into violence,
But great patriots did not stay silent.
12/14/20
Inspired by "The 'Trump Won' Farce Isn't Funny Anymore"
by Jamelle Bouie NYT Opinion 12-12-20

American politicians quickly learn
Palestinians must bow to security concerns,
An ever-expanding list of Israeli demands.
The indigenous are to get none of their land.
International law cannot be applied,
Because Israel is never denied.
America is slave to Israel.
That statement is literal.
12/14/20
*Inspired by <u>BROKERS OF DECEIT – How the U.S. Has
Undermined Peace in the Middle East</u> by Rashid Khalidi*

The evicted PLO worried about the refugee camps,
Filled with Palestinians as defenseless as lambs.
America gave the PLO explicit assurances,
That refugee safety was of the utmost urgency.
Those assurances were utterly unreliable.
For the massacres, America was liable.
So was Israel who let the murderers in
And fired star shells to help them begin.
12/15/20
*Inspired by <u>BROKERS OF DECEIT – How the U.S. Has
Undermined Peace in the Middle East</u> by Rashid Khalidi*

Only Bernie says Israel must withdraw
In accordance with international law.
There is no bigger suckup than Cruz.
Who would make Palestinians lose.
Then Muslims would resent us more.
They would want justice all the more
And sympathize with jihadi war.
4/6/16
PG 347th Posting 5/10/16
timothyjcallahan.blogspot.com

Yaalon spoke of the man whose head was blown:
Do you want a brutish army without moral backbone?
Once neutralized they should not be killed.
With restraint the soldier must be filled.
3/31/16
PG 346th Posting 4/3/16
timothyjcallahan.blogspot.com

Israel is really Palestine you know.
Israel stole it making Palestinian foes.
After all its ethnic cleansing and killing,
Israel wonders why terrorists are willing.
One thing that would decrease terror
Would be Israel correcting its West Bank error.
We want a just solution to the Palestinian question.
We believe despite Israel that is destined.
3/21/16
PG 345th Posting 3/27/16
timothyjcallahan.blogspot.com

To work for me, deny reality.
Biden's victory is but a fallacy.
I won states where they say I lost.
I made this mob and I am boss.
It's time to stop standing back and by.
Proud Boys and other MAGA men, arise!
The Second Amendment is for just such an instance.
With enough insistence, we can still win this.
12/5/20

He left the battlefield on his trusty steed:
I'm never, ever going to concede!
I'll never attend a Biden inauguration.
#presidentialoccupant will be his designation.
I will arouse a rear guard action,
And rule all through my faction.
I am victim of a vast conspiracy.
To say otherwise is heresy.
12/6/20
Inspired by "The Last Act of the Trump Drama:
Rage, Denial and Retribution" by Peter Baker
NYT White House Memo 12-6-20

Women, often Black, were sterilized without their knowledge.
Black women served as specimens at medical colleges.
Some would lose benefits if they did not "consent".
Fewer Black children is what this public policy meant.
Hundreds of Black men thought they were being treated
For syphilis, but they were being cheated.
The doctors wanted to observe the disease.
This went on for forty years.
12/7/20
*Inspired by "How Black People Learned Not to Trust"
by Charles M. Blow NYT Opinion 12-7-20*

Israeli police are not fools.
Force is one of our main tools.
Restricting it would be a loss.
We don't want officers getting soft.
We want no chilling of aggressiveness.
There is no such thing as excessiveness.
We want no accountability measures.
Killing Palestinians is our pleasure.
12/9/20
*Inspired by "Killing of Autistic Man Exposes Police Brutality
Problem in Israel" by David M. Halbfinger and
Adam Rasgon NYT front page 12-8-20*

Trump will give three trillion to the rich over a decade.
For 75 years Social Security could be paid.
Over 20 years, the cuts would add 34 trillion to the debt.
Trump hasn't released his tax returns yet.
5/12/16
*PG 352nd Posting 5/15/16
timothyjcallahan.blogspot.com*

Israel cuts down thousands of ancient olive trees.
Israelis clear the land, then seize.
What does the U.S. do about this theft?
It stares blankly at Palestinians bereft.
4/21/16
PG 349th Posting 4/24/16
timothyjcallahan.blogspot.com

My brother and the boss,
Stations of the Cross.
I always thought no way,
To see my father pray.
At home he was cruel,
In church he was a fool.
4/3/09
PG 348th Posting 4/17/16
timothyjcallahan.blogspot.com

God does not reward you for being good,
Even though he obviously could.
You're blessed for choosing Christ as your savior,
Which makes you have the proper behavior.
5/3/09
Poems 7 and 8 from pp. 34, 35 of
Poet Against Israel by Timothy J. Callahan
PG 348th Posting 4/17/16
timothyjcallahan.blogspot.com

Sunday, December 6, 2020
Poetry Group Five Hundred Ninety-First Posting 12/6/20

Violence directed at innocent civilians,
Like when the IDF kill them,
Is against international law,
And I'll tell you what's more.
Resistance against an illegal occupation,
Is allowed the occupied population.
A strike against occupying armed force,
Is internationally legal of course.
11/28/20
*Inspired by <u>BROKERS OF DECEIT – How the U.S. Has
Undermined Peace in the Middle East</u> by Rashid Khalidi*

Yad Vashem is Israel's Holocaust memorial,
Whose leaders should be apolitical and cordial.
Likud nominated Effie Eitam for chairman.
He is neither tolerant nor caring.
He wants to expel Palestinians from the West Bank.
For the conflict we have men like him to thank.
Yad Vashem should keep the moral high ground.
Leave the chair vacant until a better person is found.
11/29/20
** Inspired by "Israel's Pick to Lead Holocaust Memorial
Stirs Controversy" by Isabel Kershner
NYT International 11-29-20*

Reagan was much more predisposed toward Israel,
Than was Jimmy Carter the liberal.
Republican ranks were full of neoconservatives,
Anti-Soviet and pro U.S.-Israel servitude:
The Fourth Geneva Convention does not apply to Palestine.
Therefore, the West Bank is not really occupied.
So "settlements" are not against international law.
We will never let the Cold War thaw.
"Settlements" are only "obstacles to peace".
There's no reason building them should cease.
11/30/20
*Inspired by <u>BROKERS OF DECEIT – How the U.S. Has
Undermined Peace in the Middle East</u> by Rashid Khalidi*

Begin said the Camp David Accords
Do not a Palestinian state award,
Despite their autonomy provision,
Which he reads with extreme restriction.
No Palestinian self-determination
That would threaten Israel's position.
Any "autonomy" would be for people, not land.
Someday they will have no place to stand.
12/1/20
*Inspired by BROKERS OF DECEIT – How the U.S. Has
Undermined Peace in the Middle East by Rashid Khalidi*

Trump should not have promised the Sudanese,
That from 9/11 claims, they'd get immunity,
Because Congress is not about to grant it.
Sudan now sees that Trump took advantage.
Foreign banks will be reluctant to invest.
So much liability hangs over Sudan's head.
Why should the Sudanese make nice with Israel,
When the U.S. plans to keep them miserable?
12/2/20
*Inspired by "New Accord Between Sudan and Israel
May Unravel, Officials Say" by Lara Jakes
NYT International 12-2-20*

He didn't freeze when I told him to freeze.
I shot the other when he sneezed.
Another admitted he had a gun.
He didn't have time to produce one.
One day a suspect got up and ran.
I shot him down with the gun in my hand.
7/12/16
*PG 361st Posting 7/17/16
timothyjcallahan.blogspot.com*

Zionists hold the peace process hostage.
Persecuting Palestinians is their process.
Their control over Washington makes them smug.
They kill Palestinians and shrug.
5/16/16
*PG 353rd Posting 5/22/16
timothyjcallahan.blogspot.com*

Modeled on the fight against apartheid,
BDS takes the Palestinian side.
Pompeo calls the movement anti-Semitic.
His first impulse is to protect Israel the Wicked.
Labeling BDS anti-Semitic suppresses
People's rights of freedom of expression.
We have the right to participate in the movement or not.
Calling it anti-Semitic is rot.
11/22/20
*	Inspired by "Pompeo Trip to Israel Delivers Parting
Gifts, Delighting Hard-Liners" by David M. Halbfinger
and Isabel Kershner NYT International 11-20-20*

Falsely labeling "settlement" products "Made in Israel",
Enables it to benefit from making millions miserable.
The brutal occupation quietly pays off.
People buy products they don't know the source of.
Israel has no incentive to change its bad behavior.
If only the new president could be the Palestinians' savior.
Israel wants to maintain the status quo.
Americans don't know enough to say no.
11/22/20
*	Inspired by "Pompeo Trip to Israel Delivers Parting
Gifts, Delighting Hard-Liners" by David M. Halbfinger
and Isabel Kershner NYT International 11-20-20*

Christian fundamentalism Pompeo deeply believes.
With Palestinians he never grieves.
He is of the people of one book.
At Palestinian grievance, he never looks.
His head is into the supernatural;
He disregards the factual.
God tells him Palestinians are depraved,
But at the Second Coming, Jews will be saved.
11/23/20
*Inspired by "Pompeo Trip to Israel Delivers Parting
Gifts, Delighting Hard-Liners" by David M. Halbfinger
and Isabel Kershner NYT International 11-20-20*

Five Days after the Camp David Accords were signed,
Carter wrote a side letter to Begin, though not inclined.
Wherever "Palestinian people" occurs in the text,
Call them "Palestinian Arabs" at best.
That term denies them peoplehood,
Which for Zionism is good.
11/24/20
*Inspired by BROKERS OF DECEIT – How the U.S. Has
Undermined Peace in the Middle East by Rashid Khalidi*

The wounded man posed no danger,
But the sergeant was a changer
Of wounded men to dead.
He shot him in the head.
Now manslaughter is the charge
Against the inhumane sarge.
7/25/16
PG 363rd Posting 7/31/16
timothyjcallahan.blogspot.com

Palestinians want territorial contiguity,
The same as you and me.
They want a homeland on their own land.
They don't want to be better than.
I write for Palestinian territory,
Most people ignore me.
I say they are the new Irish,
But those words fall on silence.
7/16/16
PG 361st Posting 7/17/16
timothyjcallahan.blogspot.com

Standing in Stratford-on-Avon,
I wonder how many acorns
Made oak trees back to back
To when Shakespeare heard that quack.
10/17/09

I went with a whore in Denver once,
But I wouldn't let her take off my guns.
Another time I was bending over
And one of my guns fell out of the holster.
A homeless bum tried to pick it up:
I put six shots through his beggar cup.
10/16/09
**Poems 7 and 8 from pp.36,37 of*
Poet Against Israel by Timothy J. Callahan
PG 360tht Posting 7/10/16
timothyjcallahan.blogspot.com

Sunday, November 22, 2020
Poetry Group Five Hundred Eighty-Ninth Posting 11/22/20

Bibi can no longer brag the U.S. is in his pocket
American bone has been pulled from the Israeli socket.
Biden will preserve a future Palestinian state.
Unilateral annexation will forever wait.
Maybe he'll punish Israel for its brutal occupation
That would lift the Palestinian population.
Trump's Israel favoritism is over.
U.S. policy will be balanced and sober.
11/14/20
*Inspired by "Biden's Victory Means Demotion for
Netanyahu and Less Focus on Israel"
NYT Election News Analysis by David M. Halbfinger*

In spite of his initial challenge
To the paradigm without balance,
President Carter meekly accepted
Begin's language at Camp David.
The Palestinians were promised
Israeli controlled "autonomy".
The military occupation was continued.
Palestinians are prayed for by St. Jude.
The colonization kept on.
Jimmy Carter leapt on.
11/15/20
*Inspired by <u>BROKERS OF DECEIT – How the U.S. Has
Undermined Peace in the Middle East</u> by Rashid Khalidi*

A secret letter to P.M. Rabin from President Ford,
Showed just how much Israel was adored.
Any time America wanted to make a move,
It had to be something Israel would approve.
Kissinger was afraid of this just enough
To have left it out of his memoirs voluminous.
Any proposed American peace proposal
Was subject to immediate Israeli disposal.
11/16/20
*Inspired by BROKERS OF DECEIT – How the U.S. Has
Undermined Peace in the Middle East by Rashid Khalidi*

Look, if you can't get Trumpists to wear a mask,
How you gonna move them away from the fossil fuel past?
Vaccines, if not cooperation, will get us through this yet,
But climate change poses an existential threat.
Why should a fracker fix the leaks in his wells?
What the hell's in it for me? the fracker yells.
And why should I wear a mask to help strangers?
Let every man face his own dangers.
11/17/20
*Inspired by "Covid, Climate and the Power of Denail"
by Paul Krugman Opinion NYT 11-17-20*

No, I meant he's the founder of ISIS, I do.
What can I say to convince you?
Also, Obama is a Muslim.
The founder of ISIS was him.
8/17/16
*PG 366th Posting 8/21/16
timothyjcallahan.blogspot.com*

Militant settlers and their rabbis boiled.
They kept the angry mobs well oiled.
The right made Rabin out to be a monster.
Rabin was shot by one such mobster.
He wanted to trade land for peace.
For that goal his life ceased.
8/10/16
*Inspired by "Trump's Ambiguous Wink Wink"
by Thomas L. Friedman NYT OpEd 8/10/16
PG 365th Posting 8/14/16
timothyjcallahan.blogspot.com*

The most important thing is to end the Occupation.
Show Palestinians on a U.S. TV station.
See what we enable Israel to do.
Americans should have a clear view.
Enabling Israel's stealing and killing,
We make terrorists more willing.
The world suffers for Israel's greed,
And ignores Palestinian need.
8/5/16
*PG 364th Posting 8/7/16
timothyjcallahan.blogspot.com*

Sunday, November 8, 2020
Poetry Group Five Hundred Eighty-Seventh Posting 11/8/20

If Israel could vote in Tuesday's election,
Trump would be its popular selection.
He showered gifts on its far right leaders,
Who feed the other-peoples'-land eaters.
Between himself and Bibi, Biden would keep distance.
He would understand Palestinian resistance.
Israel too will benefit from the two state solution,
Which would bring about a lasting peace resolution.
11/1/20
Inspired by "R.I.P., G.O.P."
NYT Editorial Sunday Review 10-25-20

Even though 1956 was an election year,
Eisenhower condemned Israel without fear.
It had invaded the Sinai Peninsula,
With France and Britain invincible,
At the same time the Soviets invaded Hungary.
Israel took the focus off Soviet thuggery.
Attention turned to Western neocolonialism,
And away from totalitarianism.
11/2/20
Inspired by BROKERS OF DECEIT – How the U.S. Has
Undermined Peace in the Middle East by Rashid Khalidi

Palestinians have been colonized and dispersed.
With an occupation, they are cursed.
From the U.S., Israel usually got what it wanted,
Which was never a just resolution of the conflict.
Israel's lawyer has been the United States,
Enabling "settlers" to create accomplished fates,
Which make the two-state solution more distant.
To changing the status quo, Jews are resistant.
11/4/20
*Inspired by <u>BROKERS OF DECEIT</u> – How the U.S. Has
Undermined Peace in the Middle East by Rashid Khalidi*

Under the administrations of Johnson, Nixon, and Ford,
Palestinians were ignored and Israel adored.
Ford went furthest in his rejection of the PLO.
He had Kissinger and Israel strike a secret memo:
The PLO must recognize Israel's right to exist.
No parallel demand on Israel was the gist.
Carter was the first to recognize Palestinian rights.
On actualizing them, he set his sights.
11/7/20
*Inspired by <u>BROKERS OF DECEIT – How the U.S. Has
Undermined Peace in the Middle East</u> by Rashid Khalidi*

To Al Aqsa and its surroundings,
UNESCO did something astounding.
It voted the site Islamic.
Israelis will now bomb it.
10/17/16
PG 375th Posting 10/23/16
timothyjcallahan.blogspot.com

The only solution is to transfer Arabs from here to there,
To Jordan, Lebanon or anywhere.
We must evict them from their farms.
Soon all Palestine will be ours.
Not a single village will be let off.
Our Jewish leadership is not soft.
Wherever Arabs go to get out of our way,
We will cleanse those places someday.
10/5/16
PG 373rd Posting 10/9/16
timothyjcallahan.blogspot.com

You are so trickable.
I find you despicable.
You traded the cow for beans
Forgetting your family's needs.
Plant the beans and see if they grow.
Maybe they will, but I'm saying no.
Mother, you are full of doubt.
Wait till you see my beans sprout.
Such a beanstalk will you see
That you'll stop disparaging me.
9/15/16
PG 370th Posting 9/18/16
timothyjcallahan.blogspot.com

Republicans lack philosophical underpinning.
This November, they will not do much winning.
Their shrinking base of support pledges allegiance
To authoritarian populism and white grievance.
Trump accelerated his party's demise.
Democratic ideals Republicans despise.
Republicans stood back and stood by,
Enabling President Trump's lies.
10/25/20
Inspired by "R.I.P., G.O.P."
NYT Editorial Sunday Review 10-25-20

Presidential authority in foreign affairs
Is theoretically extensive if one dares.
But in practice that authority is circumscribed
By domestic political reality vibes.
Presidents can't solve the Palestinian problem,
Because Congress is owned by the Israel lobby.
Most presidents don't get deeply involved.
Will the conflict ever be resolved?
10/26/20
Inspired by <u>BROKERS OF DECEIT – How the U.S. Has</u>
<u>Undermined Peace in the Middle East</u> by Rashid Khalidi

Republicans, like Israelis, regard greed as a virtue.
If you are poor or Palestinian, they will hurt you.
Republicans want the rich to pay the least possible,
Whether through tax evasion or statutes illogical.
Israelis need more than eighty percent of Palestine.
They build more settlements by design.
Republicans support West Bank colonization.
From the lobby they get Zionist qualification.
10/27/20

On his walk to his school for adults with disabilities,
Iyad al-Hallaq met with Israeli police villainy.
Their leader fired at his feet up the Via Dolorosa.
They found him cowering in a sanitation enclosure.
A teacher told police the man was harmless.
Mr. al-Hallaq was also arms-less.
But police shoot Arabs like varmints.
So even though the commander ordered ceasefire,
One of his officers had a murderous desire,
And shot Iyad in the torso twice.
Try him for manslaughter the court advised.
10/31/20
*Inspired by "Manslaughter Charge Is Urged
for Israeli who killed Unarmed Autistic Palestinian"
by David M. Halbfinger and Adam Rasgon
NYT International 10-22-20*

The Hagana rolled barrel bombs down hills.
Many Palestinians were killed.
Flame throwers were also used,
Against Palestinians abused.
10/28/16
*Inspired by The Ethnic Cleansing of Palestine by Ilan Pappe
PG 376th Posting 10/30/16
timothyjcallahan.blogspot.com

They worked hard for Palestine's ending,
A systematic mega-operation of ethnic cleansing.
The outcome was never in doubt.
In fact, it was a rout.
10/26/16
*Inspired by The Ethnic Cleansing of Palestine by Ilan Pappe
PG 376th Posting 10/30/16
timothyjcallahan.blogspot.com

You will not be younger than you are today.
Time marches on, act without delay.
Help Hillary get out the vote.
Trump is hoping that you don't.
10/10/16
PG 374th Posting 10/16/16
timothyjcallahan.blogspot.com

Sunday, October 25, 2020
Poetry Group Five Hundred Eighty-Fifth Posting 10/25/20

President Trump often makes bad matters worse.
The Israeli-Palestinian conflict was not the first.
His peace plan was a gift to the Israeli right.
It worsened the Palestinians' plight,
And made it impossible for the U.S. to be a broker.
The rest of the world thinks our country is a joker.
Too bad the two-state solution wasn't one of Putin's goals.
Trump would attempt it despite the political tolls.
10/19/10
Inspired by "His Incompetent Statesmanship"
by Serge Schmemann NYT Sunday Review 10-18-20

Trump won't divest himself from ownership of
His family business because money is his first love.
The Trump International Hotel in D.C.
On corruption runs lucratively.
Favor-seekers spend gobs of cash
For hobnobbing loose and fast.
Their spending shows their pro-Trump sentiments,
As they schmooze for benefits.
10/20/20
Inspired by "His Unapologetic Corruption"
by Michelle Cottle NYT Sunday Review 10-18-20

For the pleas to condemn violence, Trump is to blame,
Because violence is so often committed in his name.
Trump has been invoked in many acts of violence.
He promotes it or sits by in silence.
Our president is a liar, a racist, a reprobate.
In society, his behavior replicates.
Even the children of minorities,
Are harassed horridly.
10/20/10
Inspired by "His Demagogy" by Jesse Wegman
NYT Sunday Review 10-18-20

Sudan will be off the list of terrorism state sponsors,
More good news since the fall of al-Bashir the monster.
But lifting this harmful designation
Comes with conditions from the administration.
Sudan must recognize Israel before Election Day,
No matter what the Sudanese populace will say.
Because of Trump's political goal
In Sudan, the Islamists might regain control
10/21/20
Inspired by "Sudan Exults at U.S. Removal of
Terror State Designation" by Abdi Latif Dahir
NYT International 10-21-20

They won't be opening embassies in one another's capitals.
Fully normalized relations will not be happening.
Sudan's government did just enough to get off the list,
Of state sponsors of terrorism so dissed.
To do more would spur pro-Palestinian protests,
In a country in deep economic distress.
Trump bullied Sudan to start down a path,
That will arouse the Sudanese people's wrath.
10/24/20
*Inspired by "Sudan and Israel Pursue Economic
Bond, Falling Short of Normalized Ties"
by Lara Jakes, Declan Walsh, and Adam Rasgon
NYT International 10-24-20*

Land is worth dying for because it's the only thing that lasts.
Palestinians died in vain for it in the past.
The United States should help them more.
Show Muslims we want justice not war.
10/31/16
*PG 377th Posting 9/6/16
timothyjcallahan.blogspot.com*

Maklef ran the cleansing of Haifa.
His men were population wipers.
He ordered they kill any Arab encountered:
We are their neighborhood trouncers.
Any door that does not give
Blow open with explosives.
Torch all things inflammable.
Your conduct should be damnable.
11/3/16
*Inspired by The Ethnic Cleansing of Palestine
by Ilan Pappe
PG 376th Posting 11/6/16
timothyjcallahan.blogspot.com*

Sunday, October 18, 2020
Poetry Group Five Hundred Eighty-Fourth Posting 10/18/20

On Arab TV Prince Bandar bin Zionist spoke.
Saudi support for Palestinians he further broke.
He admits that they have a just cause,
But for Israel he reserves his applause.
Although unjust, Israeli leaders have known success,
While Palestinian leadership has been feckless.
Bandar got support from the Crown Prince Butcher,
Who takes his orders from Jared Kushner.
10/10/20
Inspired by "Saudi Royal on TV Criticizes
Palestinian Leadership" by Isabel Kushner
and Ben Hubbard NYT 10-7-20

Low in the polls, high on steroids, he could blow a gasket,
As he runs around the White House maskless.
He carelessly puts at risk his most devoted.
I could shoot someone on Fifth Avenue, he has been quoted.
He calls U.S. troops "losers and suckers".
Liberals are commie motherfuckers.
The caronavirus wipes out seniors furiously.
Think how much we'll save in Social Security.
10/11/20
Inspired by "Do Trump Supporters Disgust Him?"
by Mark Lebovich NYT Sunday Review 10-11-20

Truman's understanding of the world was limited.
The country went from experience to innocence.
Truman had been an artillery officer showing bravery.
At the same time, Roosevelt was assistant secretary of the Navy.
He knew the importance of the vast Arab lands.
Truman knew only the adulation of his Zionist fans,
Whom he badly needed to get elected.
Arab goodwill was not selected.
10/13/20
*Inspired by <u>Brokers of Deceit – How the U.S. Has
Undermined Peace in the Middle East</u> by Rashid Khalidi*

Truman listened most to people like himself,
Calculating always what politically would help.
Middle East strategy and national interest,
Were to winning elections a hindrance.
He didn't listen to the Pentagon or Department of State,
Who warned of decades of Arab hate.
He was impervious to advice from intelligence services.
He had a low opinion of international experts.
10/13/20
*Inspired by Brokers of Deceit – How the U.S. Has
Undermined Peace in the Middle East by Rashid Khalidi*

Truman did what was politic in domestic terms.
About Arab views he never wanted to learn.
Four American diplomats from Arab capitals,
Whose urgent concern was palpable,
Were kept waiting to meet him till after Election Day.
He would have lost Zionist votes the other way.
Because the diplomats pressed the Arab point of view,
Knowing what ignoring it would do.
10/14/20
*Inspired by Brokers of Deceit – How the U.S. Has
Undermined Peace in the Middle East by Rashid Khalidi*

Obama calls for the two-state solution.
Nitwityahoo treats him like a nuisance,
Although he should be grateful,
Because Obama dished out a plate full.
$38 billion over ten years will we give
So Palestinians will die and Israelis live.
It's the most generous deal ever.
Will Nitwityahoo reciprocate? Never.
9/15/16
PG 370th Posting 9/18/16
timothyjcallahan.blogspot.com

See the statistics of this warming planet,
Which cannot reproduce itself, can it?
See rising seas, freakish storms, and deadly droughts.
Republicans don't care what it's all about.
9/8/16
PG 369th Posting 9/1/16
timothyjcallahan.blogspot.com

Sunday, October 11, 2020
Poetry Group Five Hundred Eighty-Third Posting 10/11/20

Camp David provisions relating to Palestinian autonomy,
Were not implemented, which was no anomaly.
Reagan policymakers thought they could end this impasse,
But dealing with the Israelis was a grim task.
The carnage in Beirut ended with an American brokered ceasefire.
The Palestinians were ejected which was Israel's desire.
The Reagan Plan read more objectively the autonomy accords,
But on helping Palestinians, the Israelis shut the door.
This was not the first or last time America acquiesced
To Israel's perpetuation of the mess.
10/3/20
*Inspired by Brokers of Deceit – How the U.S. Has
Undermined Peace in the Middle East by Rashid Khalidi*

The wealthy aren't paying what they owe.
Our tax system doesn't tell them no.
Rental and proprietorship income and capital gains,
Full reporting the wealthy feign.
They have the most opportunity to shirk liability.
Shady deductions have new viability.
Cracking down on illegal tax evasion
Should be the first order of the next administration.
10/4/20
*Inspired by "Why the I.R.S. is Outgunned"
by Natasha Saren NYT Sunday Review 10-4-20*

Truman was the last president without a college education,
Ignorance contributed to his historic miscalculation.
Roosevelt promised the Saudi King that Palestinians
would be consulted.
Under Truman this is not what resulted.
He denied that Roosevelt had made Ibn Sa'ud any promise,
Until the State Department produced the correspondence.
Had FDR's pledges been scrupulously respected,
Middle East peace would have been effected.
10/5/20
*Inspired by _Brokers of Deceit – How the U.S. Has
Undermined Peace in the Middle East_ by Rashid Khalidi*

President Trump's Trumpublican administration,
Has been infected by its own misinformation.
The White House has become an infectious place,
But don't let the boss see you with a mask on your face.
Those in power don't just use language to lie.
They must act as if, even if they die.
Don't be afraid of Covid, Trump said,
Ignoring the 210,000 dead.
10/6/20
*Inspired by "A White House Infected with Propaganda"
Michelle Goldberg NYT Opinion 10-6-20*

He says he grabs women by the twat,
But only if they're hot.
He brags about sexual assault,
And says it's not his fault:
I'm like other alpha males,
When self-restraint fails.
10/12/16
*PG 374th Posting 10/16/16
timothyjcallahan.blogspot.com*

A yacht and a group of women
Hailed for Gaza but not for swimming.
They publicized the Israeli siege.
The media has quite a reach.
Israel will treat you rotten.
But, Gaza, you are not forgotten.
10/6/16
PG 373rd Posting 10/9/16
timothyjcallahan.blogspot.com

Betrayest thou the Son of Man with a kiss?
I so much more expected a hiss.
But Adam did kiss Eve
Before setting nature to grieve.
9/15/09
*Luke 22:48
PG 372nd Posting 10/2/16
timothyjcallahan.blogspot.com

Philoctetes reeked from a festering wound.
Nevertheless Greeks came for him in June.
The bleak war at Troy called for measures stark,
Like a stinking bowman who never misses his mark.
2/15/09
*Poems 6 and 7 from pp. 40,41 of
Poet Against Israel by Timothy J. Callahan
PG 372nd Posting 10/2/16
timothyjcallahan.blogspot.com

White supremacy has always rendered Blacks an afterthought,
Now and at our founding, when they were sold and bought.
At avoiding homicide charges, police are deft,
But they shot this woman to death while she slept!
Black people push the nation to be better stewards,
Of its ideal, about which it hasn't been prudent.
American justice is not on their side,
Stemming from the original divide.
9/26/20
*Inspired by "Breonna Taylor Deserved Justice"
by Melanye Price NYT OP-ED 9-25-20*

McConnell's unabashed hypocrisy and haste
By Democratic vengeance will be chased.
The District of Columbia and Puerto Rico will be states.
Four more liberal senators await.
The Supreme Court will be expanded too.
Social progress will continue true blue.
The filibuster will be a thing of the past.
The legislative accomplishments will be vast.
9/27/20
*Inspired by "America Is In Terrible Danger"
by Frank Bruni NYT Sunday Review 9-27-20*

Trump lost more than almost all tax-filing individuals.
Running losing businesses became habitual.
But business losses are a tax deduction,
Which gave his tax liability an extreme reduction.
Trump is in a tightening financial vise.
He has debts in the hundreds of millions in size.
The tax returns don't say who the creditors are.
Are we barred from thinking the debts are to the Czar?
9/28/20
*Inspired by "President's Taxes Chart Chronic Losses,
Audit battle And Income Tax Avoidance"
by Russ Buettner, Susanne Craig, and Mike McIntire
NYT 9-28-20

In 1950, the richest paid 70 percent of their income,
In taxes, and they could afford that sum.
But by 1980, they paid only 47 percent.
More money for the rich was what GOP meant.
They paid only 23 percent in 2018.
Keeping that much money is mean.
This is an indictment of the income tax system,
Yet Republicans preach that greed is not Christian.
9/29/20
*Inspired by "The Picture of a Broken Tax System"
Editorial NYT 9-29-20

The rich get richer while the IRS gets smaller.
That leaves the rich with billions of uncollected dollars.
Republicans have slashed funding for the IRS.
Of tax law enforcement, there has been less.
Restore funding and update collection techniques.
We could squeeze a trillion from rich deadbeats.
Republicans want the rich to pay as little as they can,
Legally or underhand.
9/30/20
*Inspired by "The Picture of a Broken Tax System"
Editorial NYT 9-29-20*

The official name of Plan Dalet was the Yehoshua plan,
The Zionist master plan to cleanse the land.
Blow up the villages and plant mines in the rubble.
If they sneak back, our kill rate could double.
10/24/16
*Inspired by The Ethnic Cleansing of Palestine
by Ilan Pappe
PG 376th Posting 10/30/16
timothyjcallahan.blogspot.com*

Destroy a neighborhood and we make an impression.
That was one of Ben-Gurion's lessons.
Destroy the houses systematically.
Make your point emphatically.
The Palestinians who survive
Will run for their lives.
Do this hundreds of times,
And we will own Palestine.
10/20/16
*Inspired by "The Ethnic Cleansing of Palestine"
by Ilan Pappe
PG 375th Posting 10/23/16
timothyjcallahan.blogspot.com*

Palestinian statehood should precede
Normalization (all the Arabs agreed),
Which two Arab states no longer heed.
They are traitors to the cause in deed.
They and Trump treat Palestinians with contempt.
From fairness America has always been exempt.
The Palestinian struggle is a historical one,
Just as Israel is Zionism's son.
9/19/20
Inspired by "Trump's Middle Eastern Mirage"
by Roger Cohen NYT Opinion 9-19-20

My base will risk their lives to vote,
I'm betting most Democrats won't.
We have to stop people voting by mail.
The mail-in ballots plot must fail.
We must know the results on the night of the election.
Ballots on hand after that will face rejection.
Meanwhile, Kanye will have siphoned votes from Biden,
Thus improving my victory margin.
9/20/20
Inspired by "Taxes. Wives. Votes. It's All the
Same to Trump"by Frank Bruni NYT Sunday Review
9-20-20

Evangelicals support Israel's broadest land claims.
For the Abraham Accords, Trump should be ashamed.
Israel was finally about to annex
Land with which Palestinians thought they were blessed.
Trump and his Muslims made Bibi postpone
The Will of God on His Holy Throne.
Pray God send not a curse upon our nation.
Trump has always tried God's patience.
9/21/20
*Inspired by "Ad Depicts Trump as a Peacemaker to
Sway U.S. Jews and Evangelicals" by Michael Crowley
NYT 9-21-20*

Republicans want to jam through a nominee,
As much as that would be an anomaly.
They want to control the court for a generation.
Social progress will undergo a degradation.
Conservative ideas would have the advantage.
We would lose rights we have taken for granted.
The right believes in white minority rule.
Stacking the court is but one of their tools.
9/21/20
*Inspired by "Conservatives Try to Lock In Power"
by Charles M. Blow NYT Opinion 9-21-20*

The next president ought to make this appointment.
Republicans thought Mitch's words poignant.
The Senate does not confirm nominees in an election year.
From that new rule Republicans will never veer.
Why would we deny the voters a chance to weigh in?
Reverse ourselves, and they'd call us hypocrites again.
Our view is this: Give the people a voice.
Let the election reflect the people's choice.
9/23/20
*Inspired by "An Op-Ed From the Republicans of 2016"
by Stuart A. Thompson NYT OP-ED 9-23-20
Line 1 by Mitch McConnell; Line 3 by Ted Cruz;
Line 5 by Tom Cotton; Line 7 by Mitch McConnell

The "second Holocaust" awaiting the Jewish state
Was a myth to cover Jewish hate
The aggressor Jews were never in danger.
They were the Palestine rearrangers.
11/24/16
PG 380th Posting 11/27/16
timothyjcallahan.blogspot.com

You're the man who owns me.
You're the stone that hones me.
What would I be without you?
That only my gods knew.
6/2/09
PG 339th Posting 11/20/16
timothyjcallahan.blogspot.com
*Poems 6 and 7 from
Poet Against Israel by Timothy J. Callahan

It's more deadly than even your strenuous flus.
That's why I created my own public ruse.
I wanted to always play it down.
Anyone who wears a mask is a clown.
Just stay calm I say; it will go away.
All my evangelicals pray every day.
Don't believe your lying eyes.
I will win a Nobel prize.
9/13/20
Inspired by "Trump's Deliberate Caronavirus Deception"
by Michelle Goldberg NYT Sunday Review 9-13-20

In his first two years, Obama took pro-Palestinian stances,
But Republicans and the lobby ruined peace's chances.
Obama was pressured into a humiliating retreat.
His 2011 U.N. speech showed the retreat was complete.
It was the most pro-Israel speech Israel could have wanted,
Full of standard Israeli tropes on the conflict.
In 2012 he met for hours with Nitwityahoo about Iran.
The subject of peace with the Palestinians was banned.
In his reelection campaign, Obama was Israel's servant,
Trying to win over the Israel supporters so fervent.
9/14/20
Inspired by Brokers of Deceit – How the U.S. Has
Undermined Peace in the Middle East by Rashid Khalidi

Trump boasts he has achieved peace in the Middle East,
But he hasn't achieved peace in the least.
He has joined three little monsters in unholy matrimony,
Who were already cooperating and cozy.
Peace will only come with a sovereign Palestinian state.
The sellout of these Gulf states means we have longer to wait.
With Israel, the Arabs swore not to normalize relations,
Until the creation of a Palestine nation.
9/15/20
*Inspired by "Trump to Host Ceremony Celebrating Mideast Deals"
NYT*

A black day in the history of the people of Palestine,
Four Zionist nations proclaimed the occupation is fine.
It wasn't conflict resolution, and it won't bring peace.
It was a business deal not helping Palestinians in the least.
The Arabs should isolate Israel until it gives back,
The land it stole in the 1967 surprise attack.
Peace in the Mideast is a delusion,
Without the two-state solution.
9/16/20
*Inspired by "Israel Cements Diplomatic Links To 2 Arab States"
by Michael Crowley NYT 9-16-20*

The world must impose Palestine on the West Bank.
For 9/11, we have the greedy "settlers" to thank.
They think a supernatural being gave them Arab land.
Their selfish delusions are grand.
They inspire terrorism, but they don't care.
Only the world can make them share.
If this is done, the squatters will pout.
Their god tells them other people don't count.
9/16/20
*Inspired by "Love Triangle Spawns Peace Deal in Mideast"
by Thomas L. Friedman NYT OP-ED 9-16-20*

He supports the Zionist greed men.
His name is David Friedman.
He is the opposite of a liberal.
He's our next ambassador to Israel.
He flouts decades of American policy.
He will betray the American polity.
12/18/16
PG 384th Posting 12/25/16
timothyjcallahan.blogspot.com

Acquiring territory by war is inadmissible.
Israelis make Palestinians miserable.
Sick of Israeli greed and hate?
End the conflict with two states.
"Settlements" beyond the '67 borders
Contravene U.N. orders.
Israelis are assiduous
In killing the indigenous.
11/29/16
**Inspired by "America Must Recognize Palestine"*
by Jimmy Carter NYT OPED 11/29/16
PG 381st Posting 12/4/16
timothyjcallahan.blogspot.com

Thousands of Afghan women have assumed public roles.
Women doing what they want is one of their goals.
But all their achievements will be erased,
When the Taliban returns to govern that place.
Women will be confined to their homes.
The ways of the Taliban are well known.
They will rape women and whip them in the street.
If women show their hair, they will get beat.
They will get the rights of women granted by Islam,
Which means all they can be is a wife and mom.
9/6/20
Inspired by "Far Beyond 2001, but fearing its return"
by David Zuchino and Fatima Faizi NYT 9-6-20

The so-called "peace process" disguises an ugly reality:
The so-called "search for peace" has been a fallacy.
Don't you think that some time in the past half century,
A Palestinian state would have made its entry?
The U.S. pressures Palestinians to obey
The dictates of their oppressor in every way.
America could not do a Palestine nation,
So it engaged in conflict perpetuation.
9/7/20
Inspired by <u>Brokers of Deceit – How the U.S. Has</u>
<u>Undermined Peace in the Middle East</u> by Rashid Khalidi

Avoid disputes with our potent ally Israel.
To do otherwise makes politicians miserable.
Reluctance to engage Israel over Palestine,
Explains the half century waste of time.
Israel's friends are influential and prickly.
They ensure that peace will not come quickly.
The best we can do is conflict management.
To try to do more means political banishment.
9/8/20
*Inspired by Brokers of Deceit – How the U.S. Has
Undermined Peace in the Middle East by Rashid Khalidi*

Palestine must be sovereign without qualification.
Reverse Israeli occupation and colonization.
Israel needs justice and equity permeation.
Give Palestinians self-determination.
Palestinian refugees and their descendants
Have a just grievance, mend it.
We had had since 1967,
The means to avoid 9/11.
9/9/20
*Inspired by Brokers of Deceit – How the U.S. Has
Undermined Peace in the Middle East by Rashid Khalidi*

Trump's plan was heavily slanted in Israel's favor.
Maybe Biden will be the Palestinians' savior.
Despots abandon the Arab Peace Initiative of 2002,
Which for peace required things for Israel to do.
UAE and Bahrain legitimize the occupation,
To improve their Zionist relations.
The world should impose Palestine.
Biden should say fine.
9/12/20
*Inspired by "Bahrain Moves to Normalize Ties to Israel"
by Michael Crowley and David M. Halbfinger NYT 9-12-20

Pray away the gay is consumer fraud.
For the New Jersey Judge I applaud.
Homosexuality is not a disorder
Within New Jersey's borders.
2/16/15
*PG 258th Posting 2/22/15
timothyjcallahan.blogspot.com

Feel not compelled to breed like rabbits.
Drop sex and find new habits.
Don't ask the church for birth control.
Just keep that thing out of the hole.
Overpopulation hurts the poor.
But no birth control forevermore.
The Vatican is not malleable.
The Pope is infallible.
1/28/15
*Inspired by "Be Fruitful, Not Bananas"
by Frank Bruni NYT Sunday Review 1/25/15
*PG 285th Posting 2/1/15
timothyjcallahan.blogspot.com

Sunday, September 6, 2020
Poetry Group Five Hundred Seventy-Eighth Posting 9/6/20

Kyle shot to death two people and wounded a third.
From his idol, President Trump, he had gotten the word:
When the looting starts, the shooting starts,
As much as that breaks my heart.
To surrender to police, Kyle tried his best.
Gun across his chest, he was too white to arrest.
The right sees him as a symbol of self-defense.
Their praise of him will have a bad consequence.
More armed militiamen will attend protests,
On their lethal, Trump-inspired quest.
8/30/20
*Inspired by "Kenosha Shows Where the GOP Is Headed"
 by Jamelle Bouie NYT Sunday Review 8-30-20*

Facebook's algorithm rewards sensational, false content.
Billions of people view medical nonsense.
Facebook bolsters distrust in science and medicine.
GreenMedInfo and RealFarmacy should be jettisoned.
Facebook enables these charlatans to thrive.
It cares more about profit than viewers' lives.
Doctors' ability to counsel and provide care
Is diminished by misinformation from you know where.
8/31/20
*Inspired by "Hoaxes Are Making Doctor's Jobs Harder"
by Seema Yasmin and Craig Spencer NYT Sunday Review 8-30-20*

Full Palestinian statehood was Obama's motivation.
He said "settlement" building must end before negotiation.
The state was to be drawn roughly along the '67 frontier.
This is what previous presidents had wanted for years.
Obama wanted to abide by U.N. Resolution 242,
Defining what was fair to Palestinians and Jews.
But Republicans, the Israel lobby, and Nitwityahoo
Made sure the peace plan would not go through.
9/1/20
*Inspired by <u>BROKERS OF DECEIT – How the U.S. Has
Undermined Peace in the Middle East</u> by Rashid Khalidi*

The sellout Emiratis rolled out the red carpet,
For a planeload of Zionists, including Jared.
The message to the Palestinians was drop dead,
With the Israelis we are now in bed.
We no longer care whether you get a state.
Israel will always control your fate.
More riches we Emiratis need.
Like the Zionists, we know greed.
9/2/20
*Inspired by "In Symbolic First, Israeli Airliner Completes
Direct Flight to the U.A.E." by David M. Halbfinger NYT 9-1-20*

It's hard to fight white supremacy when the president incites it.
Stopping violence is impossible because Trump invites it.
Right-wing extremists think what they do is permissible.
Of Kyle Rittenhouse, Trump is not critical.
The militia movement seeks a second civil war,
Racism is at the movement's core.
Trump promotes civil unrest.
As inciter, he wants to be best.
The Tree of Life massacre wasn't just a blip.
White nationalists have been tightening their grip.
9/4/20
*Inspired by "Biden Condemns Violence. Why Won't Trump?"
by Michelle Goldberg NYT Opinion 9-1-20*

Devoid of penological purpose,
The death penalty is the worst.
The penalty cannot be reversed.
The person is not preserved.
He will never know the heavenliness
Of exculpatory DNA evidence.
4/1/15
*PG 295th Posting 4/12/15
timothyjcallahan.blogspot.com*

The answer to the gun problem is more guns.
When we say guns, we mean tons.
More people packing is the solution.
We can save lives by more shooting.
4/1/15
*PG 295th Posting 4/12/15
timothyjcallahan.blogspot.com*

Pastor gets ugly when he speaks of wickedness.
About sin he has a bitterness.
He shouts and trembles.
The devil he resembles.
3/24/15
*PG 293rd Posting 3/29/15
timothyjcallahan.blogspot.com

Sunday, August 30, 2020
Poetry Group Five Hundred Seventy Seventh Posting 8/30/20

We never lost the Trump supporters' credence,
In our scam to monetize their grievance.
Every penny raised will go toward wall construction.
A lie like that takes an abundance of gumption.
The president gave We Build the Wall his blessing.
About him I may soon be confessing,
Unless he signals that I'll be pardoned.
About avoiding prison I am ardent.
8/23/20
*Inspired by "Trumpism's a Racket. Steve
Bannon Knew it" by Michelle Goldberg
NYT Sunday Review 8-23-20

State needs to act above American politics,
But in Israel the Secretary loves to frolic.
Pompeo filmed a video on a rooftop in Jerusalem,
Meant to stir up evangelical enthusiasm.
Tune in to the Republican Convention tonight;
You will see him do something not right.
Mixing diplomacy and politics is taboo.
Republicans think that is no longer true.
Israel as a bipartisan issue is dead.
No more annexation Joe said.
8/25/20
*Inspired by "Mingling Partisan Politics and Diplomacy
In Israel" by Isabel Kershner and David D. Kirkpatrick
NYT 8-25-20*

The United States had long insisted,
That two separate states be listed,
And that Jerusalem be decided in negotiation.
A lasting peace was always the motivation.
But now Trump has given the city away.
Palestinians plan a capital on the eastern half someday.
Trump's "peace plan" makes the world miserable,
Because it's so biased toward Israel.
8/25/20
*Inspired by "Mingling Partisan Politics and Diplomacy
In Israel" by Isabel Kershner and David D. Kirkpatrick
NYT 8-25-20*

If only John Milton could write this poem for me,
Or if William Wordsworth could tell the story.
What I saw on MSNBC was a revolution:
Two bright people promoting the two-state solution.
Joy Reid and Susan Rice openly spoke
Of the aspirations of Palestinian folk.
I hope that night was MSNBC's start
Of coverage of an issue close to my heart.
8/28/20

The Palestinians of Gaza are inflicted,
With Egyptian and Israeli restrictions,
On the movement of people and goods,
Which ruined Gaza as they knew it would.
High unemployment and widespread poverty
Since 1948 have not been a novelty.
Israel must permit the building of an industrial zone,
And facilitate the flow of electricity to Gazan homes.
Israel must allow the export and import
Of goods and services of all sort.
Israel must end its procrastination
And fulfill its obligations.
8/28/20
*Inspired by "Gaza Goes Under Lockdown After
First Cases of Local Transmission" by Adam Rasgon
and Iyad Abuheweila NYT 8-27-20*

Republicans like to skip science.
In the supernatural, they place their reliance.
Injecting politics into science can be fatal.
That happens when Trump doesn't like the data.
He ties treatment approval to political considerations.
Chloroquine and convalescent plasma are two iterations.
"I'm not concerned with efficacy or safety.
I just want the rubes to reelect me!"
8/28/20
*Inspired by "Politicizing Science Will Cost Lives"
Editorial NYT 8-25-20*

My free will militated
Against becoming religiously affiliated.
Yet here is the distasteful twist:
I must respect what does not exist.
5/12/15
*PG 300th Posting 5/17/15
timothyjcallahan.blogspot.com*

Sunday, August 23, 2020
Poetry Group Five Hundred Seventy-Sixth Posting 8/23/20

Was Nitwityahoo's promise of annexation,
Nothing but a useful prevarication,
To keep the "settlers" and the rest of the right,
On his side in his Supreme Court fight?
He would say, no, I have only postponed,
My picking of the West Bank's bones.
Even before my charges are beaten,
On all of Judea, we will be feasting.
Palestinians will get a scraggly, patchwork "state",
Surrounded by increasing "settlers" who hate.
8/17/20
*Inspired by "Geopolitical Earthquake Hits the Mideast"
by Thomas L. Friedman NYT, Opinion 8-14-20*

UAE gives Israel international acceptance,
While ignoring any lasting peace's essence:
For a sovereign Palestinian state,
How long must the world wait?
A state of Palestine should be imposed.
The arguments of Zionists should be closed.
Save the world from future terror attacks.
Give the Palestinians some of their land back.
8/17/20
*Inspired by "Rarity for Region – Annexing on Hold in the West Bank"
by Peter Baker, Isabel Kershner, David D. Kirkpatrick,
and Ronen Bergman NYT 8-14-20*

Trump could win another term in office.
Wouldn't that be awful?
Biden could win the popular vote far and away,
But the Electoral College could grant Trump a majority.
Enough of his base is concentrated in swing states.
A minority of voters could determine the race.
Trump suppresses the opposition in places
Where enough of his base is.
8/18/20
*Inspired by "Trump Is Going for a Technical Knockout"
by Jamelle Bouie NYT OP-ED 8-5-20*

Now Israel can normalize relations
With Arab and Islamic nations,
And still maintain its brutal occupation,
Of the betrayed Palestinian population.
Now Israel will build more "settlements" and roads,
Consolidating its West Bank control,
And trying to make the two-state solution moot.
Creeping annexation is the appointed route.
8/19/20
*Inspired by "'Nobody Buys It': Palestinians see
Israel-UAE Deal as Betrayal" by Isabel Kershner
and Adam Rasgon NYT 8-15-20*

Israel and the UAE have their first lovers' spat.
UAE suddenly smells a rat.
Israel was to relinquish some of its technological edge,
At least that is what Trump and Kushner said.
F-35s and advanced armed drones
Would no longer be for Israel alone.
Israel wants to keep its qualitative military edge,
To maintain which the U.S. Congress has pledged.
8/22/20
*Inspired by 'Trump Presses Weapons Sale to The U.A.E."
by Mark Mazzetti and Edward Wong NYT 8-20-20

He speaks stream of consciousness speak.
For content he does not dig deep.
He is thinking out loud
To the delight of the crowd.
8/22/15
*PG 315th Posting 8/30/15
timothyjcallahan.blogspot.com

The collective punishment of immigrants,
In his prefrontal lobe simmering,
Is coming to the United States,
Thanks to a huge ego filled with hate.
6/20/15
*PG 314th Posting 8/23/15
timothyjcallahan.blogspot.com

No community spread in the blockaded Gaza Strip.
In or out, it's hard to make the trip.
Permits to visit Israel are even harder to get.
Gazans have waited but haven't gotten them yet.
Travel restrictions on Americans are more liberal
For family events they fly in and out of Israel.
Under the virus guise, Israel tightens Gaza closure.
No more Israel or West Bank sojourns.
Israeli hate brought about Gaza's sad fate.
One-third of Gazans wish they could emigrate.
8/10/20
*Inspired by "Covid-19 Spares Gaza, But Travel Restrictions
Prove Less Forgiving" by Adam Rasgon and Iyad Abuheweila
NYT 8-8-20*

As Israel has gone from victory to victory,
Palestinians have been shattered as a social entity.
They confront profound existential anxiety,
Rooted in their experiences this past century.
Yet Israel's phony angst is emphasized.
With Palestinians, America can't empathize.
Israel's quest for security is paramount.
Yet only Palestinian security is in doubt.
Israel has made the Palestinians miserable.
Its lobby keeps the process invisible.
8/11/20
*Inspired by Brokers of Deceit – How the U.S. has
Undermined Peace in the Middle East by Rashid Khalidi*

Israeli soldiers let Palestinians through barrier breaches,
So Arabs could enjoy themselves on Israel's beaches.
Beachgoers returning at night after a wonderful day,
Found that the soldiers had illuminated their way.
For many Palestinians, this was only the first time
They stood in Mediterranean Sea sunshine.
Yesterday, Israel shut it all down,
But those soldiers deserve renown.
8/12/20
*Inspired by "Israel Briefly Relaxes Border Rules, Letting
Palestinians Visit Beach" by Adam Rasgon and
Mohammed Najib NYT 8-12-20*

The deal was overhyped by both sides.
(Notice that Palestinians were not one of the sides.)
The UAE already was normalizing relations,
Despite the contrary sentiments of its population.
Nitwityahoo already was barred from annexing,
Because his junior partner Gantz is against it.
UAE broke the Arab peace plan and got nothing for it.
The Palestinians have a plight; it's okay for Israel to ignore it.
8/15/20
*Inspired by "Netanyahu Swerves, Eyeing Legacy"
by David M. Halbfinger NYT 8-14-2020*

Most Arab states are controlled by undemocratic regimes,
Subservient and eager to stay on the U.S. team,
And ever desirous of Israeli approval.
The leaders undergo a backbone removal.
But the Arab people revere the Palestinians,
Even though Arab leaders are servile idiots.
Palestinians must appeal over the heads of those leaders,
To the millions of sympathizers beneath them.
6/30/20
*Inspired by The Hundred Years' War on Palestine
by Rashid Khalidi

The Palestine flag will fly at the U.N.
(The U.S. voted against Palestine again.)
The U.N. adds legitimacy to their aspirations.
Palestinians have resisted Israel for the duration.
The Palestinians are tenacious.
They deserve self-determination.
9/11/15
*PG 317th Posting 9/13/15
timothyjcallahan.blogspot.com

People want to enlarge their lives
By buying guns and knives,
And to fight and die for a cause.
They want to make their bullets yours.
People feel more powerful with guns.
Especially with the bigger ones.
7/29/15
*PG 311th Posting 8/2/15
timothyjcallahan.blogspot.com

Sunday, August 9, 2020
Poetry Group Five Hundred Seventy-Fourth Posting 8/9/20

A boost in her public estimation Hillary needed,
Then under fire for various alleged misdeeds.
So that desperation was the urgent reason,
She sat next to Chelsea and Elie Wiesel
At Bill's State of the Union Address
At the Capitol in 1996.
7/31/20
*Inspired by <u>The Holocaust Industry – Reflections on the
Exploitation of Jewish Suffering</u> by Norman G. Finkelstein*

Why can't America give the Palestinians some help?
Because "Israeli security" comes before everything else.
The human rights of others and international law
By the wayside must fall.
"Israeli security" is endlessly expansive
Permeating small things and massive.
Generator parts cannot be shipped to the Gaza Strip
Nor can cement make that trip.
Will poor villages be allowed to have water cisterns?
On "Israeli security" that question turns.
8/1/20
*Inspired by <u>Brokers of Deceit – How the U.S. has
Undermined Peace in the Middle East</u> by Rashid Khalidi*

The more voters, the more likely we are to lose.
I've learned that every system can be abused.
The U.S. Postal Service will not be up to the task,
Of delivering ballots from first to last when asked.
Mail-in voting is subject to fraud and should be abolished.
So should a lot of liberal so-called knowledge.
My base will risk their lives to vote.
I'm betting Democrats won't.
8/2/20

Thousands of Israelis have taken to the streets
To oust Nitwityahoo from his undeserved seat.
He should not rule while facing corruption charges.
Of all Israeli thieves, his take was the largest.
For bribery, fraud, and breach of trust,
People call him "Crime Minister" in disgust.
His handling of the caronavirus has been miserable.
For many reasons, he is not good for Israel,
Nor for the U.S. and the rest of the world.
Too much terrorism inspiration have we heard.
8/5/20
*Inspired by "Thousands Demonstrate as Anti-Netanyahu
Protests Gain Steam" by The Associated Press NYT 8-1-2020

The Israeli guard shot the Eritrean man,
Who had picked the wrong place to stand.
The Israeli guard thought the man a terrorist.
Investigation proved he never was.
What he was though was black.
That's a color that attracts attack.
If only he could have turned himself white.
He'd be alive with his family tonight.
International observers Israel needs
To deter its cowardly misdeeds.
10/20/15
*PG 323rd Posting 10/25/15
timothyjcallahan.blogspot.com

Human caused climate change is here.
Let's not argue that another year.
Settled science is not controversial.
Teach climate change on TV commercials
10/12/2015
*PG 322nd Posting 10/18/15
timothyjcallahan.blogspot.com

Trump says vaccines should be dumped,
Including the one for mumps:
"Autism comes from vaccines.
And pediatricians are mean."
9/18/15
*PG 318th Posting 9/20/15
timothyjcallahan.blogspot.com

Sunday, August 2, 2020
Poetry Group Five Hundred Seventy-Third Posting 8/2/20

Yo ho ho and a bottle of rum.
I smell the blood of a non-English woman.
Me thinks thou art a fucking bitch,
But please to the rest of Congress don't snitch.
A.O.C. wasn't raised to take abuse from men.
She took to the House floor and humiliated him then.
Another woman might have let his sexist remarks slide.
Mr. Yoho wished he had some place to hide.
7/27/20
*Inspired by "A.O.C. and the Jurassic Jerks"
by Maureen Dowd NYT Sunday Review 7-26-20*

Between 1891 and 1911, ten million Africans died.
Belgian exploitation of Congo was why.
Ivory and rubber resources
Were capitalism's main courses.
The project was labor intensive,
But labor was not expensive.
Workers were worked to death,
Replaced at their last breath.
Only one scholarly book bears this out.
Holocaust studies in the thousands are counted.
7/27/20
*Inspired by The Holocaust Industry – Reflections on the
Exploitation of Jewish Suffering by Norman G. Finkelstein
The book mentioned in line 9 is King Leopold's Ghost
by Adam Hochschild (Boston:1998)*

To enact sterilization laws, the Nazis were not hesitant.
They explicitly invoked the U.S. precedent.
Thousands of Americans had been involuntarily sterilized.
Here was a policy the Nazis thought wise.
The Nuremburg Laws stripped Jews of the franchise,
And forbade miscegenation between Jewish and non-Jewish lives.
Long under similar disabilities were southern U.S. Blacks.
For American precedents, the Nazis did not lack.
7/28/20
*Inspired by The Holocaust Industry – Reflections on the
Exploitation of Jewish Suffering by Norman G. Finkelstein

The Nazi holocaust's abnormality springs not from the event itself,
But from the exploitative industry it spawned with Jewish help.
A crime need not be aberrant to warrant atonement,
Which in any case should be begun without postponement.
Restore the Nazi holocaust as a rational subject of inquiry.
It became a scheme lacking all purity.
7/28/20
*Inspired by The Holocaust Industry – Reflections on the
Exploitation of Jewish Suffering by Norman G. Finkelstein

The Holocaust industry's expert connivers
Shook down European countries and Jewish survivors.
In August 2000, the WJC announced with elation,
That it stood to amass $9 billion in Holocaust compensation,
Which was extracted in the name of needy Holocaust victims.
But to receive the money, the WJC didn't pick them.
It said the monies belonged to "the Jewish people as a whole".
And that the WJC was "the Jewish people as a whole".
7/29/20
*Inspired by The Holocaust Industry – Reflections on the
Exploitation of Jewish Suffering by Norman G. Finkelstein
The WJC is the World Jewish Congress

To avoid 51 counts of racketeering, violating sanctions, and tax evasion,
Billionaire Marc Rich took a long Swiss vacation.
He became a major benefactor of Jewish and Israeli groups.
The head of the ADL was one of his best paid dupes.
In fact, Foxman initiated the idea of a pardon.
Clinton did grant Rich a pardon, and it was a large one.
Ehud Barak and Shimon Peres also had Clinton's ear,
As did Rabbi Irving Greenberg so revered.
7/29/20
*Inspired by <u>The Holocaust Industry — Reflections on the
Exploitation of Jewish Suffering</u> by Norman G. Finkelstein
The ADL is the Anti-Defamation League*

If Trump cared about the defacement of that Portland courthouse,
He could have the graffiti removed right now.
To change the Covid subject, Trump welcomes street clashes.
He sends in unmarked feds to stoke the passions.
Trump's provocations are seeding the violence
Black Lives Matter protesters will not be silenced.
But every time something burns down,
President Trump gains ground.
 7/31/20
*Inspired by "Help me Find Trump's 'Anarchists' in Portland"
by Nicholas Kristof NYT Opinion 7-30-20*

Israeli bullets give us solidarity.
We move about East Jerusalem warily.
The land upon which we live and die
Is by Zionist Israel occupied.
Some youths fight to Kingdom Come.
They become schooled in martyrdom.
12/17/15
*PG 331st Posting 12/20/15
timothyjcallahan.blogspot.com*

Tonight I am nonsymptomatic.
Don't bother locking me in the attic.
I will be of no harm.
No hair covering my arms.
Tonight the moon is new,
And I can be with you.
10/23/15
*PG 323rd Posting 10/25/15
timothyjcallahan.blogspot.com

Sunday, July 26, 2020
Poetry Group Five Hundred Seventy-Second Posting 7/26/20

When something is not right, not just, not fair,
Say something if you dare.
Will this be the beating that leaves me paralyzed?
Looking into the troopers' eyes, John saw he was despised.
When ordered to disperse, the marchers would not.
Mr. Lewis's skull was cracked and so were a lot.
Televised images of billy club cracks
Galvanized support for the Voting Rights Act,
Which Johnson signed into law five months later.
John was an agitator, a real troublemaker.
 7/20/20
*Inspired by "Civil Rights Icon Turned Conscience of Congress"
by Katherine Q. Seelye NYT 7-19-20

The Holocaust dogma of eternal Gentile hatred
Means the Holocaust was climactic and fated.
This complements the Holocaust dogma of uniqueness.
Drawing comparisons shows weakness.
The persecution of non-Jews was merely accidental.
The suffering of the Gypsies was not consequential.
The oppression of others historically has been episodic.
But the persecution of Jews is always chronic.
So Israel can do whatever it sees fit,
Much of which is illegit.
7/21/20
*Inspired by *The Holocaust Industry — Reflections on the
Exploitation of Jewish Suffering* by Norman G. Finkelstein*

Before we had a museum on the Washington Mall,
Commemorating slavery, Jim Crow and all,
There was a Holocaust museum there.
To African Americans, was that fair?
Before we commemorated Native American suffering,
There was a Holocaust museum about another thing.
The Nazi holocaust was not an American crime.
So why did that museum come first in time?
7/22/20
*Inspired by *The Holocaust Industry — Reflections on the
Exploitation of Jewish Suffering* by Norman G. Finkelstein*

I heard Rachel Maddow say "Middle East peace,"
On one of her shows this week.
The camel's nose is under the tent.
The Israel lobby will make her repent.
Even for her off-hand remark,
They'll be all over her like narcs.
7/22/20

Crime among Palestinians is not an Israeli priority.
Concern for Arabs is not in Jewish biology.
About cooperation, the Israelis were teasing.
They hinder Palestinian Authority policing.
They only care about counter-terrorism operations.
For those the Palestinians got cooperation.
However, now they no longer want it.
Israel is about to step-up the conflict.
7/24/20
*Inspired by "Much at Stake For Palestinians on Police Force"
by David M. Halbfinger, Adam Rasgon and Mohammed Najib

I have no boat, so I will take
The path of sunbeams across the lake.
Wet texture sets sunshine aglitter.
The flecks of orange have the jitters.
2/10/14
*PG 253rd Posting 2/16/14
timothyjcallahan.blogspot.com

Nebuchadnezzar ate grass as do oxen.
His slender wife turned into a dachshund.
They forgot that God is all seeing,
And knocks sinners down The Great Chain of Being.
1/31/14
*PG 254th Posting 2/9/14
timothyjcallahan.blogspot.com

Violence is as American as cherry pie.
Guns are available for anyone to buy.
When TV talks of another shooting,
I grab the remote and quick mute it.
Will America always be like this?
As long as we have too many guns, yes.
11/7/13
*Line 1 by H Rap Brown
*PG 225th Posting 12/8/13
timothyjcallahan.blogspot.com

Sunday, July 19, 2020
Poetry Group Five Hundred Seventy-First Posting 7/19/20

Jewish groups need Israel as a victim of cruel Arab attacks.
For such an Israel, one can get support, donors, greenbacks.
As American Jews enjoyed greater success secularly,
They moved steadily to the right politically.
Complementing the rightward turn was an inward turn.
Alliances among the have-nots were burned.
Resources were earmarked for Jewish concerns only.
Jewish affinity for Blacks is phony.
When the Movement began demanding economic reform,
The reception among Jewish Americans was not warm.
7/11/20
*Inspired by _The Holocaust Industry – Reflections on the
Exploitation of Jewish Suffering_ by Norman G. Finkelstein

The Republican Party became a personality cult.
President Joe Biden will be the result.
Trumpublicans intend to go down with the ship.
The only honorable Republican is Mitt.
Never Trumpers want Trump defeated.
After that they won't be needed.
But what if Trumpism survives Trump's presidency?
The Never Trumpers should disband hesitantly.
7/12/20

Should women be able to have sex without risking pregnancy?
Unwanted pregnancies will be the court's legacy.
The justices eroded the birth control mandate under the ACA.
For contraceptives some poor women will have to pay.
State interference with personal health decisions
Is the court's and Trump's holy mission.
Reproductive rights should be personal, not political,
And not subject to nuns who are critical.
7/13/20
*Inspired by "Birth Control Access Is Curtailed, Again"
Editorial, and by "Sex, Sisters and Dr Donald"
Opinion by Gail Collins NYT 7-9-20

Mueller's team convicted Stone for covering up
For the corrupt Donald J. Trump,
Who had the bald temerity
To grant Stone clemency.
Does he think we cannot see,
The obvious conspiracy?
But the Trumpublicans bury their heads.
With or without him, they are dead.
7/14/20

Holocaust "uniqueness" serves as Israel's prize alibi.
Its claims on other nations cannot be denied.
Special people consider themselves specially threatened,
And this America will not soon be forgetting.
What Israel deems necessary for survival,
America will never deny it.
Right now that's four billion dollars a year,
Plus tax free private donations to Israel so dear.
7/17/20
*Inspired by The Holocaust Industry – Reflections on the
Exploitation of Jewish Suffering by Norman G. Finkelstein

From everlasting to everlasting,
Guns will be blasting.
From ammunition to ammunition,
Shooters are anti-musicians.
From target to target,
Like a person or a varmint.
All hail the almighty gun,
That gives all power to anyone.
5/19/14
*PG 259th Posting 5/25/14
timothyjcallahan.blogspot.com

You don't have to be anti-Semitic to be anti-Zionist.
I back the Palestinians out of Irishness.
I hate Israelis for what they do,
Not because they are Jews.
4/16/14
*PG 245th Posting 4/20/14
timothyjcallahan.blogspot.com

Floridians may shoot whomever they fear.
The judge and jury will say, get out of here:
That victim must have really scared you.
It's the jury's opinion that he dared you.
2/24/14
*PG 237th Posting 3/2/14
timothyjcallahan.blogspot.com

Sunday, July 12, 2020
Poetry Group Five Hundred Seventieth Posting 7/12/20

The universalist message of Bruno Bettelheim
Resonated with Jews and gentiles just fine.
But after the '67 war, unique Jewish suffering
Was not allowed to be compared to any other thing.
Unique suffering confers unique entitlement,
And Israel obviously was heaven sent.
Elie Wiesel became The Holocaust interpreter.
Israel could be a war crime perpetrator.
The Holocaust became a powerful tool.
Deference to Israel became the rule.
7/4/20
*Inspired by _The Holocaust Industry – Reflections on the
Exploitation of Jewish Suffering_ by Norman G. Finkelstein

An arbitrary and superficial selection of traits
Became the basis of racism and hate.
Traits that would be neutral in the abstract
Were used as excuses to enslave people in fact.
Africans were profitably regarded as inferior,
Because of irrelevant differences in their exterior.
African Americans are stigmatized
So they can be dehumanized.
7/5/20
*Inspired by "America's Enduring Caste System"
by Isabel Wilkerson NYT Magazine 7-5-20

Trump insists that Nitwityahoo get Gantz to agree,
Before unilateral annexation can be.
Gantz is against it, but will he hold out?
He has already broken the no partnership vow.
Trump wants Gantz to help him cover his ass,
Because people will die when annexation comes to pass.
Gantz says everything but the Covid response must wait.
This makes Trump and Nitwityahoo irate.
7/8/20
*Inspired by "West Bank Annexation Window Opens, but
Netanyahu Remains Quiet" by David M. Halbfinger
NYT 7-2-20

Was Bibi's annexation promise a ruse,
Just more cynical electoral abuse?
He did get a lot of religious right wing votes,
From religious Zionists most gross.
He diverted attention from his corruption trial,
About which the right is in denial.
But he hasn't talked to security officials on the scene
About what unilateral annexation would mean.
7/10/20
*Inspired by "West Bank Annexation Window Opens, but
Netanyahu Remains Quiet" by David M. Halbfinger
NYT 7-2-20

Hands up means don't shoot.
Of police etiquette, that's the root.
Do not create a fatal scene
When someone is surrendering.
8/19/14
*PG 262nd Posting 8/19/14
timothyjcallahan.blogspot.com

Intelligent design is religion based and can't be tested.
Fundamentalists are highly invested.
Evolution is proven in myriad ways.
But Christians stick to the old six days.
7/2/14
*Line 1 by John E. Jones III
*PG 255th Posting 7/6/14
timothyjcallahan.blogspot.com

God forsook Christ on the cross.
He took away Christ's holy force.
God looked at Jesus and averted his eyes.
Jesus had become what his father despised.
6/18/14
*PG 253rd Posting 6/22/14
timothyjcallahan.blogspot.com

Sunday, July 5, 2020
Poetry Group Five Hundred Sixty-Ninth Posting 7/5/20

Can America escape its death pact with white supremacy,
Which has been reaffirmed down through the centuries?
Lack of wealth has defined black life since emancipation.
The descendants of slaves should be paid reparations.
Jim Crow was also a system of economic exploitation.
For those hundred years also the nation should be paying.
The actualization of justice requires economic repair.
Congress should pass H.R. 40 if it cares.
6/28/2020
*Inspired by "What Is Owed" by Nikole Hannah-Jones
NYT Magazine 6-28-2020

The most successful ethnic group in the United States
Somehow victim status claims.
Dividends accrue from this specious victimhood.
Jews' preference for Israel carries more weight than it should.
They get immunity from criticism, however justified.
They slime Americans who take the Palestinians' side.
Moral corruption attends their immunity.
They deprive Palestinians of opportunity.
6/29/2020
*Inspired by The Holocaust Industry — Reflections on the
Exploitation of Jewish Suffering by Norman G. Finkelstein

Jews as military heroes in the June '67 war
Effaced the passive victim image forevermore.
Holocaust survivors had been a liability.
Now they had sainthood viability.
The Holocaust industry sprung up after
Israel brought the Arabs to military disaster.
It became a weapon for deflecting criticism
Of Israel for its Palestine cynicism.
6/29/2020
*Inspired by The Holocaust Industry – Reflections on the
Exploitation of Jewish Suffering by Norman G. Finkelstein

"I'm sick and tired of hearing about the Holocaust!"
(By Christmas, I feel the same way about Santa Clause.)
But Jesse Jackson's outburst never was forgotten,
By the Jewish elites who treated him rotten.
He dared espouse the Palestinian position,
For which he never expressed contrition.
He also represented domestic constituencies,
Who were at odds with American Jewry.
6/30/20
*Inspired by The Holocaust Industry – Reflections on the
Exploitation of Jewish Suffering by Norman G. Finkelstein
Line 1 by the Reverend Jesse Jackson in 1979

Most Arab states are controlled by undemocratic regimes,
Subservient and eager to stay on the U.S. team,
And ever desirous of Israeli approval.
The leaders undergo a backbone removal.
But the Arab people revere the Palestinians,
Even though Arab leaders are servile idiots.
Palestinians must appeal over the heads of those leaders,
To the millions of sympathizers beneath them.
6/30/2020
*Inspired by The Hundred Years' War on Palestine
by Rashid Khalidi

With the Star of David as their proud totem,
Jews fought affirmative action programs.
In all the Key Supreme Court tests,
Reflecting mainstream Jewish sentiments,
Jewish organizations filed amicus briefs,
Finding no need for affirmative action in the least.
7/1/2020
*Inspired by The Holocaust Industry – Reflections on the
Exploitation of Jewish Suffering by Norman G. Finkelstein

He was a super Zionist but not a religious Zionist.
Opposed to Palestinian rights denialists,
He was a founding member of Peace Now,
Which wants to turn swords into plows.
It advocates for the two state solution,
Without which peace is an illusion.
Sternhell wanted national rights universal,
And settler-colonial reversal.
7/3/2020
*Inspired by "Zeev Sternhell, 85, a 'Super Zionist' Wary
Of Extreme Israeli Nationalism" NYT Obituaries 7-3-20

Hey all you sellers of loose cigarettes,
The police haven't killed you yet.
But the longer you ply your trade, no doubt,
The police will come and choke you out.
12/5/14
*PG 275th Posting 12/7/14
timothyjcallahan.blogspot.com

Mental illness is not a personal failure.
But many afflicted wind up with jailors.
Could only they have been treated,
Before their crimes were completed.
 9/29/14
*PG 268th Posting 10/5/14
timothyjcallahan.blogspot.com

Sunday, June 28, 2020
Poetry Group Five Hundred Sixty-Eighth Posting 6/28/20

The same "settlers" who want mass Palestinian castration
Are against Nitwityahoo's planned annexation!
No, they are not done showing malice.
They're just worried about home values.
They aren't the majority who built near the Green Line.
The complainers squatted on land meant for Palestine.
They will live in enclaves in a Palestinian state.
So for them annexation wouldn't be that great.
6/21/20

Unilateral annexation risks Israel's security.
The Palestinians will react furiously.
It threatens Israel's progress in forging ties
With Arab states who could be allies.
Annexation will certainly ruin
Israel's standing with the European Union.
Israel's international law violation
Will lead to international isolation.
Even the United States will disapprove
Once Biden into the White House moves.
6/22/20

Trump is not attuned to the anti-racism vibes.
He has no taste for a movement for black lives.
Instead of throngs of police brutality protesters,
Trump wants slumber where racism festers:
How can I keep the continuity of white control,
And still appeal to the African-American soul?
I say the only thing they need is jobs.
With everybody working, there'll be no mobs.
6/23/20
*Inspired by "'Law and Order' for Trump's Foes"
by Charles M. Blow, NYT OP-ED 6-22-20

He feeds off the energy of the crowd,
Which he encourages to be loud.
His food is adulation and affirmation.
He eats the same in his MAGA habitation,
Where cabinet meetings start with worshipful praise.
Of insincerity, there's never a trace.
A backlash is brewing, but Trump can't sense it.
Trumpublicans laud Trumpism; the people are against it.
6/24/20
*Inspired by "The Boy Who Cried Fake News"
by Jamelle Bouie, Opinion, NYT 6-24-20

The presidential envoy extraordinaire,
About Palestinians doesn't care.
Jared Kushner lets Nitwityahoo
Do whatever he wants to do.
Maximalist Israeli positions
Are just what they were wishing.
Religious Zionism is the most selfish greed.
On all of Palestine it wants to feed.
6/24/20
*Inspired by The Hundred Years' War on Palestine
by Rashid Khalidi

"The Holocaust" is an ideological representation of the Nazi holocaust,
In which morality and the historical record get lost.
Like most ideologies, it bears some connection with reality.
The purity of its motives is the real fallacy.
The Holocaust casts Israel as a victim state,
Though greed, brutality, and racism are its essential traits.
Israeli prerogative and privilege are a given.
Palestinians are The Holocaust's ultimate victims.
6/26/20
*Inspired by The Holocaust Industry — Reflections on the
Exploitation of Jewish Suffering by Norman G. Finkelstein

I am nature, bold and brave.
Though called a mother, I am a grave.
I am brutal, and I don't take a bribe.
Most of my animals are eaten alive.
Most of my plants that bring good cheer
I put to death for half the year.
11/27/13
*Line 2 by Alfred de Vigny
*PG 255th Posting 12/8/13
timothyjcallahan.blogspot.com

Great deeds are usually wrought at great risk,
Like sailors sailing past Charybdis.
Much more do sailors fear the songs of sirens,
Which lure ships' crews to their rocky environs.
11/6/13
*Line 1 by Herodotus
*PG 252nd Posting 11/17/13
timothyjcallahan.blogspot.com

Sunday, June 21, 2020
Poetry Group Five Hundred Sixty-Seventh Posting 6/21/20

Reactionaries resist the liberation
Of marginal or powerless populations,
Who Trump thinks should know their place.
This is, of course, the sentiment of his base.
But protestors say justice needs a new beginning.
Public opinion they are quickly winning.
Trumpublicans are white supremacist relics.
Their reactionary impulses tell it:
A brutal military response
Is what they want.
*Inspired by "Reactionaries Are Having a Bad Month"
by Paul Krugman, Opinion, NYT 6-12-20
6/14/20

Security Council Resolution 2334 passed 14-1,
Because of a remarkable U.S. abstention.
It said Israeli settlement activity
Had no legal validity,
And was a flagrant violation of international law.
But the resolution should have done more.
It provided for no sanctions or coercive measure.
Israel continued building at its pleasure.
Toothless American declaratory posturing,
Further Israeli aggression was fostering.
6/15/20
*Inspired by *The Hundred Years' War on Palestine*
by Rashid Khalidi

Despite malevolent Zionist insistence,
Palestinian resistance persists.
Millions of Arabs remain in Palestine.
They were supposed to be gone by this time.
Despite the thousands killed or arrested,
The Jewish state is still contested.
No justice, no peace.
Resistance won't cease.
6/16/20
Inspired by <u>The Hundred Years' War on Palestine</u>
by Rashid Khalidi

Israel's armed might dwarfs that of all the Arabs put together.
The Palestinian people are at the end of their tether.
Inequality was essential to the creation of a Jewish state
In a densely populated, overwhelmingly Arab place,
And is vital to maintaining that state's dominance,
Where only Jews can gain prominence.
Yet equality of rights is key to a just resolution.
Israel needs a justice and equity revolution.
6/16/20
*Inspired by The Hundred Years' War on Palestine
by Rashid Khalidi

Obama made Mitchell special envoy for Middle East peace.
A final settlement they were determined to reach.
Mitchell was not beholden to Israel or its lobby.
If not undermined, he would have succeeded probably.
Chief saboteur was Zionist Dennis Ross.
His intermeddling assured Mitchell's loss.
He made side deals with Nitwityahoo,
From whom he took his cue.
Mitchell wanted Hamas in the negotiations too,
But Ross and Congress kept that from coming true.
In 2011, the Mitchell initiative died quietly.
Israel and its supporters had said "no" defiantly.
6/17/20
*Inspired by The Hundred Years' War on Palestine
by Rashid Khalidi

If you are an artist, then we're in agreement.
Forget about success; aim for achievement.
One can accomplish art by exertion,
Even as an unknown person.
Dedication makes the artist valiant,
Effort is as essential as talent.
7/18/11
Line 2 by Helen Hayes (shortened)
PG 217th 10/13/13
timothyjcallahan.blogspot.com

The Great War of Yankee Aggression
Taught Confederates a valuable lesson.
If on the battlefield one cannot win,
Simply destroy the Union from within.
10/15/13
PG 218th 10/20/13
timothyjcallahan.blogspot.com

Sunday, June 14, 2020
Poetry Group Five Hundred Sixty-Sixth Posting 6/14/20

God parted the Red Sea for the Israelites.
Police parted the protesters for the Troglodyte.
God used one of His endless supply of miracles.
The police used chemical irritants.
Trump held his bible like Moses held the tablets,
Or like a magician who just pulled out a rabbit.
He held the Holy Bible aloft.
The distant protesters coughed.
6/7/20

Sensing that his daughter was about to elope,
Mr. Ashrafi brought home rat poison and rope.
Kill yourself Romina, or I will kill you.
To God and Shariah law, I am true.
So she did run away, but the law brought her back.
Within twenty-four hours her father attacked.
He decapitated his daughter in her bed.
They buried the body together with the head.
And so Mr. Ashrafi prevented dishonor to his family.
Shariah law is a perversion of humanity.
6/8/20
*Inspired by "After a Beheading, a Shaken Iran
Asks if Women Have a Right to Safety" NYT 6-7-20*

Republicans support the most hawkish Israeli policies.
They indulge in Nitwityahoo idolatry.
Rich Zionist donors have even less use for Palestinians,
Whom, they believe, should be run off like wild Indians.
Evangelicals populate the Republican base.
They believe Palestinians to be a God-forsaken race.
Republican views match the ethos of Likud.
If they could kill all the Palestinians, they would.
6/9/20
*Inspired by *The Hundred Years' War on Palestine*
by Rashid Khalidi*

The Democratic Party's more liberal segments
Are all for Palestinian betterment.
Unfortunately, leadership doesn't share these sentiments
Much to the current party's detriment.
The Democrats have big Zionist donors too,
So the pro-Palestinian message doesn't break through.
Obama couldn't help them, though he tried.
AIPAC tells Congress what to decide.
6/9/20
*Inspired by The Hundred Years' War on Palestine
by Rashid Khalidi*

If there's ever something that might reflect poorly on Jews,
You will never hear about it on U.S. cable news,
Like the smears and innuendo Keith Ellison was subjected to
For his outspoken pro-Palestinian views.
Recall the party leadership struggle after the 2016 election.
Keith was the front-runner but not the selection.
Now he is America's prosecutor of killer policemen.
Will the Zionists dare try to slime him again?
Brutal, greedy, and racist Israeli policies,
Are never shown on American TV.
6/9/20

The retroactive legalization of thousands of Jewish homes,
Built on Palestinian land privately owned,
Will not happen says Israel's Supreme Court.
An impending injustice the court thwarted.
We need more decisions of this sort.
Could Israel's Supreme Court nullify,
The land grab planned for July?
6/11/20

Mind is a manifestation of matter.
You can't have the former without the latter.
Mind a/k/a soul can't be without brain.
Transcendentalists are insane.
Howsoever high a soul might climb,
It's hooked to a brain at all times.
10/1/13
*Line 1 from The God Delusion by Richard Dawkins
*PG 216th Posting 10/6/13
timothyjcallahan.blogspot.com

Natural selection is the blind watchmaker.
That's why it's such a time taker.
It had no pictures of "finished" creatures.
Adaption determined all life's features.
There was no eternal designer,
No omnipotent old-timer.
10/22/13
*Line 1 by Richard Dawkins in The God Delusion
*PG 276th Posting 10/27/13
timothyjcallahan.blogspot.com

Nitwityahoo and the right are greedy pigs.
He thinks he is a big swinging dick.
He pictures himself revered as a Jewish hero
But his covetous annexation will come to zero.
President Joe Biden will not recognize it.
The rest of the world will despise it.
Democrats will remove the collar and leash.
In Palestine, there will finally be peace.
5/31/20
Inspired by "Annexation Violates International Law"
Editorial NYT 5-31-20

Nitwityahoo and his greedy right wing fans
Will turn the West Bank into Bantustans.
A patchwork of simmering, unstable enclaves,
Connected by bypass roads well paved.
To armed resistance the Palestinians might relapse.
The Palestinian Authority would collapse.
Israel would rule two million people with no rights.
Israelis would be Apartheid South African whites.
6/1/20
Inspired by "Annexation Violates International Law"
Editorial NYT 5-31-20

Believe me, black folks, I feel your pain,
As I fly over you in my Presidential plane.
But when the looting starts, the shooting starts,
As much as that breaks my heart.
T'would be nobler if you suffered in silence,
Your penchant for arousing police violence.
Remember, God made you black, not me.
What's all this fuss over one policeman's knee?
6/2/20

2014 marked the third attack on Gaza in six years.
The only thing incalculable was the number of tears.
3,804 Palestinians were killed in these attacks.
A total of 87 Israelis died from people shooting back.
The lopsided 43:1 scale of these causalities
Shows that Israeli restraint is a fallacy.
The gross disproportion in firepower between the two sides,
Explains the much larger number of Gazans who died.
6/3/20
*Inspired by The Hundred Years' War on Palestine
by Rashid Khalidi

Israelis fired 1.3 million bullets in the first few days of the uprising.
Into masses of unarmed protesters, live ammunition they were firing.
Israel's air force launched more than 6,000 air attacks,
Over fifty-one days in 2014 back to back.
Its army and navy fired about 50,000 artillery and tank shells.
That kind of firepower on an urban enclave really tells.
Sixteen thousand buildings were rendered uninhabitable,
Including in Gaza City, the capital.
Forty-thousand more were to some degree damaged.
Death and destruction the Israelis well manage.
Four hundred fifty thousand Gazans were forced to leave their homes.
Israel turned Gaza into a civilian kill zone.
6/5/20
*Inspired by The Hundred Years' War on Palestine
by Rashid Khalidi*

The Arms Export Control Act of 1976,
About the use of arms is very strict.
They are to be used only "for legitimate self-defense",
Which made politicians and media tense; hence,
Israeli operations in Gaza were deemed self-defense!
To avoid prosecution for war crimes, this made sense.
6/6/20
*Inspired by The Hundred Years' War on Palestine
by Rashid Khalidi*

Poetry is unfallen speech.
It reminds Him of Eden
Before the apple feeding,
When Adam and his helpmate
Were more careful what they ate.
8/19/13
Line 1 by Abraham Coles
PG 210th Posting 8/25/13
by timothy j callahan.blogspot.com

I don't want to do God's will.
But God's will is instilled.
I do what I think he doesn't want.
"That's what I want," He taunts.
9/9/13
PG 213th Posting 9/15/13
by timothy j callahan.blogspot.com

So as not to offend white Southerners
And to placate southern governors,
The military embraced segregation.
Jim Crow underwent federalization.
Ten Southern bases are named for Confederates,
Who were American Union heretics.
They rebelled to preserve and extend slavery,
White supremacy heavily favoring.
The names of these bases should be changed.
Naming them for racists is deranged.
5/24/20
*Inspired by "Why Does the U.S. Military
Celebrate White Supremacy?"
Editorial NYT 5-24-20*

The best Palestinians are either dead or gone.
We like their existence to be non.
They are the interlopers, not us.
We are what is; they are what was.
But millions of Palestinians remain.
You wish to disappear them in vain.
They deserve a state on their own land.
Palestine is their homeland.
5/25/20

In 1993, the Oslo Accords were received with euphoria.
But in time, the Palestinians were sorrier.
The colonization continued apace.
Final status talks never were raised.
People couldn't freely move around Palestine.
 Israeli policy was to separate and confine.
Checkpoints requiring permits near impossible to get
Threw over the Occupation a labyrinthine net,
Including Jewish-only bypass roads, fences and walls.
The object was to cut off the Palestinians' balls.
5/25/20
Inspired by The Hundred Years' War on Palestine
by Rashid Khalidi

He controlled how he was covered by two leading news outlets.
The coverage was slavishly flattering from the outset.
He performed official favors for wealthy businessmen,
Who gave him expensive gifts again and again.
Nitwityahoo tries to discredit law enforcement.
From the right he enjoys total endorsement.
He delegitimizes the prosecution and judges.
Nitwityahoo says he is above them.
5/27/20

Ariel Sharon was opportunistic and reckless.
He was intent on winning the next election.
So he acted provocatively in order to get ahead.
The Second Intifada left 6,600 dead.
To the Haram al-Sharif, a visit he made.
He needed hundreds of police to feel unafraid.
It was the worst upsurge of violence since the '67 war.
Sharon won the election and so much more.
Suicide attacks hurt the Palestinians' media image,
And strengthened Israeli prerogative and privilege.
5/29/20
Inspired by <u>The Hundred Years' War on Palestine</u>
by Rashid Khalidi

They who seldom think of heaven are not likely to get thither.
They are more likely to cross the Styx River.
From Hell's wharf Satan shouts, come hither!
From flames souls cry, why did I dither?
7/16/13
Line 1 by Bishop Horne
PG 205th Posting 7/21/13
timothy j callahan.blogspot.com

Diet not going well? With this you will persist:
We gain the strength of the temptation we resist.
Because I only eat it in my dreams,
I have the power of ice cream.
7/7/13
Line 2 by Ralph Waldo Emerson
PG 205th Posting 7/21/13
timothy j callahan.blogspot.com

The ghost of the murdered haunts the steps of the malefactor.
Trayvon will always be Zimmerman's master:
"Aren't you the guy who killed that black kid?
A lot of us don't like what you did."
7/15/13
*Line 1 by Sir Walter Scott
*PG 205th Posting 7/21/13
timothy j callahan.blogspot.com

Sunday, May 24, 2020
Poetry Group Five Hundred Sixty-Third Posting 5/24/20

Goliath Israel persecutes the Palestinian David,
But Palestinian youths brave it.
The price of throwing a stone,
Might be a broken bone,
Or a rubber bullet in the eye,
Or a live round in which case they die.
Israelis ordered force, might, and beatings.
They want more than mild mistreating.
They want Palestinians dead on the ground.
On such atrocities was Israel founded.
5/17/20
*Inspired by The Hundred Years' War on Palestine
by Rashid Khalidi

 Did the PLO know
That Israel had a veto
Over any U.S. positions,
And that Israel made all the decisions?
The PLO did not grasp American disdain
For Palestinian interests and aims.
Yet America had betrayed them before
In the 1982 Lebanon War,
When America promised to safeguard the camps,
Which turned out to be a bloody sham.
5/18/20
*Inspired by The Hundred Years' War on Palestine
by Rashid Khalidi

Israel was eating the cake the two sides were supposedly dividing.
By the rules of the negotiations, Israel was not abiding.
James Baker's best efforts could not interrupt,
The unending series of "settlements" going up.
Bush withheld ten billion dollars in loan guarantees.
But the colonization did not cease.
Israel does not negotiate in good faith.
It wants to eat the whole cake.
5/18/20
*Inspired by The Hundred Years' War on Palestine
byRashid Khalidi

The key point was always security for Israel, its "settlers" and occupation.
It never really believed in a sovereign Palestinian nation.
Security in Israel's lexicon has an all encompassing meaning:
Complete domination with no one intervening.
Never an honest broker, always Israel's partner,
The U.S. inspired the 9/11 carnage.
The injustice of the Palestinian plight
Puts America in a perpetual fight.
5/19/20
*Inspired by <u>The Hundred Years' War on Palestine</u>
by Rashid Khalidi*

Just for a laugh, Pompeo went to Jerusalem,
To try to dampen annexation enthusiasm.
But his boss already lit the fuse:
A third of the West Bank Palestinians will lose.
A third intifada might hurt Trump's election chances,
And bring about BDS movement advances.
But Nitwityahoo is intent on annexing,
No matter how vexing.
5/22/20

Oslo I made the PLO a subcontractor of the occupation.
It offloaded the cost and liability of subjugating the population.
The PLO provided security for the "settlers" and occupation forces,
Against the Palestinian resistance quarters.
This straightjacket on Palestinian defiance
Was achieved with American connivance.
But now Israel annulled the Oslo agreement.
Mahmoud Abbas said what he meant.
The Israeli army will have to resume daily control
Of 2.1 million angry Palestinian souls.
They won't provide security for Israel's theft of their homeland.
A homeland on their own land is their just demand.
5/22/20
*Inspired by The Hundred Years' War on Palestine
 by Rashid Khalidi

You want to fight me? Okay fine.
You choose your weapon; I'll choose mine.
Go ahead, pick up your Bible and Torah.
I come bearing poet's laurel.
4/29/13
*PG 194th Posting 5/5/13
Poet Against Israel by Timothy J. Callahan

Kissinger had a Cold-War-driven framework for the Middle East.
He cared about the Palestinian problem the least.
His goal was to get Egypt to make a separate peace,
And make Soviet assistance there cease.
We could let the Syrians move and break the back of the PLO.
Israel will say how far into Lebanon the Syrians can go.
Kissinger colluded to crush the Palestinian movement.
He let Syrians into Lebanon to do it.
But Kissinger was nothing if not pragmatic.
His deference to Israel was not automatic.
With the PLO he had secret contacts,
Which helped U.S. interests behind Israelis' backs.
The PLO protected American lives in Beirut
And negotiated with Iran's hostage-taking group.
5/9/20
Line 5 by Henry Kissinger
Inspired by The Hundred Years' War on Palestine
by Rashid Khalidi

For ten weeks in the summer of 1982,
Israel invaded Lebanon and besieged West Beirut.
Whole high-rise apartment buildings were flattened.
The people inside didn't matter.
Near their targets, Israelis planted car bombs,
To do any would-be rescuers harm.
Mossad called it killing for killing's sake.
Israeli calls for peace are fake,
Because without justice there can be no peace.
Without a Palestine, resistance won't cease.
5/10/20
*Inspired by The Hundred Years' War on Palestine
by Rashid Khalidi

Israel invaded to defeat the PLO and expel it from Beirut,
Their hold on the West Bank to improve.
Palestinian nationalism was the ultimate target.
Of all Israel's invasions, this was the largest.
If the Palestinians could be made to lose faith in the PLO,
They would be easier to manipulate and control.
Israel was preparing to do what it wanted to do next,
All of the Occupied Territories annex.
5/11/20
*Inspired by The Hundred Years' War on Palestine
by Rashid Khalidi

President Reagan got the Israelis to stop killing once.
One angry call to Begin, and they put up their guns.
This was during the brutal West Beirut siege,
On a day when the peace treaty was already reached.
The carnage was a Ronald Reagan enrager.
He said the future relationship was endangered.
A baby with its arms blown off became the symbol of the war.
Finally, Reagan would stand no more.
5/11/20
*Inspired by The Hundred Years' War on Palestine
  by Rashid Khalidi*

Sharon told Haig what he was about to do,
In Lebanon in the summer of 1982.
Without the green light from Alexander Haig,
Israel would not have dared invade.
The invasion was a joint Israeli-U.S. military endeavor,
Their first war specifically against Palestinians ever.
The U.S. supplied the weapons that killed thousands of civilians.
It financed the IDF with billions.
It gave worthless assurances of protection,
For Palestinians after the PLO's eviction.
Snuffing Palestinian nationalism was the goal.
The U.S. played an indispensible supporting role.
5/12/20

Why did all those Marines die in their barracks?
American media knew but wouldn't share it.
They paid the price of U.S. collusion with the Israeli occupier.
American TV should have been a hue and crier.
But U.S. media is not to be critical
Of U.S. servility to Israel.
5/12/20

Trump wants the court to ignore a massive amount of history,
To keep his financial records a mystery.
Nixon and Clinton failed to withhold information.
Their defeats were national sensations.
Vance wants your business records in a criminal inquiry.
Like any other criminal, you should be worried.
In America, no one is above the law.
We will see your tax returns and more.
5/13/20

An Israeli soldier was killed by a stone,
From a Palestinian home thrown.
Why in the first place was the stone thrown?
For TV viewers this is all unknown.
Cable news is not allowed to show the conflict.
Publicity is not what Nitwityahoo wanted,
Because people might ask why the stone was thrown,
And demand that all the reasons be shown.
5/15/20

Israel depends largely on complaisant American public opinion.
On MSNBC you will never hear "Palestinian".
CNN can't show Israeli soldiers shooting teenage protestors.
By the Israeli lobby it would be pestered.
Five decades of American and international policy,
Nitwityahoo will show was so much folly.
American TV will agree,
Not to show Israeli greed.
5/15/20

Sunday, May 10, 2020
Poetry Group Five Hundred Sixty-First Posting 5/10/20

The Zionist narrative enjoyed complete dominance.
The Israel lobby gained congressional prominence.
The word "Palestine" was unmentionably ominous.
Palestine supporters were but nominal.
Yet Palestinian identity continues.
They have been badly abused,
But they refuse to lose.
A homeland on their own land
Is their just demand.
5/3/20
*Inspired by <u>The Hundred Years' War on Palestine</u>
by Rashid Khalidi*

The old will die and the young will forget.
That was the Zionists' bet, which hasn't happened yet.
The Palestine Movement appears on the world stage.
This has the Jewish "settlers" enraged.
Israel tried for decades to disappear them,
But the Europeans continue to cheer them.
The Palestinians refuse to lose.
Make Israel cut them loose.
5/3/20
*Inspired by <u>The Hundred Years' War on Palestine</u>
 by Rashid Khalidi*

In the West, Israel was a beleaguered victim of Arab hostility.
In the Arab world, that image was an impossibility.
The leaders of Arab states were fidgety,
After Israel's decisive victories.
They feared ultimate national harm,
From Israel's nuclear arms.
But the susceptible Americans were taught
That with perils Israel was fraught.
The Palestinians are a forgotten but just cause.
Americans don't know the applicable international laws.
 5/3/20
*Inspired by <u>The Hundred Years' War on Palestine</u>
 by Rashid Khalidi*

Not having the numbers or the resources,
The PLO rarely overcame Israeli forces,
But in Karameh, a Jordanian town,
PLO fighters turned an Israeli brigade around.
Of course, they were backed by Jordanian artillery,
Which was the most lethal killing machinery.
The Israelis left the battlefield in disarray.
They had near two hundred casualties in the fray.
This battle restored Arab dignity,
Coming nine months after Israel's bigger victory.
5/5/20
*Inspired by *The Hundred Years' War on Palestine*
by Rashid Khalidi*

Assassinations were a weapon in Israel's ambition
To transform a Palestine to Israel transition.
Mossad killed the leaders to try to kill the movement.
The more dead Palestinians, the more improvement,
Because "terrorists" the Palestinians were branded.
America felt the same way to be candid.
Israel aimed to eliminate the Palestinian reality
Demographically, ideationally, and politically.
5/6/20
*Inspired by *The Hundred Years' War on Palestine*
by Rashid Khalidi*

My national security advisor was set up.
With dirty cops at the top I am fed up.
My Roy Cohn wants to drop the charges.
My followers want more cartridges.
That Flynn lied is no disgrace.
They shouldn't have questioned him in the first place.
Defendants everywhere should not be hesitant
To use Flynn's case as a precedent.
A guilty plea isn't necessarily a guilty plea.
My Justice Department agrees.
5/9/20

I am the scourge of God on Israel's back.
I will make Israeli squatters pack.
They think God is on their side,
But greed is something God can't abide.
7/11/13
*PG 204th Posting 7/14/13
Poet Against Israel by Timothy J. Callahan

Sunday, May 3, 2020
Poetry Group Five Hundred Sixtieth Posting 5/3/20

 Like a passing ship indifferent to the drowning man,
America lets Israel ignore Palestinians any way it can.
Trump gave Nitwityahoo permission to annex
Thirty percent of the 20% for the Palestinians meant.
Decades of American policy Trump unwound.
Will Biden sail past as Palestinians drown?
4/26/20

For those Palestinians who escaped execution,
The alternative was destitution:
Loss of homes, jobs, and deeply rooted communities.
America acquiesced dutifully.
For three-quarters of a million Palestinians, the world turned upside down.
Their feet no longer touched their ancestral ground.
City dwellers lost their capital and properties.
It was a tragedy worthy of Sophocles.
4/26/20
*Inspired by The Hundred Years' War on Palestine
by Rashid Khalidi*

One policy that increases Israeli salivation
Is that of disproportionate retaliation.
When feda'iyin killed three Israeli civilians,
A woman and her two children,
Israeli special forces Unit 101
Under the command of Ariel Sharon
Carried out a massacre in Qibya
Reminiscent of the Nakba.
They blew up forty-five homes with the residents inside.
Sixty-nine Palestinian civilians died.
The U.N. Security Council condemned the raid
With more of them the U.N. was repaid
4/27/20
*Inspired by The Hundred Years' War on Palestine
by Rashid Khalidi*

Under cover of co-conspirators Britain and France,
Israeli troops smashed through towns and refugee camps.
Hundreds of male civilians were rounded up and shot.
These massacres were part of Israel's Suez War plot,
And were carried out after resistance ceased.
Israel lies when it says it wants peace.
News of the massacres was suppressed in Israel.
And in American media so liberal.
4/27/20
*Inspired by <u>The Hundred Years' War on Palestine</u>
by Rashid Khalidi*

The myth of the Six Day War prevails.
Israel is vulnerable never fails
To justify support for its extreme positions
And its ethnic cleansing ambitions.
But in 1967 (as now) Israel was in little danger.
It was (and is) as safe as Jesus in the manger.
Israel's lie of existential peril
Caused America's great error.
4/28/20
*Inspired by <u>The Hundred Years' War on Palestine</u>
by Rashid Khalidi*

John F. Kennedy went to Palestine,
In the early summer of 1939.
There he wrote his father a letter
To help him understand the situation better.
JFK was skeptical of the arguments of both sides.
With him this skepticism would abide.
So as president he was less susceptible
To Israel lobby pressure,
Unlike Johnson who was overly reliant,
On advisors most of whom were Zionists.
4/29/20
*Inspired by <u>The Hundred Years' War on Palestine</u>
by Rashid Khalidi*

People have to get it inside.
They can inject or imbibe
Disinfectants like bleach.
Why keep it out of children's reach?
Clean your innards like you would a counter top.
Keep it up until I say stop.
And get some UV light in there.
On the side of caution err.
4/29/20

The Arab land Israel took in its 1956 attack,
President Eisenhower made it give back.
So in '67 when it planned a preemptive strike
On Arab air forces with all of its considerable might,
Israel sought and obtained Johnson's permission
For the dastardly surprise attack mission.
Meanwhile, the U.S. reassured the Arabs without question,
That it would prevent any Israeli aggression.
This time America would let Israel forever keep
Some of the Arab land it had seized.
5/1/20
*Inspired by _The Hundred Years' War on Palestine_
by Rashid Khalidi*

No Palestinians ever existed
Golda Meir firmly insisted.
The indigenous population is a lie.
There's no one for whom to cry.
Believe in colonial settler negation.
There is no mass segregation.
5/1/20
*Inspired by _The Hundred Years' War on Palestine_
by Rashid Khalidi*

An artist never really finishes his work; he merely abandons it.
There's a world without his art, and he lands in it.
He is free of the artistic compulsion,
No further need to render emotion.
Shakespeare didn't write in his retirement.
He did not find writing a requirement.
He was not slave to some writing journal.
The role of artist is not eternal.
11/13/12
*Line 1 by Paul Valery
*PG 172nd Posting 12/2/12
Poet Against Israel by Timothy J. Callahan

Sunday, April 26, 2020
Poetry Group Five Hundred Fifty-Ninth Posting 4/26/20

The ethnic cleansing began before the state was proclaimed.
A most sinister offensive, Plan Dalet it was named,
Depopulated scores of Arab villages, towns, and cities.
The Zionist para-military men were giddy.
The Irgun and Haganah stormed with enthusiasm
The village of Dayr Yasin near Jerusalem.
They shot and killed a hundred residents.
Not one Zionist gunman was hesitant.
4/18/20
*Inspired by The Hundred Years' War on Palestine
by Rashid Khalidi

Sacrifice the Palestinians for a Jewish state,
To expel them and take their place.
A Jewish state in an Arab majority land
Violates the U.N.'s self determination plan,
Which is enshrined in the U.N. Charter.
But the U.N. was not the Palestinians' partner.
So the Jews had to make it not a majority Arab land.
They expected the U.N. would understand.
4/19/20
*Inspired by _The Hundred Years' War on Palestine_
by Rashid Khalidi

On a U.S. warship in the spring of 1945,
When he had only weeks to be alive,
FDR reassured the Saudi King
Not to worry about a thing:
The U.S. would not harm the Arabs of Palestine.
It would consult them and everything would be fine.
These pledges were quickly forgotten by Roosevelt's successor.
Truman turned out to be a Zionism blesser:
I have hundreds of thousands of Zionist constituents.
Pro-Palestinian voters are but a pittance.
4/19/20
*Inspired by _The Hundred Years' War on Palestine_
by Rashid Khalidi

Nitwityahoo plans to annex large swaths of the occupied West Bank.
For this we have scaredy-pants Gantz to thank.
He did get one concession, so he's not the worst:
Nitwityahoo can't do it until July first.
At one time, Gantz wanted international consensus.
But now he's not so contentious.
Gantz thinks being deputy is neato,
Though he doesn't get a veto.
4/21/20

Telling the Palestinians to quit and sit,
Nitwityahoo made a commitment,
To annex more Palestinian land.
Trump already told him he can.
Israel and America are colluding
To conclude the dream of the two-state solution.
This dream will never die because it is just.
Full Palestinian sovereignty is a must.
4/21/20

He is denied notoriety; he's blacklisted.
He wants more readers, but can only wish it.
The Israel lobby won't let his blogspot out,
Yet right now his poems should be shouted.
Nitwityahoo wants to annex more of Palestine.
If Americans knew better, they would not say fine.
Israel is content to inspire world terror.
Over-feeding it has been America's error.
Read about it at his blogspot.com.
He welcomes the publicity bomb,
And knows how bad it will be.
It's worth it if it makes people read.
4/21/20

Supposedly, he's better than progressives are fearing.
But the time of Nitwityahoo's annexation is nearing.
What is Joe Biden doing to stop it?
He prays the poet against Israel would drop it.
America is party to a great sin.
In ignominy it will live.
We killed the Palestinians and took their land.
The Israel lobby should be banned.
4/22/20

Judeo-Christians notice later or sooner,
That the Holy Bible completely lacks humor.
Why does God hate comicality?
Is laughter a spiritual malady?
In Heaven at table when God makes a gaffe,
Not one soul present ever dares laugh.
2/17/13
Line 2 by Alfred North Whitehead
PG 185th Posting 3/3/13
Poet Against Israel by Timothy J. Callahan

Sunday, April 19, 2020
Poetry Group Five Hundred Fifty-Eighth Posting 4/19/20

Ignorance makes people weak and vulnerable.
About Israel Americans are gullible,
So they send billions to that country.
In return they get worse than nothing.
Anti-Americanism is the steady crop
Of America's annual money drops.
Every payment is a gamble.
Take 9/11 for example.
4/12/20

If you wish to colonize a land in which people are already living,
Make clear to them that their end is your beginning.
The colonial enterprise produced resistance
Against the Zionists and the British.
Herzl believed it wouldn't from his great distance.
The Zionists ethnically cleansed with insistence.
Herzl never knew how brutal that would be.
What would he say if he was there to see?
4/12/20
*Inspired by <u>The Hundred Years' War on Palestine</u>
by Rashid Khalidi*

Under pressure from the Zionist movement,
And Churchill's support most pertinent,
The British Army formed a separate Jewish Brigade Group,
(For Palestinian volunteers, the British did not do it.)
Which provided training, combat experience and resources
To supplement the already considerable Zionist forces.
This would help them in the coming conflict,
Which the Palestinians never wanted.
4/13/20
*Inspired by The Hundred Years' War on Palestine
by Rashid Khalidi*

The Palestinians faced the para-state of the Jewish Agency.
Their own central state system was in latency.
The Mandate granted the Jews vital arms of governance.
It was an anti-Palestinian covenant.
They had no centrally organized military force.
They were doomed to lose, of course.
Irish patriots kept a clandestine parliament.
Outfought and out-administered, the British went.
The Dail Eirann still meets today.
The Palestinians haven't gotten their state.
4/14/20
*Inspired by The Hundred Years' War on Palestine
by Rashid Khalidi*

The Israelis flatter Trump deliriously,
Because he doesn't take the Palestinians seriously.
His so-called "Peace Plan" to end the conflict
Gives Nitwityahoo everything he wanted.
Trump is wrong about Palestine like everything else.
He cares only about Jewish money and himself.
The Palestinians have Bernie's heart, and he's not afraid to show it.
Biden better find a heart, and I hope he knows it.
4/14/20

An artist is a creature driven by demons,
One of which demands achievements.
Another says, remember and weep.
The artist begins grimly to reap.
A third sneers, you must hold me at bay,
To get to say what you want to say.
12/18/12
*Line 1 by William Faulker
*PG 180th Posting 1/27/13
Poet Against Israel by Timothy J. Callahan

The U.N. and World Court say Israel is a cheater:
No territorial acquisition by force is ever legal.
This is a corollary of the U.N. Charter.
The world should oppose Israel harder.
Forcible land grabs are unlawful.
Why does the world dawdle?
Israel is a U.N. member state
But the U.N. Charter it hates.
4/4/20
Inspired by <u>The Hundred Years' War on Palestine</u>
 by Rashid Khalidi

I like to be home,
Writing pro-Palestinian poems.
Consummate righteous underdogs,
Who have slogged a long slog,
Palestinians deserve a sovereign state.
My fervor will not abate.
America, you are party to a great sin.
Turn and seek justice again.
4/4/20

Herzl thought about the future state reflectively:
Removal of the natives must be done circumspectly.
We must expropriate gently their private property.
Don't let them know their future's in jeopardy.
This condescending attitude toward Arab intelligence and rights
Was continued by America in the Palestinian plight:
The Palestinians are not worthy of being taken seriously.
The Israelis persecute them fearlessly.
4/5/20
*Inspired by <u>The Hundred Years' War on Palestine</u>
 by Rashid Khalidi

A land without a people for a people without a land.
That was the greatest lie in the history of man.
But the former governor of Arkansas wanted to believe it.
He had a lingering doubt and wanted to relieve it.
So Huckabee went over there and about Palestine he tread.
There's really no such thing as the Palestinians, he said.
That was upon his return in March 2015.
Not one Palestinian had he seen.
Compared to Jews, he believes Arabs are lesser beings,
So are women, Mike says, again not seeing.
4/6/20
*Line 6 by Fmr Gov. Mike Huckabee
*Inspired by <u>The Hundred Years' War on Palestine</u>
 by Rashid Khalidi

In Ireland, he earned the nickname Bloody Balfour,
But the Palestinians came to curse him more.
His infamous "Declaration" took their national rights.
Confiscation and persecution it invites.
The words "Arabs" or "Palestinians" were never used
Yet they were robbed in favor of the Jews.
A declaration of war by the British Empire,
Palestinian land to acquire.
That was the Balfour Declaration,
An invitation to invasion and segregation.
4/7/20
*Inspired by The Hundred Years' War on Palestine
by Rashid Khalidi

The British tied Palestinians to trucks and locomotives.
Discouraging rebel attack was the motive.
They learned this tactic fighting the Irish until 1921,
The year the Irish rebellion won.
Demolishing the homes of the relatives of rebels,
They also learned in Ireland from the devil.
They put down the Great Arab Revolt.
This land is not for you, the Palestinians were told.
Who were treated as if they had no national existence,
And no collective rights, just subsistence.
4/8/20

Make Biden say "Palestinians" on television.
Let him tell how many are dead, wounded, or imprisoned.
Mr. Biden, what would you do to further their cause?
Will you make the imposition of a Palestine U.S. law?
That last questions is a joke, because I know you won't.
You, Trump, and Nitwityahoo are in the same boat.
Not supporting the Palestinians is wrong.
You will push America's sin along.
4/9/20

Senator Sanders never groveled to billionaires.
He was not the first choice among millionaires.
But those who support universal human dignity
Support him vigorously and significantly.
The ideological struggle he won.
He showed Biden how it's done,
Who now has his own public option plan,
And believes healthcare is a universal right of man.
4/9/20

The impudent artist vowed:
I am here to live out loud.
I can take the mask off reality.
The keepers of the mask rail at me.
I show the brainwashed what they did not know:
That Israel is America's most harmful foe.
The Zionists hate me for living loudly.
I accuse Israel, and I say so proudly.
*Line 2 by Emile Zola
*PG 171st Posting 11/25/12
Poet Against Israel by Timothy J. Callahan

Israel has attacked Lebanon bountifully.
In '93, it launched Operation Accountability,
A ferocious assault on population centers.
The Israelis were Lebanese life enders.
One hundred-twenty dead, 300,000 displaced.
Fifty-five villages damaged or erased.
In '96, Israel launched Operation Grapes of Wrath
Another Lebanese civilian bloodbath.
In an ambulance 6 women and girls were killed.
The Israeli killers were thrilled.
In Qana, the IDF shelled the U.N. compound.
Over a hundred dead bodies were found.
3/30/20
*Inspired by <u>Beyond Chutzpah – On the Misuse of Anti-Semitism
and the Abuse of History</u> by Norman G. Finkelstein*

You said peace with the Palestinians should be our top priority.
Yet you have submitted to Likud's hierarchy.
Nitwityahoo is a corruptor, an inciter, a racist.
Now, Benny Gantz, we see your two faces.
We wanted an alternative to Nitwityahoo,
But now he has you.
3/30/20

Trumpublicans have always been science deniers.
They give credence to holy liars,
Like Jerry Falwell Jr.,
Whose views are quite peculiar.
He said the virus was a hoax
To give Trump's chances a poke.
Against medical advice, he reopened Liberty U.,
And created a potential viral hot spot too.
Trumpublicans deny the theory of evolution
But endorse increasing pollution.
Their science denial led to virus denial,
Which turned up death's dial.
3/31/20
*Inspired by "This Land Of Denial And Death"
by Paul Krugman NYT OP-ED 3-31-20*

Israelis deny Palestinians their right to self-determination.
They prefer to use expulsion and extermination.
The Jewish state was imposed on Palestinians against their will.
The military occupation is imposed on them still.
No morality or law could justify this violation.
Palestine suffered a Zionization,
Which would not have succeeded
Without America to feed it.
4/1/20

The Zionists pushed for the U.N. Partition Resolution,
Which would have hurt Palestinians in its execution.
Most of the coastal and all the interior plains
Were awarded to the new Jewish state,
Which was to get 55.5 percent of Palestine.
This the Palestinians could not abide.
But those American Zionists really tried.
With Truman they wouldn't let it slide.
He received a letter and phone call bombardment
Which was also directed at the State Department.
4/1/20
*Inspired by <u>Beyond Chutzpah – On the Misuse of Anti-Semitism
and the Abuse of History</u> by Norman G. Finkelstein*

In November '67, the Security Council unanimously approved
United Nations Resolution 242,
Calling for the withdrawal of occupying forces
And giving the Palestinians divorces.
It emphasizes the inadmissibility
Of keeping stolen territory.
The whole world agreed
To curb Israeli greed.
4/2/20
*Inspired by <u>Beyond Chutzpah – On the Misuse of Anti-Semitism
and the Abuse of History</u> by Norman G. Finkelstein*

At my funeral, this will be true:
You will see me, but I won't see you.
You may caress my hair,
Though I feel nothing there.
I hear no sound,
Though you cry out loud,
For I am gone,
Yet here to look upon.
6/26/13
*PG 204*th* Posting 7/14/13
<u>Poet Against Israel</u> by Timothy J. Callahan

Sunday, March 29, 2020
Poetry Group Five Hundred Fifty-Fifth Posting 3/29/20

American Jewish elites did not become enamored
Of Israel until Palestine was a second time hammered,
Until the '67 war of conquest and occupation,
Until the world condemned Israel's confiscation.
Becoming a Zionist became personally and politically expedient
Promoting Israel's conquest was the main ingredient
These elites rediscovered the Nazi Holocaust
To justify the Palestinians' perpetual loss.
3/21/20
*Inspired by <u>Beyond Chutzpah – On the Misuse of Anti-Semitism
and the Abuse of History</u> by Norman G. Finkelstein*

ome old, instinctive Arab antipathy is a false rendering.
There were few hostilities until Zionism engendered them.
Jews had lived in the Arab world for centuries.
Zionism meant they had to leave eventually.
But if Jews had shared the land from the beginning
Then both peoples would be winning.
3/23/20
*Inspired by <u>Beyond Chutzpah – On the Misuse of Anti-Semitism
and the Abuse of History</u> by Norman G. Finkelstein*

Jewish soldiers broke the children's heads with sticks.
Into the crying mothers they thrust their dicks.
Other women and children were put on trucks.
Each of these women was finger-fucked
Because the Jewish soldiers were looking for jewelry
This was the right of post-Holocaust Jewry.
The ones with the most brutal desires
Were the eager Holocaust survivors.
3/23/20
*Inspired by <u>Beyond Chutzpah – On the Misuse of Anti-Semitism
and the Abuse of History</u> by Norman G. Finkelstein and
Inspired by <u>The Ethnic Cleansing of Palestine</u> by Ilan Pappe

The fewer Arabs remaining, the better.
Carry out that order to the letter.
Yes, Jews too committed Nazi acts.
Zionists tried to hide that fact.
The fear of Zionist attacks
Drove thousands of Arabs back.
3/24/20

Israel started the June '67 Six Day War.
Land acquisition was what it was for.
Israel says its back was against the wall
But the Arabs didn't want war at all.
If Israel wanted to avoid hostilities,
It had several possibilities,
Like restoring UN forces to the Egyptian border.
Israel wouldn't have had to spend a quarter.
The World Court offered to arbitrate
The closing of the Tiran Straits.
A two week moratorium was proposed by U Thant,
But peace Israel did not want.
3/24/20
*Inspired by _Beyond Chutzpah – On the Misuse of Anti-Semitism
and the Abuse of History_ by Norman G. Finkelstein

To recover Israeli-occupied Sinai,
In 1971 Egypt offered to sign
With Israel a peace treaty.
Israel rebuffed Egypt's entreaty.
The world warned that war was inevitable.
To the world, Israel's greed was incredible.
And so, in October '73 there was a war.
Israel kept the Sinai for not much more.
But it retained Golan,
Which in 1967 was also stolen.
3/24/20
*Inspired by _Beyond Chutzpah – On the Misuse of Anti-Semitism
and the Abuse of History_ by Norman G. Finkelstein

In the 1930's, the Zionist movement attacked civilians.
Later, Israel bombarded Arab towns and villages.
The Irgun engaged in uninhibited killing
Of the aged, women, and children.
Kill the prisoners came the word.
The line of the impermissible was blurred.
Even before the glorious founding of Israel
The Jews made the Palestinians miserable.
3/24/20
*Inspired by <u>Beyond Chutzpah – On the Misuse of Anti-Semitism
and the Abuse of History</u> by Norman G. Finkelstein*

In 1966, an Israeli armored brigade
Went to Samu to lay waste.
The soldiers razed 125 homes
And everything in the school zone.
They destroyed a workshop and a medical clinic
Before the mission was finished.
They killed 18 Jordanian soldiers.
Israeli soldiers are vultures.
America's UN ambassador sighed,
The attack could not be justified.
3/25/20
*Inspired by <u>Beyond Chutzpah – On the Misuse of Anti-Semitism
 and the Abuse of History</u> by Norman G. Finkelstein*

Mr. President, let compassion be your guide.
Let the sanctions on Iran slide,
At least temporarily
And of course warily.
That country is overwhelmed by cases,
Grief is painful in all races.
Smooth the way for IMF emergency funding
To do otherwise would be blundering.
Show the people we are on their side.
Let the economic sanctions slide.
3/26/20
*Inspired by "Lifting Sanctions on Iran" Editorial
NYT 3-26-20

Some insights of the saint stem from his days as a sinner.
That sinner was a saint beginner.
So forgive sinners for what they do.
Someday one may pray for you.
1/8/13
*Line 1 by Eric Hoffer
*PG 179th Posting 1/20/13
Poet Against Israel by Timothy J. Callahan

My international audience must wonder
At the publishing world's blunder:
Hasn't this American poet paid his dues?
Is everyone in New York afraid of the Jews?
2/20/13
*PG 184th Posting 2/24/13
Poet Against Israel by Timothy J. Callahan

Good taste handicaps any creative functioning,
And should be restricted to fine luncheoning.
I will be no slave to propriety.
Martyred Palestinians rely on me.
5/27/13
Line 1 by Salvador Dali
PG 189th Posting 6/2/13
Poet Against Israel by Timothy J. Callahan

Sunday, March 22, 2020
Poetry Group Five Hundred Fifty-Fourth Posting 3/22/20

I hated Trump before I loved him.
When I loved him, I said no one was above him.
However, now that he is gone,
And other Republicans bombed,
I hate Trump again.
I'm ready to be reasonable, just say when.
Think of the Trump years as an aberration.
His madness is not for the duration.
3/15/20

Sometimes the army demolishes houses with the occupants still inside.*
Under the rubble, some cry before they die,
Because many times no warning is given,
That this is no longer a place for living.
Some of the buried were rescued; others were not.
Palestinian rescuers were shot.
Bulldozers drove over the rubble
Under which the still living huddled.
3/15/20
*Inspired by *Beyond Chutzpah – On the Misuse of Anti-Semitism
and the Abuse of History* by Norman G. Finkelstein*

The aim of the Jews was not to exploit, but to dispossess
Land or water, Palestinians get less and less
Jewish "settlements" expropriate Palestinian resources.
Fair? Israel says of course it is:
We are the master-race over these natives,
Whom we righteously hateth.
After their land we lust.
All of it is for us.
3/16/20

The problem with the Palestinian economy is closure,*
Which is a lot of fun for Israeli soldiers.
Who restrict movement of Palestinians and goods.
They'd kill all the Palestinians if they could.
At checkpoints they make people wait for hours.
Putting them in cages is within their powers.
If you get out of a car, you might be shot.
Israel's effect on traffic is to clot.
3/16/20
*Inspired by _Beyond Chutzpah – On the Misuse of Anti-Semitism
and the Abuse of History_ by Norman G. Finkelstein

Every Palestinian is a security threat.
Why aren't they all dead yet?
It's not for lack of trying.
I love to watch a Palestinian dying.
Nitwityahoo is always my choice.
To my patriotism he gives voice.
Someday we will expunge them all.
Then we will take down the wall.
3/16/20

Israel's occupation stimulated Palestinian nationalism,
This is in accord with healthy rationalism,
Because the Israelis have been so oppressive.
About stealing land they are obsessive.
Palestinians deserve a sovereign state.
Their dignity and that of the Jews should equate.
The world has been telling us this for so long:
Not supporting the Palestinians is wrong.
3/17/20

Only 11 percent of the wall runs along the Green Line.*
The rest cuts off 15 percent of the West Bank by design.
The wall enclosed "settlements" for eventual annexation..
That eventuality will soon be a realization.
Palestinians also live in the cut off land,
In their own private Bantustan.
Ultimately, Israel will move them.
Americans will not rue them.
3/18/20
*Inspired by <u>Beyond Chutzpah – On the Misuse of Anti-Semitism
and the Abuse of History</u> by Norman G. Finkelstein

Israel forces transfers on secret evidence.*
Related to a terrorist? We call that malevolence.
You will be plucked from your West Bank home,
And dropped into Gaza where you know no one.
The Supreme Court of Israel agrees on this:
The state can force transfers as much as it pleases.
That exalted court has also ruled,
That house demolitions are not racism fueled,
And can be conducted on short notice,
With collective punishment as the stated motive.
The Fourth Geneva Convention is irrelevant,
When it comes to Greater Israel development,
Israel is not bound by international law.
Its Supreme Court simply knows more.
3/18/20
*Inspired by _Beyond Chutzpah – On the Misuse of Anti-Semitism
and the Abuse of History_ by Norman G. Finkelstein

 A house is worth more in an occupation*
To knock them down Israel hastens.
When the troops arrive, you have an hour,
To save anything within your power.
After that the bulldozer begins.
The blameless family cringes.
Thousands of times houses have been destroyed,
Once places of sadness and joy.
3/8/20
*Inspired by _Beyond Chutzpah – On the Misuse of Anti-Semitism
and the Abuse of History_ by Norman G. Finkelstein

House demolition as a form of punishment*
Demonstrates Israel's Hunnishness.
It is against the Geneva Convention,
And the Hague Regulations not to mention.
Only Iraq under Saddam Hussein
Did the same.
3/8/20
*Inspired by _Beyond Chutzpah – On the Misuse of Anti-Semitism
and the Abuse of History_ by Norman G. Finkelstein

Liberals and Fake News are out to get me
I respond better when people pet me.
The Coronavirus is under control,
Although it has taken a toll
On my precious stock market.
Why am I always the target?
This is Chinese revenge for trade barriers.
Why do I shake hands with virus carriers?
Limiting spread could minimize damage.
There's nothing I do better than manage.
3/10/20

House demolitions constitute collective punishment.
Bulldozers make families' fortunes plummet.
People not accused of any crime are punished.
These barbarities show Israelis are Hunnish.
The families bore no blame for the suspects' acts.
The consciences of Israelis are lax.
Collective punishment violates international law,
But Israelis dispute that call.
3/10/20
*Inspired by Beyond Chutzpah – On the Misuse of Anti-Semitism
and the Abuse of History by Norman G. Finkelstein*

Due to discriminatory access to building permits,
Palestinians couldn't build "legally" though they yearn for it.
They "break the law" because they need more housing.
The arrangement with Israel is Faustian,
Because any day the army could bulldoze your abode
For a "settlement" or a Jewish-only bypass road.
Demolishing homes violates international covenants,
To which Israel is a party but thinks it's above them.
3/11/20
*Inspired by <u>Beyond Chutzpah – On the Misuse of Anti-Semitism
and the Abuse of History</u> by Norman G. Finkelstein*

Hundreds of thousands of fruit trees have been uprooted.*
Sometimes before destruction, houses are looted.
Criticism from America has been muted.
Israel is not what it's reputed.
People return to the ruins for what can be salvaged
From Israeli mechanized malice.
Palestinians aren't given time to harvest crops,
Before the bulldozer's blade drops.
3/11/20
*Inspired by <u>Beyond Chutzpah – On the Misuse of Anti-Semitism
and the Abuse of History</u> by Norman G. Finkelstein*

If he's afraid of Israel, he shouldn't be president.
That's why about Biden you should be hesitant
He's afraid to say "military occupation"
Toward Palestinians he has no commiseration.
Bernie Sanders is not afraid of Israel.
He hates how it makes Palestinians miserable.
He will bring justice to where it never existed.
Palestinians will be proud of all these years they resisted.
3/11/20

Political liquidations have the effect
Of stimulating terrorist attacks.
That Israelis want peace is a fable.
They want all the land on the negotiating table,
Which they at all costs try to avoid.
Giving land for peace would not bring them joy.
So when Hamas tries to make an agreement,
Israel assassinates a Hamas leader.
Then Hamas attacks with vengeance.
Israeli leaders created this.
3/1/20
*Inspired by <u>Beyond Chutzpah – On the Misuse of Anti-Semitism
and the Abuse of History</u> by Norman G. Finkelstein*

In the decades after the occupation began,
Torture of Palestinians was not banned.
Detainees were handcuffed, hooded and hung by the wrists.
They were beaten severely with clubs and fists.
Electric shock and sexual assault,
Banging heads repeatedly against walls.
America's Abu Graib pales in comparison.
The Israelis don't find it embarrassing.
3/1/20
*Inspired by <u>Beyond Chutzpah – On the Misuse of Anti-Semitism
and the Abuse of History</u> by Norman G. Finkelstein*

"Settlement", occupation, and apartheid won the Israeli election
A plurality of Jews made Nitwityahoo their selection.
He intends to annex part of the West Bank.
He got permission from the chief Yank.
But can he form a government while under indictment?
If not, there's hope for Jewish enlightenment.
In two weeks he will sit in the defendant's chair.
But about corruption, Israelis don't care.
3/3/20

 Being arrested in the Territories is bad fortune.
The detainee knows he will be tortured.
Hooded, he can't see the blows coming,
Hit in the testicles, the head, the stomach.
This has happened to thousands of boys and men.
If they ask for mercy, they are beaten again.
Israel is a fascist state.
Which America should berate.
Only in Israel was torture legally sanctioned,
Which doesn't make the Jews anxious.
 3/3/20
*Inspired by Beyond Chutzpah – On the Misuse of Anti-Semitism
and the Abuse of History by Norman G. Finkelstein

If the detainee is in a coma, he's not faking.
He got that way from violent shaking.
Rotational acceleration of the head
Makes detainees brain damaged dead.
This is another GSS tradition.
Blame the death on a preexisting condition.
3/3/20

Nitwityahoo proved once again that ugly campaigns are effective
Smearing Gantz with personal invective was his objective.
Rumors and innuendo the premier spread.
Gantz is immoral and dishonest, he said.
Yet in two weeks Nitwit will be tried for corruption.
That he won't do jail time is the assumption.
The sad thing is not just the reelection of Nitwityahoo.
It's that the majority of Jews think like him too.
3/4/20
*Inspired by "Israelis Stick With Netanyahu"
by Shmuel Rosner NYT OP-ED 3/4/20

Democratic socialists want a civilized society
In which all have dignity and security.
Healthcare is a human right.
Its realization is within sight.
The oldest candidate is ahead of his time.
But by cable news he was slimed.
Biden is afraid to say "occupation".
He's against a Palestine nation.
The Israel lobby already owns him.
It has de-backboned him.
3/4/20

Beaten and humiliated, Palestinians never got leniency.
They are treated as if they're meaningless.
Jews join the Border Police to get the chance
To beat up Arabs whenever they can
Israel did nothing regarding complaints.
The Israeli people are far from saints.
America is responsible for the persecution.
Israel and America underwent a fusion.
3/4/20
*Inspired by <u>Beyond Chutzpah – On the Misuse of Anti-Semitism
and the Abuse of History</u> by Norman G. Finkelstein

Religious fundamentalists preach that it's unGodly
For women to have autonomy over their bodies.
Men are lower than angels, and women lower than men.
Like the beasts below them, women must be penned.
10/23/12
*PG 168th Posting 11/4/12
<u>Poet Against Israel</u> by Timothy J. Callahan

An Israeli F-16 dropped a one ton bomb
On Shehadeh's apartment building home,
Killing him and 14 Palestinian civilians.
Israeli pilots are especially hideous.
He never cared that 9 of them were children:
Palestinians are here so we kill them.
All I felt was the release of the bomb.
Other than that I felt happy and calm.
2/22/20
*Inspired by <u>Beyond Chutzpah – On the Misuse of Anti-Semitism
 and the Abuse of History</u> by Norman G. Finkelstein*

The soldiers provoked Palestinians to throw stones.
If the jeeps hadn't come they would have gone home.
The soldiers enticed minors like mice to a trap
When the children came close, the IDF opened up.
It is a kind of sport to remove.
Palestinians always lose.
The Jews knew the Palestinians would not run
When they saw the jeeps come.
 2/22/20
*Inspired by <u>Beyond Chutzpah – On the Misuse of Anti-Semitism
and the Abuse of History</u> by Norman G. Finkelstein*

An army that kills so many children
Has no restraint on killing.
Israel dehumanizes Palestinian kids.
The soldiers who shoot them are glib.
The soldiers are taught not to feel guilty,
Even though their souls are filthy:
Palestinian life is worthless they say.
Better to kill them before they mate.
2/23/20

Rachel Corrie tried to save a Palestinian house
With the bulldozer, she decided to joust.
The bulldozer driver intended to hurt.
Soon Rachel fell down the moving mound of dirt.
He pushed her beneath the scoop and then the blade.
What a mess of Rachel's body this made.
He thought reversing it was fine.
He drove over her a second time.
*Inspired by <u>Beyond Chutzpah – On the Misuse of Anti-Semitism</u>
<u>and the Abuse of History</u> by Norman G. Finkelstein

The departure of the ambulance was coordinated with Israeli administration,
But the doctor and crew were headed for tribulation.
Israeli soldiers opened fire causing an explosion.
The doctor burned to death at the end of his sojourn.
The soldiers are Zionist zombies in a trance.
They blow up ambulances cleared in advance.
Israel does not abide by medical neutrality.
Its soldiers know only brutality.
2/25/20
*Inspired by <u>Beyond Chutzpah – On the Misuse of Anti-Semitism</u>
<u>and the Abuse of History</u> by Norman G. Finkelstein

House demolition is captured for TV viewers,
It renders hundreds homeless not accused of wrongdoing.
Assassination is another brutal tool
Against international rules.
Is he the one? Say yes.
Kill him with no attempt to arrest.
Undercover forces have a license to kill.
They don't have to ask victims to stand still.
Shooting them in the back is brave.
Think how much court time we save.
2/26/20
*Inspired by <u>Beyond Chutzpah – On the Misuse of Anti-Semitism</u>
<u>and the Abuse of History</u> by Norman G. Finkelstein

Sunday, February 23, 2020
Poetry Group Five Hundred Fiftieth Posting 2/23/20

The U.N. published a list of 112 companies
(which did not put Nitwityahoo at ease)
Doing business with "settlements" on Palestinian land.
These companies make money any way they can.
Airbnb, TripAdvisor and Expedia
Are among the list's greedier.
To do business with illegal "settlements" is to aid
The commission of war crimes today.
2/17/20

The U.N. is committed to its longstanding pledges
That there'd be two states with pre'67 edges.
Entrenching the occupation is Trump's plan's theme
And strengthening the apartheid regime.
Israel wants an end to the question of Palestine.
With Trump's "peace plan", that is fine.
Any Palestine would look like Swiss cheese.
The "settlements" are a pock-marking disease.
2/17/20

Trump knows Palestinians want a better economy,
But ignores the fact that they want autonomy.
The borders were to resemble those of pre-'67,
But Trump says annexation is a given.
Any state would be a mimic.
Sovereignty would be limited.
Anti-Americanism abounds.
Terrorism knows no bounds.
2/17/20

Elie said everything about Jews is unique
Like anti-Semitism and the Holocaust by the Nazi freak.
This "uniqueness" allows Israel unique moral dispensation.
The IDF can succumb to any bloody temptation.
One of the main reasons Israelis are such bastards
Is that they don't think they're bound by moral standards.
2/17/20
*Inspired by _Beyond Chutzpah – On the Misuse of Anti-Semitism
 and the Abuse of History_ by Norman G. Finkelstein

Israel's brutal repression of the Palestinians evokes
Hostility towards Israel expressed here in tropes.
Building illegal Jewish "settlements"
Elicits anti-Zionist sentiments.
But when there's hope for justice, take the early Oslo years,
Anti-Semitism declines and Israel gets cheers.
The diminishment of anti-Semitism is in Jewish hands.
Give back some of the Palestinians' land.
2/20/20
*Inspired by <u>Beyond Chutzpah – On the Misuse of Anti-Semitism
and the Abuse of History</u> by Norman G. Finkelstein

A charge of anti-Semitism is used to deflect
Legitimate criticism from those who want a check
On Israel's mistreatment of the indigenous.
Israel's persecution of Arabs has been hideous.
American cable news has a proclivity
For ignoring war crimes in the name of sensitivity:
We wouldn't want to offend our viewers.
God forbid, there might be fewer.
2/20/20

The IDF use excessive force
Killing a lot of civilians of course.
They used helicopter gunships
To go on murderous gun trips.
Extrajudicial execution was the goal
But many bystanders got full of holes.
The helicopters are courtesy of the USA,
Meant to be used in any way.
2/21/20
*Inspired by <u>Beyond Chutzpah – On the Misuse of Anti-Semitism
and the Abuse of History</u> by Norman G. Finkelstein

The IDF (as usual) unjustly
Took Jamal al-Sabbaagh into custody.
He posed no threat to those who detained him.
There was no rule of law to save him.
The IDF shot him dead,
With a bullet to his head.
Israeli soldiers are mirthless
They say Palestinian life is worthless.
2/21/20
*Inspired by <u>Beyond Chutzpah – On the Misuse of Anti-Semitism
and the Abuse of History</u> by Norman G. Finkelstein

Sunday, February 16, 2020

Israel was expected to keep some "settlement" blocs,
In exchange for land swaps.
Isolated, interior "settlements" would be vacated.
The Palestinian dream of statehood would be placated.
But that is not what the AmerIsrael plan calls for.
Israel stole land and will be allowed to steal more.
The Jordan Valley should not be annexed in its entirety.
But AmerIsrael practices land piracy.
Trump makes a joke of Palestinian aspirations.
Nitwityahoo likes to see their exasperation.
2/10/20

Bernie wants a country that helps workers, not just the 1%.
When he said justice, this is part of what he meant.
Do unto others what you would have them do unto you.
That's Bernie's spirituality and what he will do.
He's unafraid to talk about the Palestinian plight.
Biden is afraid of Israel to Israel's delight.
No lobby has a hook in Bernie.
Come with him on this reparative journey.
2/10/20

Those few Americans who know of Israel's ways
Are more sympathetic to the Palestinian case.
They sympathize because they are informed.
But knowledge of Israel is not the norm.
The reality of the conflict evokes hostility to Israel.
Palestinians are ignored by cable news so liberal.
Exposing Israel is now anti-Semitic.
Why doesn't the poet against Israel get it?
2/10/20

For conflating Palestinians with Nazis, Israel is keen.
But no comparisons of Israel to the Nazi regime.
Israel's army uses roundups, internment camps and watch towers.
All these are vestiges of Nazi power.
Israelis align with supporters of the far right.
In Trump's Zionism, Israel delights.
Over the Palestinians, they call themselves master-race.
They ethnically cleanse at a faster pace.
2/15/20
*Inspired by _Beyond Chutzpah – On the Misuse of Anti-Semitism
and the Abuse of History_ by Norman G. Finkelstein

Imagine an army of dicks like him.
He and his party of tea won't win:
"The Investor class will save this country,
If we just give the rich more money."
10/12/12
PG 165th Posting 10/14/12 from
Poet Against Israel by Timothy J. Callahan

I write poems the old fashioned way:
Their sound is as important as what they say,
Because sound enhances sense.
Sound makes sense clench.
10/15/12
PG 166th Posting 10/21/12 from
Poet Against Israel by Timothy J. Callahan

Sunday, February 9, 2020
Poetry Group Five Hundred Forty-Eighth Posting 2/9/20

It's an AmerIsrael agreement having nothing to do with peace.
Palestinian resistance will never cease.
Trump green-lighted Israel's newest land grab.
Palestinians he likes to jab.
Anti-Americanism will rise.
We are Israel's patsy in the world's eyes
The "Sunday Review" had nothing about this.
The media believes ignorance is bliss.
2/2/20

Nitwityahoo boasted they'd vote on Sunday
(Yet the cabinet didn't vote, and here it is Monday)
To annex a substantial amount of the West Bank.
For this opportunity, he has Trump to thank.
But Trump told him to wait till after the election.
Will Nitwityahoo defy Trump? That's the question.
To get the most votes
Nitwit cannot coast.
He must annex by Election Day,
Or far right voters might stay away.
2/4/20

Zionism has the advantage of a biblical coat.
On Israel the evangelicals dote.
Superstition outweighs the scientific world view.
Palestinians must be annulled by the Jews,
Who deny them the right of national existence.
Until a Palestinian state, Israel will face resistance.
Whose side do you think a Jesus would be on?
Not near as many Palestinians would be gone.
2/4/20
*Inspired by <u>Beyond Chutzpah – On the Misuse of Anti-Semitism
and the Abuse of History</u> by Norman G. Finkelstein*

Trump's so called "peace plan" will not bring peace.
Palestinian resistance will not cease
Until both sides are sovereign states.
What ethnic cooperation awaits.
But not under Donald Trump's watch.
His attempt at peace he botched.
But his political objective will come true:
Israelis will reelect Nitwityahoo.
2/8/20

The Israelis are killing teenage protestors again.
There will be peace, but I don't know when.
Trump took 30% of the 20%
That was for the Palestinians meant.
They were not offered sovereignty,
But a decrease in poverty.
2/8/20

She who complains, sins.
In every conception the state wins.
Her body is the state's until delivery.
Paul Ryan calls this chivalry.
8/18/12
*Line 1 by Saint Francis de Sales
PG 160th Posting 9/9/12 from
<u>Poet Against Israel</u> by Timothy J. Callahan

Down you mongrel, Death! Back into your kennel!*
Bold words, but the kennel is mental not metal.
I range at will. Where I go I kill.
I am voracious and cannot get my fill.
7/6/12
*Line 1 by Edna St. Vincent Millay
PG 161st Posting 9/16/12 from
Poet Against Israel by Timothy J. Callahan

Sunday, February 2, 2020
Poetry Group Five Hundred Forty-Seventh Posting 2/2/20

Herzl said Jews weren't safe except in a state of their own.
That this is also true of Palestinians is well known.
Jews vow never again to be victims.
Palestinians? Jews kick them.
Israel delegitimizes honest critics
Who also are Israel's victims.
America does Israel's bidding
And so a large share of the sinning.
1/26/20

Trump's Middle East peace plan won some applause.
It is a plan to liquidate the Palestinian cause.
No sovereign state or a roadmap to one.
Of Trump's plan, Palestinians will have none.
Trump aligns the U.S. with Israel's far right positions.
A Democratic president will reverse Trump's decision.
Only a Palestinian state will end the conflict.
That is what the world has long wanted.
1/28/20

According to Trump's peace plan long awaited,
None of the Jewish "settlements" would be vacated.
Palestinians would get a reduction in poverty
And maybe a small state with limited sovereignty.
Israel will annex more Palestinian land.
Nitwityahoo's reelection will be grand.
Trump's rich Jewish donors will reward him.
Republican Jews can afford him.
2/1/20

Must I leave my guns at the Gates of Zion?
Heaven wouldn't be heaven without my shooting iron.
Or perhaps God is an NRA member.
Then my guns I will never surrender.
8/5/12
PG 158th Posting 8-26-12 from
Poet Against Israel by Timothy J. Callahan

There is no coming to consciousness without pain.
Consciousness is both a blessing and a bane.
Staying asleep seems a better thing,
Than waking and remembering.
 7/7/12
*Line 1 by Carl Jung
PG 160th Posting 9-9-12 from
Poet Against Israel by Timothy J. Callahan

Sunday, January 26, 2020
Poetry Group Five Hundred Forty-Sixth Posting 1/26/20

It is standard Israeli policy
To steal Palestinian property.
Israelis favor mass killings
Of Palestinian civilians.
Committing crimes against humanity
Does not detract from that nation's vanity.
A charge of apartheid? Israel pooh-poohs it.
Israel tells the world, get used to it.
1/20/20

One means of torture that seldom fails,
Is shoving a needle under someone's fingernails.
I want maximal pain . . . the most excruciating, intense, immediate pain.
For the conflict, the Palestinians are to bla
Palestinian villages are automatically destroyed
Because of the actions of one village boy.
Targeted assassination reduces collateral damage.
It can even be performed on the Sabbath.
1/20/20
*Inspired by *Beyond Chutzpah – On the Misuse of Anti-Semitism
and the Abuse of History* by Norman G. Finkelstein
Line 2-3 by Alan Dershowitz

The time has come when
Republicans will sell out again.
The Senate will not convict Trump,
Who tells Republicans how high to jump.
They are afraid of his retribution.
They are averse to election losing.
With obsequiousness they trick him.
Republicans won't convict him.
1/21/20

Israel critics in the U.S. are novelties.
Chomsky is a brave critic of Israeli policies.
Israel apologists call him an anti-Semite;
We showed that Israel is a sepulcher white.
Jewish American liberals are in the vanguard.
Noam Chomsky writes with the gift of a bard.
Academia is on the Palestinian side.
It doesn't like to see justice denied.
1/21/20
*Inspired by Beyond Chutzpah – On the Misuse of Anti-Semitism
and the Abuse of History by Norman G. Finkelstein*

The vast majority of Palestinians killed have been civilians.
Israeli soldiers are reckless villains.
A large proportion of the dead were children.
Israeli soldiers are indiscriminate killers.
To be against Israel is to be anti-racism
And anti-Israel disgracism.
Oppose Israel and be anti-imperialism.
Come to Gaza for the realism.
1/21/20

Into Jenin the IDF slammed
Jenin is a large refugee camp.
Thousands homeless and hundreds dead.
For killing Arabs the soldiers were bred.
Most of the home destruction was done after the fight.
Just for the hell of it and out of spite.
Israel held up humanitarian aid for ten days.
It likes to cause the most pain when it invades.
1/21/20
*Inspired by _Beyond Chutzpah – On the Misuse of Anti-Semitism
and the Abuse of History_ by Norman G. Finkelstein

Why did Adam have a navel?
When God did him a favor
And spared him time in the womb?
God has a navel too I presume.
9/18/12
*Line 1 from Omphalos by Philip Gosse,
discussed in The Greatest Show On Earth (p. 214) by Richard Dawkins
*PG 163rd Posting 9/30/12 from Poet Against Israel by Timothy J. Callahan

Does the dignity of the service compensate for the holes in his chest?
None of the gathered bereaved say yes.
At the center of the service is a member of the service.
If he could talk, he'd say I don't deserve this.
10/23/12
*PG 169th Posting 11/11/12 from Poet Against Israel by Timothy J. Callahan

The fate of Jews is more important than that of Palestinians,
And it's always okay to kill their civilians.
No justification exists for Zionism except a racist one.
Racism explains the taking at the point of a gun,
And the denial of basic human rights.
Racists created the Palestinian plight.
1/12/20

Finkelstein and others were very critical
Of Dershowitz's The Case for Israel.
The book was an academic fraud,
Though it held the public awed.
The author appropriates large swaths
Of another hoax book from the past.
He stitched together evidence out of whole cloth.
A misinformed public is the cost.
1/13/20
*Inspired by <u>Beyond Chutzpah – On the Misuse of Anti-Semitism
and the Abuse of History</u> by Norman G. Finkelstein*

Anti-Semitism is any challenge to Jewish interests.
Israelis complain that Israel is not finished.
Critics of Israeli hegemony
Are labeled a public enemy.
No one can criticize Israel anymore.
A charge of anti-Semitism bars the door.
Most critics lack any animus toward Jews.
The just don't want the Palestinians to lose.
1/14/20
*Inspired by Beyond Chutzpah – On the Misuse of Anti-Semitism
 and the Abuse of History by Norman G. Finkelstein*

When peace gets favorable press
And war a bad name,
Then Israel gets depressed,
But never takes any blame.
In 1982, when Israel felt peace pressure,
It started a war in Lebanon for good measure.
Critics were not motivated by anti-Jewish animus.
They recoiled at another bloody Israeli tantrum.
1/15/20
Inspired by <u>*Beyond Chutzpah – On the Misuse of Anti-Semitism
and the Abuse of History*</u> *by Norman G. Finkelstein*

Sick of criticism, Zionists changed the equation.
They called Israel "the Jew among nations".
So criticizing Israel became anti-Semitic.
Valid criticism and anti-Semitism were wedded.
Israel and Jews want to appear as victims.
Israel's victimhood is promoted by Christians.
1/15/20
**Inspired by* <u>*Beyond Chutzpah – On the Misuse of Anti-Semitism
and the Abuse of History*</u> *by Norman G. Finkelstein*

You can have faith in a tree.
Trust one and you will see.
A tree will always be there
Whenever you need to share.
You can lose yourself in green
The most beautiful color ever seen.
Climb into her upper branches.
In the wind she sings and dances.
9/20/12
**PG 163rd Posting 9/30/12 from
Poet Against Israel by Timothy J. Callahan*

Defend your faith when you hear
There is something wrong with the atmosphere.
Liberals say earth is getting warmer.
These blasphemers say this is God's warning.
If God is telling us anything,
It's that the sky is tainted by mankind's sin.
We are living in the End of Days.
Christ will return in clean air or haze.
9/13/12
*PG 164th Posting 10/7/12 from
Poet Against Israel by Timothy J. Callahan

Sunday, January 12, 2020
Poetry Group Five Hundred Forty-Third Posting 1/12/20

A moral and a legal right is meaningless unless it can be exercised.
Israeli wrongs need to be rectified.
The Palestinian refugees have a right of return.
How to satisfy it the U.S. must learn.
Evacuated "settlements" could be given instead,
Of the exact land from which they fled.
The refugees can be given their own homes,
Just as I have shown.
1/6/20
*Line 1 by Norman G. Finklelstein from Beyond Chutzpah —
On the Misuse of Anti-Semitism and the Abuse of History

A 1989 U.N. General Assembly Resolution,
Reaffirming the two-state solution,
Passed 151 to 3.
Almost the whole world agrees,
That a Palestine should exist
By an adjacent Israel kissed.
This will bring Middle East peace.
Anti-Americanism would eventually cease.
1/6/20
*Inspired by _Beyond Chutzpah – On the Misuse of Anti-Semitism
and the Abuse of History_ by Norman G. Finkelstein

The Euro-American conquest of North America,
Or the apartheid regime in South Africa.
Israel comes out on the wrong side of the analogy.
Israel's greatness is fallacy.
The right is wrong everywhere but Israel.
There the worst thing is a liberal.
We don't want most; we want it all.
Around the Palestinians we'll build more walls.
1/8/20
*Inspired by _Beyond Chutzpah – On the Misuse of Anti-Semitism
and the Abuse of History_ by Norman G. Finkelstein

The Jews voided the two millennia of non-Jewish habitation.
"Historical rights" is their time manipulation.
Two thousand years they lived outside of Palestine.
They have to share and shouldn't whine.
They have no right to that land but in mystical terms.
Time to ameliorate real world concerns.
Only a Palestinian state will end the conflict,
What the civilized world has long wanted.
1/8/20

Israel holds out as long as possible in defiance of international law.
Its creation fundamentally flawed.
The Jews created sufficient facts on the ground.
The hands of the clock turned round and round.
Then they said reality cannot be reversed.
The Palestinians must be cursed.
Palestine is Israel now
Which can't be changed no how.
1/8/20
*Inspired by Beyond Chutzpah – On the Misuse of Anti-Semitism
 and the Abuse of History by Norman G. Finkelstein*

Nazi/Holocaust movies arouse cynicism.
They make Jews not Palestinians the victims.
Exploitation of anti-Semitism can delegitimize
Israel critics who rightly criticize.
Israel must withdraw from the Occupied Territories,
Then spend a decade showing it is sorry.
The end of anti-Semitism is within Israel's grasp.
To sovereignty let the Palestinians pass.
1/8/20
*Inspired by Beyond Chutzpah – On the Misuse of Anti-Semitism
and the Abuse of History by Norman G. Finkelstein*

Abraham, I have a task for you.
Lord, don't ask what I can't possibly do.
But that is exactly what I am telling you to do.
And I hope you enjoy the spectacular view.
Up yon mountain you and Isaac will tread.
When you get to the top, cut off his head.
7/14/12
*PG 153rd Posting 7/22/12 from
Poet Against Israel by Timothy J. Callahan

Sunday, January 5, 2020
Poetry Group Five Hundred Forty-Second Posting 1/5/20

In Israel's June '82 Lebanon fight,
Its brutal practices came to light.
Lebanon did not censor Western journalists,
Who reported that the Israelis were murderous,
Killing thousands of civilians,
Backed by U.S. billions.
Israel stood aside and let its Christian allies
Turn refugees into food for flies.
12/29/19
*Inspired by Beyond Chutzpah – On the Misuse of Anti-Semitism
and the Abuse of History by Norman G. Finkelstein

Palestinians were ethnically cleansed in 1948
To make way for the new Jewish state.
Morally, this was a major crime.
Palestinians will not return any time.
Why can't they have just 20 percent of
The ancient homeland they are bereft of?
12/29/19
*Inspired by Beyond Chutzpah – On the Misuse of Anti-Semitism
and the Abuse of History by Norman G. Finkelstein*

The establishment of a state religion is forbidden.
A.G. Barr keeps the Constitution well hidden.
Religious authoritarianism is his thing.
Christian nationalists he begins.
He wants taxpayers to fund Christian schools,
Though he knows that's not cool.
He wants President Trump treated like a king.
To his bible and his guns he clings.
12/30/19
*Inspired by "Barr Thinks America Is Going to Hell"
by Katherine Steward and Caroline Frederickson
NYT OP-ED 12-30-19*

Zionists say in 1948 Palestinians became refugees,
Because Arab radio instructed them to flee.
Later, scholars studied the radio archives:
No such broadcasts were ever alive.
More Zionist mythology needed to be dispelled.
A forest of rotten falsehoods was felled.
1/1/20
*Inspired by Beyond Chutzpah – On the Misuse of Anti-Semitism
and the Abuse of History by Norman G. Finkelstein*

Of all his themes, payback for injustices suffered
By the Palestinians, whom AmerIsrael smothered,
Is the most recurring notion in bin Laden's speeches,
Which went out to the world's farthest reaches.
Unconditional support for Israel imposes secondary costs,
Like the thousands on 9/11 lost.
3/12/19
*Inspired by _The Israel Lobby and U.S. Foreign Policy_
by John J. Mearsheimer and Stephen M. Walt
*PG 500th Posting 3/17/19
timothyjcallahan.blogspot.com

Imagine the Immaculate Conception:
No original sin since inception.
She grew up the Blessed Virgin Mary.
On his way out, Jesus popped her cherry.
4/9/12
*PG 139th Posting 4/15/12 from
Poet Against Israel by Timothy J. Callahan

Sunday, December 29, 2019
Poetry Group Five Hundred Forty-First Posting 12/29/19

Israelis call the two-state solution a delusion:
Justice for Palestinians is an illusion.
But under intense international pressure,
Israel has been forced to take measures.
Like postponing the building of "settlement" projects.
Stopping further Zionism is not farfetched.
The two-state solution is more than a slogan.
Al Aqsa mosque is more than a token.
12/23/19

Begin knew he was lying at Camp David.
The meeting was not Carter's favorite.
Both men had said with vehemence
There'd be no "settlements" before the peace agreement.
Back home, Begin ordered more "settlement" building.
Carter realized that Begin was a villain.
No President could stop the "settlements".
Carter was too much of a gentleman.
12/23/19
*Inspired by The Israel Lobby and U.S. Foreign Policy
by John J. Mearsheimer and Stephen M. Walt*

On June 8, 1967, the Six Day War was well underway.
Israel decided to bomb an American ship that day.
The USS Liberty was an intelligence ship.
Israeli aircraft and boats tried to make it flip.
Thirty-four U.S. sailors were killed.
That is what Israel willed.
The Israelis said it was an accident,
But that's not what the attack meant.
12/23/19
*Inspired by The Israel Lobby and U.S. Foreign Policy
by John J. Mearsheimer and Stephen M. Walt*

President Kennedy put himself in political jeopardy,
When he gave Israel U.S. weaponry.
He was trying to dissuade Israel from a nuclear arsenal
But thinking Israel would be amenable was farcical.
Israel badly wanted the product of Dimona.
It did not care if the world made it a loner.
It wanted offensive weapons from the U.S.
The country that would always say yes.
12/25/29
*Inspired by The Israel Lobby and U.S. Foreign Policy
by John J. Mearsheimer and Stephen M. Walt*

We will find out what it meant,
That Sanders did the most events
In California, delegate rich.
The people like Bernie's pitch.
Knock on doors and make phone calls.
His win won't be close at all.
Vote and get a friend to vote.
Bernie could gloat, but he certainly won't.
He will pick a cabinet of the brightest and best.
He will lead the people's fairness quest.
12/26/19

Does an indicted Prime Minister deserve another term?
Should Nitwityahoo's career be adjourned?
Half the Israelis want him reelected.
In Nitwityahoo they see their hate reflected.
The other half want centrist Benny Gantz.
Israel's reputation he could enhance.
Israelis on both sides want annexation.
They don't want a Palestinian nation.
12/27/19

The truth crows as clearly as a rooster.
Justice will prevail now or in the future.
It took the Irish 600 years
Of blood, sweat, starvation and tears
To get their land back.
May Palestine come quicker than that.
3/8/12
*PG 135*th* Posting 3/18/12 from*
Poet Against Israel by Timothy J. Callahan

Sunday, December 22, 2019
Poetry Group Five Hundred Fortieth Posting 12/22/19

Helping Israel should no longer mean defending it uncritically.
Cut military and financial aid to Israel fittingly.
Cut out the politicians who take lobby contributions.
Make it U.S. policy to impose a two-state solution.
Only one candidate would do these things:
Bernie would, and Middle East peace bring.
12/15/19

Without Jewish Americans, Israel would not have been established.
They controlled politicians in order to have it.
But America's own interests suffered.
America subverted itself to another.
We enabled the Israeli occupation.
Preventing a Palestinian nation.
The 9/11 attacks
Were by Arabs getting back.
12/15/19
Inspired by The Israel Lobby and U.S. Foreign Policy
by John J. Mearsheimer and Stephen M. Walt

The state of Israel is the result of a racist endeavor.
Jews everywhere are associated with it forever.
Trump's order equates anti-Zionism with anti-Semitism.
No wonder he came in for college student criticism.
Israel is bad and many students know it.
They are pro-Palestinians and want to show it.
If Jewish students are offended or scared,
They should write or call you know where
And tell Mr. Nitwityahoo
Palestinians deserve a state too.
12/16/19

Is it fair that Jews take all the land and Palestinians get none?
No, it's not, and Israel should be shunned.
Could the conflict end without a Palestinian state?
No, because the dignity of the two peoples would not equate.
What would happen if Israel allowed a Palestinian state?
The rest of the world would call Israel great.
12/17/19

Which of the two progressive candidates,
Will win? – You have to wait.
Two liberal titans in the same primary contest.
Both of them walking into that long sunset.
Warren has been overtaken by Sanders on the left.
Warren in a Sanders administration would be a gift.
Bernie will end the Israeli-Palestinian conflict,
By giving the Palestinians what they have long wanted.
12/17/19

The wellbeing of Israel is in U.S. interests on moral grounds,
But its presence in the Occupied Territories is out of bounds.
West Bank "Settlements" are a huge mistake.
Aid to Israel needs to hit the brakes.
Much anti-Americanism we have created.
Unconditional aid to Israel is outdated.
Only a Palestinian state will end the conflict.
A long time ago we should have done it.
12/20/19
*Inspired by _The Israel Lobby and U.S. Foreign Policy_
by John J. Mearsheimer and Stephen M. Walt

What if Joseph and Mary never married?
What if Holy Mary miscarried?
That wouldn't be what God expected.
He had a plan and that would have wrecked it.
Or could the fetus that would have been Jesus
Somehow to salvation lead us?
*PG 129th Posting 2/5/12 from
Poet Against Israel by Timothy J. Callahan

Israelis want to ethnically cleanse the West Bank,
An easy task with bombers and tanks.
Due to Israeli vanity and bloodthirsty insanity,
The Jews will commit another crime against humanity.
This heinous act will not end the conflict,
But the U.S. Congress will say we want this.
The Israel lobby is the pied piper of Congress.
Look at all these years of cleansing progress.
12/9/19
Inspired by The Israel Lobby and U.S. Foreign Policy
by John J. Mearsheimer and Stephen M. Walt

The lobby undermined some of Israel's interests unwittingly.
It regrets the loss of the Democrats bitterly.
But the Trumpublicans are still under the spell.
Their votes on Israel they willingly sell.
Congress always puts Israel on top.
Anti-Americanism is the steady crop.
World terrorism grows from that.
Nitwityahoo has been chief rat.
12/9/19
Inspired by The Israel Lobby and U.S. Foreign Policy
by John J. Mearsheimer and Stephen M. Walt

The Israel lobby's control of Congress is sinfulness.
Campaign finance reform would reduce its influence.
Publicly financing elections would break the link.
Elected officials could stare down the lobby and not blink.
Deliberations would be more open on Capitol Hill.
Legislators would not fear the lobby's chill.
Give Congress members freedom and solace.
Purge private money from the electoral process.
12/9/19
*Inspired by <u>The Israel Lobby and U.S. Foreign Policy</u>
by John J. Mearsheimer and Stephen M. Walt*

The Jews who founded Israel were underhanded.
Most Americans don't understand it:
Why are the Palestinians so upset?
They provoke Israel, which they then regret.
Don't they know they are defeated?
Many times they have been beaten.
12/10/19
*Inspired by <u>The Israel Lobby and U.S. Foreign Policy</u>
by John J. Mearsheimer and Stephen M. Walt*

Reject politicians' pro-Israel platitudes.
Palestinian history will change your attitude.
The lobby stifles open dialogue.
We want sunlight; they want fog.
Campaign contributions from pro-Israel PACs
Convince politicians to hide the facts.
The media keeps Americans in the dark.
The consumers are easy marks.
12/10/19

The Israel lobby hates sensible moderates.
Any criticism of Israel the lobby can't tolerate.
Critics are marginalized and smeared.
New voices are forced to yield.
The lobby hates open discussion and free speech.
The truth about Israel remains out of reach.
Israeli leaders are guilty of war crimes.
Cable news thinks ignorance is fine.
12/11/19
*Inspired by _The Israel Lobby and U.S. Foreign Policy_
by John J. Mearsheimer and Stephen M. Walt

Trump says anti-Semitism includes anti-Israel sentiment.
He discards the First Amendment and applies censorship.
The U.N. has resolved that Zionism is racism.
Build a Palestinian state to end anti-Semitism.
Trump makes colleges adopt policies that will chill
The valid critics of Israel's ill will.
12/14/19

Darling, I feel the eyes of Our Lord.
His eyes have unmade my sword.
Take heart, my love. Yes, God is a voyeur.
But praise mercy, He's not a joiner.
12/14/11
*PG 128th Posting 1/29/12 from
Poet Against Israel by Timothy J. Callahan

To begin the Palestinian Earthly heaven,
The Jews must withdraw from what they stole in '67.
President Sanders will use the full leverage at his disposal.
The West Bank will be interior Palestine and Gaza the coastal.
Under two states violence would decrease.
Sympathy for terrorists would cease.
Israel will support the solution of two states
Or U.S. aid will quickly abate.
Only Bernie could throw this much shade.
Of Israel, Biden is afraid.
11/30/19

If a Democratic president told the "settlers" to move,
And Israel fought this nail and tooth.
Israel's dominance of the U.S. could be blown.
Israel would proceed as a colonial power on its own.
If Israel is too greedy to give up its colonies,
America should walk away saying don't follow me.
Palestinian blood stains America's hands.
We helped kill them and steal their land.
12/2/19

To get *Roe v. Wade*, women made a lot of noise.
They fought for their right of reproductive choice.
And now under Trump that fight has resumed.
Republicans more than ever want to control women's wombs.
With two appointments, Trump moved the Supreme Court to the right.
That court will soon be the venue of the fight.
The same court that giveth can taketh away.
Get out and support a Democrat today.
12/3/19

The University of North Carolina at Chapel Hill
Spent millions against the student body's will
For the upkeep of a Confederate statue.
The $2.5 million went to that group.
Neo-Confederates are white supremacists.
The Democratic Party is their nemesis.
Spend money on the descendants of slaves,
The university's reputation save.
12/4/19
*Inspired by "A Subsidy for White Nationalism"
by William Sturkey NYT OP-ED 12-4-19*

Denying Palestinians political rights has not made Israel safer.
Billions in unconditional aid hasn't been a favor.
After over fifty years, the Palestinians are still stateless.
Israel put them on the forever wait list.
America underwrites the "settlement" building,
And the Palestinian civilians killing.
Anti-Americanism provokes terror attacks.
Bought legislators stab us in the back.
12/4/19

Oh Father, I fear the nails.
My constant faith failed.
I wish I could pass this cup
And still have all your love.
Please keep me from
Thy Will be done.
10/24/11
*PG 115th Posting 10/30/11 from
Poet Against Israel by Timothy J. Callahan*

Can I master my fate or is it too late?
Is mastering fate even a human trait?
Jonah fled God's fate but wound up following it.
He had his pride, but a whale kept swallowing it.
10/19/11
*PG 118th Posting 11/20/11 from
Poet Against Israel by Timothy J. Callahan

Sunday, December 1, 2019
Poetry Group Five Hundred Thirty-Seventh Posting 12/1/19

America should use its considerable leverage,
To make the selfish Israelis generous.
A sovereign Palestine should be our policy.
Palestinians deserve liberty and equality,
Which they will have only in their own land.
Back to Israel the "settlers" will be remanded.
Why must the Jews have all of everything?
To life under occupation, the Palestinians cling.
11/24/19
*Inspired by The Israel Lobby and U.S. Foreign Policy
by John J. Mearsheimer and Stephen M. Walt

Israel's value to the U.S. is reduced by its pariah status in the region.
Muslims who detest the occupation are legion.
Israel is prohibited from "coalitions of the willing".
Other nations recoil at Israel's Palestinian killing.
America adheres to a blind allegiance to an uncooperative partner.
This fidelity made America Israel's martyr.
About the 9/11 attacks,
The reporting was lax.
11/24/19
*Inspired by The Israel Lobby and U.S. Foreign Policy
by John J. Mearsheimer and Stephen M. Walt

In July, President Trump boasted a taunt:
The Constitution gives me the right to do what I want.
I bribed Zelensky with millions in aid,
To turn some lemons into lemonade.
I was trying to fix the upcoming election.
Voters should make me their selection.
We could put Clinton, Obama, and Biden behind bars.
Putin says such was done in the days of the Czars.
11/25/19

Hey man, I'll give you this for that.
I want dirt on the Bidens that knocks Joe flat.
Announce the investigation on TV,
Then millions in military assistance you'll see.
I will even invite you to the White House,
But on the Bidens, you must pounce.
Nothing moves until you move.
Be my pawn, not a fool.
11/25/19

Israel has chosen one-state with apartheid.
It rejected the idea of an 80/20 divide.
All these years and the Israelis don't get the gist.
Under apartheid, Palestinians will continue to resist.
They want a homeland on their own land.
They don't give a damn about Yahweh's plan.
11/25/19

The U.S. should treat Israel as a normal state.
Israel's and America's interests are not the same.
America's policy is now and long was
To heavily support Israel no matter what it does.
No more annual multi-billion dollar handouts.
Israel can support itself no doubt.
When Israel behaves badly, there should be a supposition
That Israel will face U.S. opposition.
11/26/19
*Inspired by <u>The Israel Lobby and U.S. Foreign Policy</u>
by John J. Mearsheimer and Stephen M. Walt*

President Sanders will take a harder line
(And this will be way past time)
On Israeli war crimes.
The West Bank will have a new design.
One that includes a Palestinian state.
Only Bernie can shape that fate.
It's a shame how long we've had to wait.
With Bernie, a just peace will not be too late.
11/26/19

American Jews are falling out of love,
With the Jewish state once held high above.
They reject the Israel-right-or-wrong line.
They want the creation of a Palestine.
Not a liberal democracy, Israel can't emulate the U.S.
Israel is an occupying force, no less.
Israel's Zionism is militaristic,
But like us, they are capitalistic.
We don't have much in common with Israel,
A land which makes millions miserable.
11/17/19
Inspired by "Difficult Love – Why are American Jews
at odds with Israel" by Judith Shulevitz
<u>*The New York Times Book Review*</u> *11-17-19*

I can tell you in terse verse,
That when I owned Miss Universe,
Ukraine was always well represented.
When the women were dressing, I entered.
Now I want a Biden investigation.
Re-election is my destination.
Yovanovitch wouldn't look cute in a bathing suit.
All other issues are moot.
11/18/19

From Israel, America should keep its distance,
No more billions of dollars in assistance.
Treat Israel not as a special case, but as a normal state.
Billions to Israel causes anti-American hate.
Israel does not deserve support in light of what it does.
Israel today is not what it once was.
It has an advanced and diversified economy.
Israel can afford to be an autonomy.
11/18/19
*Inspired by The Israel Lobby and U.S. Foreign Policy
by John J. Mearsheimer and Stephen M. Walt

America should use its considerable leverage
To give the Jews and Palestinians severance.
Israel must withdraw from the land it has occupied.
The "settlements" are war crimes; Israel has no alibi.
The U.S. does Israel no favors by avoiding the two-state solution.
The avoidance is due to lobby-legislature collusion.
The U.S. Congress subsidizes the occupation.
The Palestinians deserve a new nation.
11/18/19
*Inspired by The Israel Lobby and U.S. Foreign Policy
by John J. Mearsheimer and Stephen M. Walt

The justice for Palestinians movement just hit a wall.
Trump says "settlements" are not inconsistent with international law.
The Fourth Geneva Convention forbids occupiers
From putting their civilians in the land occupied.
The International Criminal Court calls the "settlements" war crimes.
The Palestinians Israel deprives.
When Nitwityahoo annexes the West Bank,
We will have the Trump administration to thank.
11/20/19

The whistle-blower is hearsay, said the Republicans quite galled.
He was not even on the July 25th call!
When presented with two witnesses who had listened in,
The Republicans were happy, right? Guess again.
Now they want to know who the whistle-blower is.
They want to make abject misery his.
11/20/19

This is the policy with which China wound up:
Round up everyone who should be rounded up.
In re-education camps Muslims are interned,
Not to be released until love of Communism they learn.
Some will need years of indoctrination
To rid them of religious preoccupation.
11/20/19

You can close your eyes to reality but not to memories.
With unwanted memories my mind hemorrhages.
To stanch the flow, I press the wound.
That will stop the memories soon.
Forgetting them is much harder than remembering.
I wish I was not at their engendering.
7/26/11
*PG 104th Posting 8/4/11 from
Poet Against Israel by Timothy J. Callahan
**Line 1 by Stanislaw J. Lec

Sunday, November 17, 2019
Poetry Group Five Hundred Thirty-Fifth Posting 11/17/19

The richest today pay much less of their income,
In taxes than the richest paid in 1961,
When federal, state, and local added up to 51.5 percent.
In 2011 the wealthiest paid 33.2 percent.
Collect more from those who have the most.
Let universal healthcare be our country's boast.
11/11/19
*Inspired by "The Billionaires Are Getting Nervous"
Editorial, Sunday Review, NYT 11-10-19*

In the Lebanon war, the U.S. was Israel's savior.
The world harshly condemned Israel's behavior.
There was no strategic or moral rationale
To support Israel's mass murder most foul.
The lobby kept the U.S. and Israel aligned.
Historians have not been kind.
The lobby hurt Israel and the U.S.
Whatever it asks, the U.S. says yes.
11/11/19
*Inspired by The Israel Lobby and U.S. Foreign Policy
by John J. Mearsheimer and Stephen M. Walt*

The lobby makes it hard for U.S. leaders to pressure Israel,
Which prolongs the Israeli-Palestinian conflict so miserable.
Islamic terrorists use the conflict as a recruiting tool.
Slave to Israel, America plays the fool.
Widespread anti-Americanism is the result
From the lobby our country must revolt.
11/11/19
*Inspired by <u>The Israel Lobby and U.S. Foreign Policy</u>
by John J. Mearsheimer and Stephen M. Walt*

Most people want to see higher taxes on the rich,
Except for the likes of Moscow Mitch.
A majority want increased social programs,
But not that sycophant Lindsay Graham.
Trump's base votes against its own self-interest.
We want to end racism. They are against this.
11/12/19

Nothing could justify or explain
The billions of U.S. dollars Israel claims.
And why must the money be unconditional?
Why do we pay to keep Gaza unlivable?
The Israel lobby steers the ship of state.
Can we free ourselves, or is it too late?
To criticize Israel, politicians get wobbly.
No one can withstand the Israel lobby.
11/12/19

America enables Israel's refusal
To feel the aspirations of the loser.
The lobby makes America willing
To finance illegal "settlement" building.
Washington cannot convince Israel
To stop making so many miserable.
The U.S. helped the losers of World War II.
Why can't Israel help the vanquished too?
11/12/19
*Inspired by <u>The Israel Lobby and U.S. Foreign Policy</u>
by John J. Mearsheimer and Stephen M. Walt

Trump's efforts to hinder the House investigation
Will not get him to his "perfect" destination.
Brave witnesses are defying his instructions.
No thanks to Trump, justice functions.
Hiding the truth about conversations and events
Is itself an impeachable offense.
11/13/19
*Inspired by "What Is the President Hiding?"
by Neal Katyal NYT OP-ED 11-13-19

I could just pull the trigger
And in an instant be bigger,
Because that would prove what I'm made of,
Shooting the man I'm afraid of.
12/19/11
*PG 123rd Posting 12/25/11 from
Poet Against Israel by Timothy J. Callahan

Trump does not prioritize the two state solution,
But a peace plan without it is an illusion.
Kushner thinks money can buy anything,
Like no Palestine with Nitwityahoo as king.
Palestinians will have justice only in their own land.
This Palestinian dream Israel bans.
Trump is cushy with the Israeli right.
He doesn't care about the Palestinian plight.
11/3/19

Despite all Trump's belligerence and finery,
Candidates criticized him in the primary.
Senator Ted Cruz called Trump a "pathological liar".
Trump called himself an American Obama denier.
"Con artist" was Senator Rubio's description.
That could be Trump's tombstone inscription.
He's a "race-baiting, xenophobic, religious bigot" said Senator Graham.
That these three changed their minds is a sham
11/4/19

The lobby tried to give Amnesty International and Human Rights Watch a
bad name,
For their critical reports on Israel's bombing campaign.
AIPAC had sent out press releases,
Saying civilian security increases,
Because the IDF conducts only surgical strikes,
Avoiding civilians, which liberals like.
This purported care turned out not to be the case.
Hundreds of civilians died in that place.
11/4/19
*Inspired by <u>The Israel Lobby and U.S. Foreign Policy</u>
by John J. Mearsheimer and Stephen M. Walt*

Nitwityahoo incites Israelis to vilify one another,
Israelis are impatient for someone other.
Benny Gantz is forming a new government.
His accession will bring a positive trend.
The right in Israel encourages haters.
If you talk peace in Israel you're a traitor.
If you see that Arabs are human beings
The right says you're not seeing.
11/5/19

Israel offered a company the job of building a rail line.
That Spanish company politely declined.
The project was to be built on stolen Palestinian land.
All companies should ban Israel's light rail plan,
And not operate in the "settlement" blocks,
Or for complicity in abuse they will be mocked.
Stand up to Israel's clampdown.
Palestinians are sovereignty bound.
11/6/19

We will make you what you are not.
No more improperly using what you've got.
Together we will pray away the gay.
 In a month of Sundays, you'll wake up straight.
Amongst all men's minds, yours will be cleanest.
Jesus Christ will bless your penis.
7/16/11
*PG 101st Posting 7/24/11 from
Poet Against Israel by Timothy J. Callahan

His poetry is discursive
And dangerously subversive.
If he ever gets a following,
Our people will be shadowing.
We will stop his chattering.
9/9/11
*PG 120th Posting 12/4/11 from
Poet Against Israel by Timothy J. Callahan

Sunday, November 3, 2019
Poetry Group Five Hundred Thirty-Third Posting 11/3/19

When the second Lebanon war commenced,
Global criticism of Israel was dense.
The U.S. gave Israel extraordinary diplomatic protection,
Much to the world's vexation.
America's U.N. ambassador John Bolton
Was to the Israeli delegation golden.
He vetoed a resolution condemning Israel,
For making the Lebanese miserable.
He worked against any U.N. imposed cease-fires,
To give Israel time to satisfy its murderous desires.
10/27/19
Inspired by The Israel Lobby and U.S. Foreign Policy
by John J. Mearsheimer and Stephen M. Walt

AIPAC wrote the resolution supporting Israel.
The Lebanese were dead or miserable.
Pelosi wanted to add something humane and functional:
"All sides to protect civilian life and infrastructure."
But AIPAC strongly objected to this particular clause.
That language did not make it past Boehner's jaws.
10/28/19
Inspired by The Israel Lobby and U.S. Foreign Policy
by John J. Mearsheimer and Stephen M. Walt

Van Hollen urged Secretary Rice to seek a cease-fire,
And send peace-keepers to Lebanon most dire.
The lobby was furious with him for daring to criticize Israel.
It decided to make the congressman miserable.
He had to apologize to all the Jewish groups:
I did not mean to criticize Israel, whoops.
He went on a five-day trip to Israel, accompanied by
Three pro-Israel activists and from AIPAC some staff guy.
The goal was to chastise Van Hollen and to remind
Other members of the cost of getting out of line.
 0/28/19
*Inspired by <u>The Israel Lobby and U.S. Foreign Policy</u>
by John J. Mearsheimer and Stephen M. Walt*

Bernie says the U.S. should demand more from Israel.
For peace, a Palestinian state is critical.
If Nitwityahoo annexes more land,
Further aid to Israel will be banned.
The party platform will include an evocation:
Israelis, end the occupation.
Castro would put a U.S. consulate in East Jerusalem.
I wish more democrats had their enthusiasm.
Biden wouldn't say the word "occupation",
And nothing about a Palestinian nation.
10/29/19

Bush warned Israel not to topple down
The democratically elected government in Lebanon.
The Israelis told Bush his position was unacceptable.
To backing down to Israel, Bush was susceptible.
The Israel lobby criticized Bush.
About Beirut, he no longer pushed.
The government there was American backed,
But not really in fact.
10/29/19
*Inspired by The Israel Lobby and U.S. Foreign Policy
by John J. Mearsheimer and Stephen M. Walt*

Much to the Israeli soldier's joy,
He shot to death an unarmed Palestinian boy.
But much to this killer's regret, it was videotaped.
From a BBC documentary, he could not escape.
An Israeli court put him in jail for one month.
Israeli soldiers can do what they want with their guns.
10/31/19

Chairman Xi puts snitches in college classrooms.
Free thinking there seldom blooms.
One professor lamented the loss of term limits.
Mao's Cultural Revolution modern China mimics.
She was fired thanks to the student informant.
Teaching in Chinese colleges is torment.
11/1/19

Israel killed many children, dads, and moms,
By, among other things, dropping cluster bombs.
The senate tried to ban them in civilian areas,
But the Israel lobby said I dare ya.
AIPAC lobbied hard against the legislation.
The ayes lost, and it was never again mentioned.
11/1/19
*Inspired by <u>The Israel Lobby and U.S. Foreign Policy</u>
by John J. Mearsheimer and Stephen M. Walt*

U.S. policy did not reflect the public's views,
Except for those of evangelicals and Jews.
Fifty-four percent said Israel should do more
To avoid killing civilians in the Lebanon war.
Sixty-five percent said the U.S. should take neither side.
Yet we supported the attacks on the hundreds who died.
America cheered as the IDF hustled.
The rest of the world was disgusted.
America's prerogative is a fallacy.
The Israel lobby sets foreign policy.
11/1/19

*Inspired by <u>The Israel Lobby and U.S. Foreign Policy</u>
by John J. Mearsheimer and Stephen M. Walt*

If Israel and the lobby were not pressing their case,
Then for war with Iran, Congress would have no taste.
Our war with Iraq was once Israel's goal,
For which America paid a heavy toll.
A nuclear Iran is preferable to a war to stop it.
The Iraq War was bad, but Iran would top it.
10/20/10
Inspired by The Israel Lobby and U.S. Foreign Policy
by John J. Mearsheimer and Stephen M. Walt

Iran helped the U.S. topple the Taliban,
By providing advice on targets in Afghanistan.
Iran facilitated U.S. cooperation with the Northern Alliance,
The only group that showed the Taliban defiance.
Iran helped with search and rescue missions,
All the while nursing an ambition:
To normalize relations with the U.S.
Did Bush reach out? Guess.
10/21/19
Inspired by The Israel Lobby and U.S. Foreign Policy
by John J. Mearsheimer and Stephen M. Walt

Trump's explanations are not in accord with the facts.
Mulvaney told the truth then tried to take it back.
There was a quid pro quo, but it isn't needed.
Trump asked for an investigation from a foreign leader
Into Trump's political rival and son.
Trump will do anything when he runs.
And he is trying to please his loan shark,
Who happens to be a Russian oligarch.
If Trump can prove Ukraine not Russia messed with our election
Then he could wipe out the Russian Sanctions every section.
This would be an ideal way of paying off his debt.
Putin wonders why Trump hasn't done it yet.
10/22/19

Corruption and evasion will be enshrined,
If we don't impeach Trump at this time.
Some future president, dumb and decadent,
Might make use of Trump's bad precedents.
There'd be political influence in our foreign policy.
The U.S. Government would be of lower quality.
Impeach this president, brazen and bizarre.
Let heroes like Elijah Cummings be your North Star.
10/23/19
*Inspired by "No, We Won't Just 'Get Over It'"
by Charles M. Blow NYT OP-ED 10-21-19

The U.S. blindly supported Israel in the Second Lebanon War.
The negative opinion of the world they ignored.
The sharp rise in anti-Americanism
Increased global terrorism.
Arab public opinion became deeply hostile to the United States.
We supported Israel in another bloody disgrace.
Arabs hate us more for the Palestinian plight.
The Israel lobby makes us misuse our might.
10/25/19
*Inspired by <u>The Israel Lobby and U.S. Foreign Policy</u>
by John J. Mearsheimer and Stephen M. Walt

Under a tree I am happy and mellow.
Above me sunshine turns green to yellow.
These leaves in the breeze sound like seas.
Seas are nice, but I prefer trees.
Nor could a ship match a tree
 In windblown majesty.
10/22/11
*PG 114th Posting 10/23/11 from
Poet Against Israel by Timothy J. Callahan

Sunday, October 20, 2019
Poetry Group Five Hundred Thirty-First Posting 10/20/19

The Palestinian cause should be endorsed.
The Israel lobby prevents that, of course.
As for TV, the Palestinians are ignored.
Producers fear that people might be bored,
The lobby forbids Palestinians on TV.
Israel doesn't want Americans to see
What Israel has done
To the indigenous ones.
10/11/19

Iran deliberately selected an American oil company.
Reconciliation it was trumpeting.
But this good faith offer went nowhere.
This friendly overture was impaled.
Clinton banned U.S. companies from working Iran's oil fields.
The Israel lobby had a lot to do with that deal.
The influence of the lobby cannot be overstated.
Iran rightly resents how long the Palestinians have waited.
10/13/19
Inspired by The Israel Lobby and U.S. Foreign Policy
by John J. Mearsheimer and Stephen M. Walt

Trump is the new doctrine and Trumpublicans bought it.
Whatever Trump says the Trumpublicans will laud it.
White supremacy they strongly defend.
Race relations they don't want to mend.
His base gives Trump blind devotion.
The mention of Obama stirs their emotions.
The Trumpublicans are racists.
Nothing Trump says is too tasteless.
10/14/19
*Inspired by "Trumpism's Infinite Vulgarities"
by Charles M. Blow NYT OP-ED 10-14-19*

Khatami wanted to do as a good president does.
He was even more enthusiastic than Rafsanjani was.
Likewise, the U.S. wanted to engage,
Rather than keep Iran in a cage.
AIPAC drafted and circulated a 74-page paper.
Israel disapproved of the rapprochement caper.
The best interests of the nation were in dialogue
But the pipes of Congress became clogged.
10/14/19
*Inspired by <u>The Israel Lobby and U.S. Foreign Policy</u>
by John J. Mearsheimer and Stephen M. Walt*

In my great and unmatched wisdom,
I turned northern Syria into bedlam.
The Kurds were suckers for believing in us.
Backing our allies is not a must.
The Russians will end up in charge there.
Anything to help the Great Russian bear.
10/16/19

Four years into the Iraq War,
Congress didn't want wars no more.
So it tried to attach a provision to a spending bill,
Which would leave war in Iran up to the legislators' will.
This was popular legislation on Capitol Hill,
Which the Israel lobby sought to kill.
Israel wanted an Iran war to be imminent,
Solely up to the American President.
Thanks to AIPAC and Eliot Engel, the language was removed.
The power of the lobby this proves.
10/17/19
*Inspired by <u>The Israel Lobby and U.S. Foreign Policy</u>
by John J. Mearsheimer and Stephen M. Walt*

In summer 2006, Israel launched a major air campaign.
Eleven hundred Lebanese died in pain,
Most of whom were civilians, a third of them children.
Afterwards, Israel was seen as more of a villain.
Hezbollah's prestige was significantly enhanced.
Its alliance with Syria and Iran advanced.
Anti-Americanism was rife.
The U.S. backed Israel in the fight.
10/18/19
*Inspired by <u>The Israel Lobby and U.S. Foreign Policy</u>
by John J. Mearsheimer and Stephen M. Walt*

Sunday, October 13, 2019
Poetry Group Five Hundred Thirtieth Posting 10/13/19

America wants justice everywhere but Palestine.
The injustice there reaches war crime.
Unconditional aid to Israel is unjust.
Palestinian dreams will not rust.
Two states for two peoples is the remedy.
Only this way will there cease to be enmity.
The denial of Palestinian dreams,
Keeps terrorists' dreams green.
10/5/19

President Trump wants the Mexicans to dig a moat,
In which snakes and alligators will soak.
Asylum seekers who try to swim across
Will find their lives lost,
In big chunks swallowed whole,
The animal bites on, then rolls.
The spikes on the top of the fence
Are designed to pierce human flesh.
10/6/19

Rachel Maddow explains what's going on.
Trump's self-incrimination blows on.
She is more than a beloved cable news host.
She is the voice of reason from coast to coast.
But she can't cover the Palestinian plight,
Not even quickly one night.
I think she would if she could.
Something stops her from doing what she should.
10/6/19
Inspired by "I'm Trying to Explain What's Going On"
by Amanda Hess, NYT Magazine 10-6-19

Trump extorted Ukraine to investigate Biden,
But the impeachment inquiry should be widened.
After this impeachment, expect another and another
As new corruption is uncovered.
Impeach Trump repeatedly if necessary,
And keep an eye on his mercenaries.
As Trumpublicans subvert patriotism for party,
The American people see.
10/7/19
*Inspired by "Impeach Trump, Repeatedly"
by Charles M. Blow NYT OP-ED 10-7-19

The wealthiest pay taxes at a lower rate,
Than the masses they love to berate.
The tax code is no longer progressive.
Tax cutters for the rich, Republicans are regressive.
Serious attempts to collect taxes usually succeed.
Good government is stronger than greed.
10/7/19
*Inspired by "The Rich Really Do Pay Lower Taxes Than You"
by David Leonhardt, NYT OP-ED 10-7-19

In 1967, Israel took from Syria the Golan Heights,
And dissolved the Golan Syrians' rights.
Israel drove 80,000 people from their homes.
They left behind their ancestors' bones.
Then the Israelis built dozens of "settlements".
Israelis are not ladies and gentlemen.
10/8/19
*Inspired by The Israel Lobby and U.S. Foreign Policy
by John J. Mearsheimer and Stephen M. Walt

In no way have we abandoned the Kurds.
(Remember, that claim is just words.)
My bipartisan critics are just jerks.
If the Kurds are good fighters, let them face the Turks.
(Originally, I said I'd wreck Turkey's economy,
But that notion will never recur to me.)
On our allies the Kurds, I had to pivot,
To keep Erdogan from buying more Russian equipment.
10/9/19

Israel's supporters said Syria has Saddam's WMD.
They said such baseless things for free.
They wanted, as soon as possible, a war against Syria.
This was lobby and neoconservative delirium.
We were still fighting in Iraq,
But Israel said Syria should be attacked.
Eliot Engel pushed the Syrian Accountability Bill.
President Bush signed it against his will.
And despite pressure, he never enforced it.
Truth was at stake and the CIA was a better source of it.
Bush knew that Syria had helped us against al-Qaeda.
He could not be a Syria invader.
10/9/19
*Inspired by The Israel Lobby and U.S. Foreign Policy
by John J. Mearsheimer and Stephen M. Walt

Their sacrifices were an enormity,
But they didn't help us with Normandy.
With our help, ISIS they slew,
But they didn't help us in World War Two.
With the Kurds, I have become bored.
Hang them out for the Turkish hordes.
I wash my hands of any genocide,
As God is my guide.
10/11/19

Sunday, October 6, 2019
Poetry Group Five Hundred Twenty-Ninth Posting 10/6/19

What Trump does to America is bad.
The leader of the free world is mad.
Unpredictability is bad for business.
What do you think this is?
Trump has been waging a war on competence.
He aims to drive out the very best.
When those who know what they're doing resign,
Trump hires hacks and says everything is fine.
9/28/19
*Inspired by "Bad for Trump but Good for the Economy"
by Paul Krugman NYT OP-ED 9-27-19*

The Democrats must impeach this malignant fraudster.
The people do not want congressional dawdlers.
Trump's betrayals already have validation.
He confessed to the central allegation.
The government witnesses will remember
And Trump will be impeached in November.
Will the Senate try this presidential glitch?
Like so much else, that's up to Moscow Mitch.
Trumpublicans believe in political expediency.
They will argue tediously for leniency.
9/30/19
*Inspired by "Impeach the Malignant Fraudster"
by Charles M. Blow NYT OP-ED 9-30-19
line 1 by Mr. Blow*

Trumpublicans believe only in political survival.
They don't care exactly how Trump tried to smear a rival.
Trumpublicans will rally round Trump,
Their legacies headed for history's dump.
9/30/19

Bernie proposes corporate tax rate increases,
Until the remuneration injustice ceases.
Companies must narrow the gap between what they pay
Their CEOs versus the workers everyday.
Pay no attention to that Trumpublican behind the curtain.
With Sanders, the rich will bear more of the burden.
10/1/19

We should not have let the Israelis think it was up to them.
America should have decided what, where, and when.
Condition aid on the creation of a Palestinian state.
The U.S. should be Israel's boss, not its mate.
We need an Israel and America separation.
Use the billions saved to pay slavery reparations.
African Americans are owed forty acres and a mule.
Using money earmarked for Israel will be cool.
That will make the "settlers" move.
10/1/19

Someone whose ideas and prose I admire,
Has found a new way to inspire.
He mixes some of my words with his,
As I have mixed some of his with mine.
His artful column, I never miss.
You can find him in The Times.
Often I am inspired by his views.
He gives me clever words to use.
10/3/19

Hong Kong fights for its relative autonomy.
Beijing hates challenges to its authority.
Communism forbids diversity of thought,
Which is what the British founders brought.
The people of Hong Kong exercise free speech,
While the right to do so may be out of reach.
Will the dictator order another Tiananmen Square?
How much will the rest of the world care?
10/3/19

Israel pushed the U.S. to become an Iraq invader.
Sharon wanted this sooner rather than later.
He told Bush that putting off the attack
Would only make it harder to invade Iraq.
His spokesman repeatedly stressed
That Saddam wanted more WMD, not less.
Get those American troops moving
Our claims of WMD proving.
10/3/19
*Inspired by The Israel Lobby and U.S. Foreign Policy
by John J. Mearsheimer and Stephen M. Walt*

Sunday, September 29, 2019
Poetry Group Five Hundred Twenty-Eighth Posting 9/29/19

Nitwityahoo is the ultimate partisan:
Israel is not a state of all its citizens,
But of the Jewish people – and only it.
Arab Palestinian citizens of Israel should git.
In accordance with the Nation-State law we passed,
Arab emigration is our sacred task.
One-fifth of Israel's population,
We would like to drop from the nation.
9/23/19
Lines 2-3 by Benjamin Netanyahu

We will decide the next premier,
And to bring the world some cheer,
It won't be Nitwityahoo.
It's Benny Gantz, that's who.
And although we can't be part of his government,
Because he made no Palestinian state covenant,
We stand to get more hospital beds,
And Bibi's political career is dead.
9/23/19
*Inspired by "We Are Ending Netanyahu's Grip on Israel"
by Ayman Odeh NYT OP-ED 9-23-19*

President Trump thought that dirt on Biden was gettable.
The complaint was of "urgent concern and credible",
And was supposed to go to Congress within a week.
However, our legislators have not had a peek.
Fortunately there have been plenty of leaks.
Trump and Zelensky discussed a quid pro quo.
Trump's reaction was "So?"
9/24/19

Senator Sanders pushes his wealth tax with vigor.
Warren's plan is good, but Bernie's is bigger.
Larger sums would support new social programs.
A Democratic Senate would end the log jams.
Wealth and income inequality would be reduced.
Class warfare would end in a truce.
Billionaires would still be billionaires.
If they're taxed more, who cares?
9/25/19

The President's words raised urgent concern.
About them the Congress must learn.
So I wrote a complaint, sent it up the line.
It is unlawfully delayed by the DNI.
Missiles were discussed, but Trump needed a favor:
Zelensky, be my political savior!
Biden and his son must have done something wrong.
Start an investigation and make it long.
9/25/19

Can I blow the whistle on you?
No, what did I do?
Extort a foreign leader for dirt.
But I want Joe Biden hurt.
You can't do it that way.
How do I get people to obey?
Try being honest and fair.
I just can't get there,
And whistleblowers are spies.
Put bullets between their eyes.
God's help beseech
You are being impeached.
9/26/19

In a state of newfound wonderment,
Rivlin asked Nitwityahoo to form a government.
This was a remarkable turnaround.
Most expected Gantz to wear the crown.
Nitwityahoo will make the most of it.
He'll quash his indictment and boast of it.
And even if he is criminally charged,
As premier he remains at large.
9/28/19

It is only by risking that we live at all.
When I put to sea, there's the chance of a squall.
That doesn't stop me from sailing my boat.
And despite the squalls, staying afloat.
4/17/11
*PG 90th Posting 5/8/11
*Line 1 by William James
Poet Against Israel by Timothy J. Callahan

The dead bury the dead.
And snatch the wounded from their beds.
Abundant dead perform these tasks.
The army of the dead is vast.
10/27/10
*PG 93rd Posting 5/29/11 from
Poet Against Israel by Timothy J. Callahan

He was lost in more than his metaphor.
He forgot what he was talking for.
Something about body bags being battle flags.
He staggered while he swaggered
And then became a tripping hazard.
5/9/11
*PG 93rd Posting 5/29/11 from
Poet Against Israel by Timothy J. Callahan

Only a few had the guts to strongly hint or say,
That pro-Israel hardliners brought about the war anyway.
Chris Matthews, Robert Novak and Maureen Dowd
Were among this heroic, little crowd.
Robert Novak deserves special mention,
Because of his little poetic invention.
He called it "Sharon's War" even before it began.
Bob Novak was an extraordinarily brave man.
9/13/19

*Inspired by The Israel Lobby and U.S. Foreign Policy
by John J. Mearsheimer and Stephen M. Walt

The arguments were specious, the "facts" artificial.
They made war seem necessary and beneficial.
The neoconservatives were at the top.
Opponents of the war were called "soft".
Israel's and America's fates are linked.
When Israel goes low, America sinks.
9/13/19
*Inspired by The Israel Lobby and U.S. Foreign Policy
by John J. Mearsheimer and Stephen M. Walt

Nitwityahoo resorts to fear-mongering
To get the far right pondering,
What would happen if Arabs had some power?
Get out and vote, don't cower!
He wants to videotape Arabs in polling places.
To suppress the vote he hastens.
His hate-speech Chat Box was suspended by FaceBook.
Nitwityahoo is a flagrant crook.
9/15/19

Bernie wants to end homelessness and limit rent increases
On the country's residential leases.
A national standard will define the cap.
Nobody else has a plan like that.
Bernie's childhood apartment was rent-controlled.
It would stay that way even if the building sold.
9/15/19

Nitwityahoo meets with AG Weinstein in October.
Neither man will leave the nobler.
Their task is to suppress an eruption
Of hundreds of thousands of dollars in corruption.
Weinstein drags out the investigation.
Guilt is neither man's sensation.
On the evidence, they cast doubt.
With witnesses they can do without.
9/16/19

In the campaign to win support for invading Iraq,
Manipulated intelligence said Saddam might attack.
Scooter Libby pressured CIA analysts
To find the go-to-war catalyst.
He contributed to the UN speech by Powell
Full of falsehoods most foul.
9/16/19
*Inspired by The Israel Lobby and U.S. Foreign Policy
by John J. Mearsheimer and Stephen M. Walt*

It used to be that all Arab citizens could do was sigh.
They want tangible improvements in their lives.
This time their parties will vote as a bloc
On one-sixth of the electorate they have a lock
They picked up three new parliamentary seats,
Arab politicians in the belly of the beast.
9/18/19

A lie in the campaign for invading Iraq
Was that Saddam was about to attack.
The government called him an imminent threat.
We had to get our military set.
CIA analysts were squeezed to make the case for war.
Afterall, what's an intelligence agency for?
9/18/19
*Inspired by The Israel Lobby and U.S. Foreign Policy
by John J. Mearsheimer and Stephen M. Walt*

Okay, so I'm not the world's greatest reader.
But I wouldn't say something inappropriate to a foreign leader.
Of course I called the president of Ukraine.
There's a lot of equipment he's about to obtain.
So I was thinking maybe he could do something for me,
Like gnaw at Biden's family tree.
9/20/19

Sunday, September 15, 2019
Poetry Group Five Hundred Twenty-Sixth Posting 9/15/19

"How to Fight Anti-Semitism" is the piece,
And I hate to be a tease,
But nowhere are the Palestinians mentioned.
That omission kindles resentment.
Give the Palestinians a homeland of their own.
Israel would receive the most good will ever known.
Israel must do something good
Like it could and should.
9/2/19
*Inspired by "How to Fight Anti-Semitism"
by Bari Weiss NYT Sunday Review 9-8-2019*

Trump is a plutocrat posing as a populist.
His highest value in life is opulence.
He enriches himself and his rich advisors.
The top one percent's wealth grows wider.
The middle class is not his concern.
For total plutocracy he yearns.
9/9/19
*Inspired by "Democrats Need to Get More Ruthless"
by David Leonhardt NYT OP-ED 9-9-19*

The hurricane may get a little piece of a great place.
I'm talking about Alabama in your face.
It could even be in for at least some very strong winds.
Dorian could then turn around and hit 'bama again.
Let me show you on this map.
Our weather services are crap.
I believe in diem carpe.
I will use my trusty Sharpie.
9/9/19
*Inspired by "Maps Don't Lie, or Shouldn't"
by Charles M. Blow NYT OP-ED 9-9-19*

So many Republicans aren't running for reelection.
Freedom from Trump is their predilection.
They're done answering for Trump's cruelties and chaos.
Many Republicans have borne a political cost,
For the shenanigans of the boss.
Republicans will remain the minority in the House.
It's either quit or quietly grouse.
9/9/19
*Inspired by "The Republicans are Dropping Like Flies"
by Frank Bruni NYT Sunday Review 9-8-19*

Nitwityahoo employs anti-Arab racism in electoral races
He wanted to put cameras in Arab polling places,
Hoping most Arab voters would not show their faces.
A Palestinian state would be an oasis.
Voting irregularities would quickly decline,
If the voting was done in Palestine.
Palestinians will have justice in their own land,
A homeland on their own land is their just demand.
9/10/19

No one trusts Trump's judgment and discretion.
What has he told Putin? – that's the question.
Foreign sources are afraid to share information.
Trump made America an unreliable nation.
Will the world trust us when we behead this dunce?
No, because we elected someone like him once.
9/10/19
Inspired by "Psst! Don't tell Trump"
by Michelle Goldberg NYT OP-ED 9-10-19

They have a perverted sense of justice, I'll tell you that.
They don't realize that they are rats.
They ethnically cleansed someone else's land,
And got a superpower to satisfy their demands.
Now they are poised to annex the West Bank.
How did we get here? We have the Israel lobby to thank.
9/10/19

Again Nitwityahoo promises annexation days before an election.
He wants all the far right to make him their selection.
Annexation of occupied territory is a war crime.
Will someone hold him accountable this time?
Trump would recognize a West Bank annexation,
And denial of a Palestinian nation.
If Trump grants the land theft recognition,
A Democrat will reverse that decision.
9/11/19

Nitwityahoo needs far-right votes to survive.
Promises of annexation he contrives.
He boasts Trump will let him do it.
Only Palestinians will rue it.
He needs reelection to quash the indictment.
Covering his ass is his biggest incitement.
9/13/19

Sunday, September 8, 2019
Poetry Group Five Hundred Twenty-Fifth Posting 9/8/19

Justice in the Occupied Territories never was.
Palestinians care more than America does.
Americans don't know what Palestinians know,
That Israel abuses them both.
Americans don't know they're complicit
In Israeli violence illicit.
American history has been stained.
Our country has been rightly blamed.
9/2/19

Why did the United States invade Iraq
Sending soldiers back and back?
Saddam was no threat to the United States.
The threat was to the Jewish state.
The Israel lobby was the without which.
Bush threw the first pitch.
Neoconservatives played their roles
In getting the U.S. in a deep hole.
9/2/19
*Inspired by The Israel Lobby and U.S. Foreign Policy
by John J. Mearsheimer and Stephen M. Walt*

Saddam Hussein and Osama bin Laden were hostile to each other.
They were Cain and Abel type brothers.
Bin Laden's people were in Afghanistan, not Iraq.
Saddam had nothing to do with the 9/11 attacks.
But America became an Iraq invader
When it should have focused on al Qaeda.
So why did America attack Iraq?
Between Israel and America there is no crack.
9/4/19
*Inspired by The Israel Lobby and U.S. Foreign Policy
 by John J. Mearsheimer and Stephen M. Walt

Following the revelation that there were no WMD in Iraq,
AmerIsrael had a lot to take back.
The Senate Intelligence Committee and the Knesset issued reports
Showing that much of the intelligence Israel gave was false.
Israel fed Washington reports of WMD.
British and American intel agreed.
9/4/19
*Inspired by The Israel Lobby and U.S. Foreign Policy
 by John J. Mearsheimer and Stephen M. Walt

Will the Israelis commit another error,
Or will this election end the Bibi era?
He will be indicted soon
For paying off a TV tycoon
For ultra-positive coverage in the news.
Their justice system abides this abuse.
Israelis, dump Nitwityahoo.
His policies betray you.
9/6/19

Major gas and oil producers will not listen
To Trump's loosening of regs regarding methane emissions.
Auto makers don't like Trump's weakened emissions regulations
Car companies are not for environmental degradation.
Despite Trump, they will play by the Obama-era rules.
American business does not abide fools.
9/6/19

How will you feel when you are overtaken,
And find out you are God forsaken?
How much you could have done while alive
To praise Him and His love revive.
But now you descend fully aware:
You are burning alive and God doesn't care.
12/5/10
*PG 71st Posting 12/26/10 from
Poet Against Israel by Timothy J. Callahan

I don't care if you believe, because it's true:
Jesus and I will have a heavenly rendezvous.
We both know where; only He knows when.
He told me not to ask Him again.
9/30/10
*PG 73rd Posting 1/9/11 from
Poet Against Israel by Timothy J. Callahan

Sharon made the peace process a farce
By refusing to negotiate with Abbas,
Which led to a Palestinian Authority loss:
The electoral winner in Gaza was Hamas.
This is exactly what Sharon wanted
To ease the pressure of the conflict.
The U.S. wouldn't ask Israel to associate
With Hamas or negotiate.
8/26/19
Inspired by The Israel Lobby and U.S. Foreign Policy
by John J. Mearsheimer and Stephen M. Walt

Nitwityahoo turned up the heat to win votes.
Two Hezbollah fighters are toast.
Allegedly they were helping Iranians prepare killer drones,
Meant to rip the flesh from human bones.
The next day an Israeli drone exploded
In a Beirut neighborhood favoring Hezbollah.
Israel thinks it can attack,
Without getting anything back.
8/26/19

I am America and America is me!
The Danish prime minister can't hit me for free.
She called my Greenland ambitions "absurd."
For her, "nasty" is the right word.
The tariff retaliation by President Xi
Was aimed directly at me.
Jerome Powell won't misuse the Federal Reserve
To give me the rate cuts I deserve.
Only Kim Jong-un sends me love letters.
They always make me feel better.
My pal Putin knows what I'm going through.
When people laugh at me, I get blue.
8/26/19
*Inspired by "Trump's Paradigm of the Personal"
by Charles M. Blow NYT OP-ED 8-26-19*

Americans would withhold aid to Israel if it resisted
An end to the conflict and America insisted.
Only a Palestinian state will end the struggle,
But the Israel lobby swings its cudgel:
No one puts pressure on Israel to negotiate.
A Palestinian state Jews will not co-create.
8/27/19

Secretary of State Condoleezza Rice
Tried to get the parties to sit down and make nice.
Olmert refused to discuss any settlement's outlines.
Abbas realized there'd be no talking this time.
Neither man appeared with her at the press conference.
Rice learned that dealing with Israelis is monstrous
But she returned, offering to mediate in March.
Prime Minister Olmert was predictably harsh.
Once more the secretary was punked.
It was her seventh visit to Israel in eight months.
8/28/19
*Inspired by The Israel Lobby and U.S. Foreign Policy
by John J. Mearsheimer and Stephen M. Walt*

The ballrooms are among the biggest in Florida,
And Doral has no illegal gardeners.
The tap water there tastes like wine.
(I am the second coming of the divine.)
And what we have also is Miami.
If that's not a fun town then damn me.
The next Group of 7 will take place at Doral,
Which will boost my income and morale.
8/28/19

The Bush administration would have pushed harder for peace.
The Israel lobby made the momentum decrease.
Rice met with the leaders of 15 major Jewish groups.
The promises she made were like jumping through hoops:
The administration would refrain from putting pressure on Israel.
She would not suggest ways to make Palestinians less miserable.
These concessions greatly limited the secretary's results,
But she avoided Israel lobby revolts.
8/28/19
*Inspired by The Israel Lobby and U.S. Foreign Policy
by John J. Mearsheimer and Stephen M. Walt

The lobby moved quickly like a leopard,
To neutralize Bush administration efforts.
Elliott Abrams helped thwart ongoing steps.
Real pressure Israel would never get.
Bush could have withheld money from Israel,
Until it makes the Palestinians less miserable.
This is interest group politics at work
Nationwide the lobby members lurk.
8/30/19

*Inspired by The Israel Lobby and U.S. Foreign Policy
by John J. Mearsheimer and Stephen M. Walt

Sunday, August 25, 2019
Poetry Group Five Hundred Twenty-Third Posting 8/25/19

Bush's Road Map called for no "settlement" activity,
But Israelis built them at liberty.
They continued assassinating Palestinian leaders.
They were content to be guilty pleaders.
Bush called the attacks heavy handed.
Israel was slow to stop them, to be candid.
The President of the United States complained,
But the Israelis were not restrained.
8/17/19
*Inspired by The Israel Lobby and U.S. Foreign Policy
by John J. Mearsheimer and Stephen M. Walt*

The Congresswomen planned to tour the West Bank,
But at the last minute, their tickets were yanked.
Trump was afraid of what they'd report
Instances of dehumanization, which Trump supports.
Members of Congress should be granted access
To a country we pay billions in taxes.
Israel warrants extra oversight.
It created the Palestinian plight.
8/17/19

Trump urged Nitwityahoo to be a stern sentry:
Grant not the Congresswomen entry.
Nitwityahoo said only Tlaib can come in and on condition
That she not exercise her B.D.S. ambitions.
But she would not harm the dignity of her cause.
Israel brought about another American loss.
Congress gives Israel over $3 billion a year.
For them to boycott our Congress members is weird.
8/20/19

The Palestinians deserve statehood and sovereignty,
But they have been victims of Israeli robbery.
Two states for two peoples must be the guiding light.
A Palestinian state is still within sight.
"Settlers" close to Israel can stay.
Those in the interior must go away.
That means three out of four "settlers" will remain,
But a sovereign state the Palestinians will gain.
8/21/19
*Inspired by "How Mideast Peace Process Became a Farce"
by Thomas L. Friedman NYT OP-ED 8/21/19

In November 2004, Arafat died; Abbas was elected in 2005.
The time was perfect for the peace process to revive.
Abbas renounced terrorism and recognized Israel.
He was eager for negotiations, which is critical.
Newly elected, Bush was full of political capital
But the lobby kept Bush's power solely Israel-adaptable.
Bush did nothing to help Abbas negotiate a state.
Abbas's power base began to abate.
8/24/19
*Inspired by The Israel Lobby and U.S. Foreign Policy
by John J. Mearsheimer and Stephen M. Walt

That old time religion
With the Holy Spirit pigeon
Just sets me on fire.
Damn me if I'm a liar.
6/4/10
*PG 88th Posting 4/24/11
Poet Against Israel by Timothy J. Callahan

Why does God's mercy have a limit?
Why does God's mercy have a limit?
I asked, but the Old Man gets livid.
We've always wanted to replace Him,
But no one has the nerve to face Him.
12/3/09
*PG 90th Posting 5/8/11
Poet Against Israel by Timothy J. Callahan

What the mozzarella!
What the mozzarella!
She's going out with another fella!
Oh, how will I get her back?
Bring her some Monterrey Jack.
7/6/10
*PG 91ˢᵗ Posting 4/11/10 from
Poet Against Israel by Timothy J. Callahan

Sunday, August 18, 2019
TENTH YEAR ANNIVERSARY -- Poetry Group Five Hundred
Twenty-Second Posting 8/18/19

In the fall of 2001, Bush wanted a Palestinian state.
His administration thought it was not too late.
He wanted anti-Americanism reduced.
That's why he wanted the conflict defused.
Support for terror groups would be undermined.
There would be justice in Palestine.
But Bush could not get Israel to change.
On all his plans the lobby rained.
Instead Bush backed Israel's hard-line,
Which kills the remnants of Palestine.
The lobby was a central reason for the shift.
Israel and the U.S. could not long have a rift.
8/12/19
Inspired by The Israel Lobby and U.S. Foreign Policy
by John J. Mearsheimer and Stephen M. Walt

The crowd even booed Deputy Secretary of Defense Wolfowitz.
He inferred Israel and Palestine would be a perfect fit.
When he referred to Palestinian suffering and the need for a state,
The crowd shouted "Down with Arafat" with hate.
Bush sent Secretary of State Powell to start negotiations
But with Arafat, the Israelis wanted no association.
The balance of power shifted while Powell was still there.
Washington decided that Israel did not have to share.
If a country's weight is measured by its influence on events,
Then Israel is a superpower not the U.S.
8/13/19
*Inspired by The Israel Lobby and U.S. Foreign Policy
by John J. Mearsheimer and Stephen M. Walt

Bush objected to Israel's so-called security fence.
On the road to peace, the fence made no sense.
The Fence (wall) is a "fact on the ground."
Meant to bog peace negotiations down.
It incorporated more of the West Bank.
It was built inside Palestine's western flank.
Thousands of Palestinians were divided.
Bush remembered America is one-sided.
8/15/19
*Inspired by The Israel Lobby and U.S. Foreign Policy
by John J. Mearsheimer and Stephen M. Walt

Each desperate to look tough to his own base,
Trump gave the order; Nitwityahoo obeyed.
The two Congresswomen were banned.
Their journey over before it began.
Trump ingratiated himself with the Trumpublicans
Many of whom are country bumpkins.
Nitwityahoo needs the far right,
All of whom are pure white.
8/16/19

Cultists want to force women through pregnancy,
Then leave the mothers in beggary.
But the fathers face no penalty;
Fathers are men you see.
3/15/11
*PG 86th Posting 4/10/11
<u>Poet Against Israel</u> by Timothy J. Callahan

You would see the tables turned,
If men had eggs and women sperm.
The right to an abortion would equal the right to a gun.
The fight about abortion rights would finally be done.
4/15/11
*PG 87th Posting 4/17/11
Poet Against Israel by Timothy J. Callahan

Sunday, August 11, 2019
Poetry Group Five Hundred Twenty-First Posting 8/11/19

Playing the anti-Semitism card stifles discussion.
The power of the accusation crushes.
Myths about Israel survive unchallenged,
Because coverage of the Middle East is not balanced.
Pro-Israel organizations have amassed political muscle.
American legislators are easily hustled.
8/3/19
*Inspired by The Israel Lobby and U.S. Foreign Policy
by John J. Mearsheimer and Stephen M. Walt*

The lobby helped make the case for war with Iraq.
It was a war for Israel, that's a fact.
Israel wants regional transformation.
It wants to be more of a nation.
America must do Israel's bidding.
The Israel lobby is not kidding.
The U.S. must make terrorism dry up,
But Israel makes terrorists rise up.
8/3/19

American subservience to Israel caused anti-Americanism,
Which in time became radical Islamic terrorism.
America should have distanced itself from Israel.
Israel's enemies make us miserable.
America should have created a Palestinian state.
At no point (including now) was it ever too late.
The Palestinian plight moved bin Laden,
To kick America out of the garden.
8/5/19
*Inspired by The Israel Lobby and U.S. Foreign Policy
by John J. Mearsheimer and Stephen M. Walt*

The lobby exerted influence on U.S. policy in the Middle East.
The resulting actions did not bring peace.
America should have acted in line with national interest.
Instead it succumbed to lobby applied stress.
8/5/19
*Inspired by The Israel Lobby and U.S. Foreign Policy
 by John J. Mearsheimer and Stephen M. Walt*

Republicans appeal to racial ill will.
All racists vote for Republicans still.
Trump appeals to white supremacists,
Protestors are punched off the premises.
Trump's followers generally have guns.
What they lack is compunction.
They are heavily armed haters
Shooting down the "invaders."
8/6/19
*Inspired by "Trump, Tax Cuts and Terrorism"
by Paul Krugman, Opinion page 8/6/19*

The first year after 9/11, Bush and Sharon clashed.
Bush wanted to help the Palestinians fast.
But the lobby pressured Bush to change course.
Israel was allowed to use merciless force.
Israel's foes were said to be America's foes.
Israel got the victory, America the woes.
The U.S. adopted Israel's preferences and justifications:
The only remedy for Palestinians is suffocation.
8/8/19
*Inspired by The Israel Lobby and U.S. Foreign Policy
 by John J. Mearsheimer and Stephen M. Walt*

From the greatest candidate to the least,
Bernie was the only one who said "Middle East."
The next President cannot be afraid of Israel.
We have enabled it to make Palestinians miserable.
That policy has not been due to American liberals.
President Sanders will have the stature and standing.
A Palestinian state will have a smooth landing.
The whole world wants the Palestinians to have a state.
The "settlements" do not make it too late.
They will be handed over as reparations.
They will join Palestine's restoration.
8/9/19

Sunday, August 4, 2019
Poetry Group Five Hundred Twentieth Posting 8/4/19

Israel boasts that B.D.S. is having no effect,
But warns Israelis that it is a strategic threat.
B.D.S. protests the denial of Palestinian rights.
It tries to lessen the pain of the people's plight.
Representatives Omar and Tlaib are its most vocal backers.
President Trump says their voices don't matter.
If we had more legislators like these two in the past
The 9/11 attacks would not have come to pass.
7/28/19
B.D.S. is the Boycott, Divest from and Sanction Israel movement

Could you charge the President with a crime after he leaves?
I could arrest him for obstruction; that's what I believe.
What about for his Russian conspiracy?
I'll pick him up for that and tyranny.
7/29/19

The Israel lobby boasts of its own power,
But attacks those who call attention to it within the hour.
The lobby's most powerful weapon is a false charge
Of anti-Semitism which tells you who you are.
Criticize Israel and you are an anti-Semite.
It's worse if you sympathize with the Palestinian plight.
7/30/19

"Settlements" are illegal barriers to peace.
This is what most of the world believes.
"Settlements" will have to be evacuated
And turned over to the U.N. immaculate.
A Palestinian state will have to be imposed.
The Jewish "settlers" will have to go.
They will better understand ethnic cleansing
The Arabs thirst for freedom quenching.
Nitwityahoo says no "settlement" will be uprooted.
That's true, but the "settlers" will be booted.
8/1/19

A charge of anti-Semitism is a potent weapon.
People's criticism of Israel must be kept in.
No one wants to be tarred with that brush.
Criticism of the lobby must remain hushed.
The lobby will smear a critic's career.
Israel and its lobby America fears.
8/2/19
*Inspired by The Israel Lobby and U.S. Foreign Policy
by John J. Mearsheimer and Stephen M. Walt

Sometimes I don't talk to my cat for days.
The food she refused on the floor lays.
Of course I find something she will eat.
But when I serve it, I do not speak.
8/6/10
*PG 61st Posting 10/17/10 from
Poet Against Israel by Timothy J. Callahan

The law takes no account of trifles,
Nor of machine guns, pistols, and rifles.
Arm yourself to spill the blood of tyrants.
And the tree of liberty hydrate.
9/27/09
*PG 63rd Posting 10/31/10 from
Poet Against Israel by Timothy J. Callahan

What we pray to ourselves for is always granted.
Every seed germinated that I ever planted,
Because I am both the soil and the sower.
I am both the supplicant and bestower.
8/27/10
*PG 34th Posting 4/11/10 from
Poet Against Israel by Timothy J. Callahan
Line 1 by Ralph Waldo Emerson

Sunday, July 28, 2019
Poetry Group Five Hundred Nineteenth Posting 7/28/19

The Israel lobby is good at orchestrating pressure.
When Israel is covered, it takes measures.
Like a widespread letter writing campaign,
Which drives network executives insane.
Or thousands of phone calls in a day,
To make writers and editors obey.
The media would rather not cover Israel.
The lobby makes everyone so miserable.
7/22/19
  *Inspired by The Israel Lobby and U.S. Foreign Policy
by John J. Mearsheimer and Stephen M. Walt*

Pro-Arab voices are conspicuously absent.
Tell me where free thinking went.
Part of our First Amendment is denied.
The Israel lobby cannot be defied.
Academia is the last place
Where Israel can be criticized without disgrace.
There is a deep-seated commitment to freedom of speech.
Many colleges are beyond the lobby's reach.
7/19/19
*Inspired by The Israel Lobby and U.S. Foreign Policy
by John J. Mearsheimer and Stephen M. Walt*

The barrier runs through the West Bank, east of the '67 line.
That's a war crime the International Court won't deny.
The land is in Palestinian jurisdiction – technically.
Knowing this Palestinians built recklessly.
Because the Israelis demolished ten apartment blocks
The Palestinian Authority they mock.
7/23/19

Alan Dershowitz wrote a book entitled "The Case for Israel"
Finkelstein wrote "Beyond Chutzpah" which was critical.
Dershowitz threatened the UC Press,
Trying to get the book suppressed.
He even wrote to Governor Schwarzenegger
But he was not a publication changer.
Finkelsteins's book was finally issued.
Alan went through a box of tissues.
7/23/19
*Inspired by The Israel Lobby and U.S. Foreign Policy
 by John J. Mearsheimer and Stephen M. Walt
UC Press is The University of California Press

The world should end the occupation.
Palestinians deserve a nation.
Boycott is a legitimate form of protest.
We used it against Nazi Germany no less.
Apartheid South Africa was boycotted.
Soon the white racists got it.
Boycotts were used by the Civil Rights Movement.
They were part of America's improvement.
On Israel's cruel dehumanization,
Boycotts shed illumination.
7/24/19

Philoctetes reeked from a festering wound.
Nevertheless Greeks came for him in June.
The bleak war at Troy called for measures stark,
Like a stinking bowman who never misses his mark.
2/15/19
*PG 17*th* Posting 12/13/09 from
Poet Against Israel by Timothy J. Callahan

When God told me He was gay
When God told me He was gay,
I wasn't quite sure what to say:
God, I've had gay friends before,
One of whom I truly adored!
12/23/09
*PG 20*th* Posting 2/3/10 from
Poet Against Israel by Timothy J. Callahan

I feel about this saloon
I feel about this saloon
The way Moonies feel about the moon.
If I can't drink here as I have hitherto,
I don't know what I will do.
10/7/09
*PG 34*th* Posting 4/11/10 from
Poet Against Israel by Timothy J. Callahan

Sunday, July 21, 2019
Poetry Group Five Hundred Eighteenth Posting 7/21/19

The adopted Senators will do fine,
So long as they follow AIPAC's line.
Money is the politician's Lord.
AIPAC can punish and reward.
Talk pro-Israel and be merry,
Or they'll finance your adversary.
7/13/19

When Howard Dean said we should act as an honest broker,
The Israel lobby saw a bad joker.
Dean wanted to bring the two sides together.
This was not an AIPAC approved endeavor.
Even-handedness is not wanted
For the Israeli-Palestinian Conflict.
7/13/19
*Inspired by The Israel Lobby and U.S. Foreign Policy
by John J. Mearsheimer and Stephen M. Walt

In the aftermath of 9/11, President Bush called for a Palestinian state.
Little did he know how long we would have to wait.
George W. Bush knew why we had been attacked.
The U.S. consistently stabbed Palestinians in the back.
7/13/19
*Inspired by The Israel Lobby and U.S. Foreign Policy
by John J. Mearsheimer and Stephen M. Walt

Ethiopian-Israelis need international help.
They want to be as Israeli as anyone else.
Their Judaism is over 2,500 years old.
Down through the centuries they kept hold.
Now they are shot by Israeli cops,
Because their complexion is too dark.
Israeli police make racism deadly,
Even when the Ethiopian is friendly.
7/15/19

Israel's education minister promotes conversion therapy.
In Israel, superstitious people are not a rarity.
Though debunked by the medical establishment,
Many Jews find conversion heaven-sent.
Rome changed the course of mighty rivers.
Israel is the new sexual orientation giver.
Conversion therapy is dangerous.
Youths say, it deranges us.
7/15/19

Go back to the country you're from.
You should have been born deaf and dumb.
Who are you to try to change our country?
Members of Congress, don't tell me.
But you all are female and brown.
Bow down then get out of town.
You're not the America I know,
Where an old, white man says stay or go.
7/15/19

We should hate Confederates the way Russians hate Czarists.
That goes especially for general Nathan B. Forrest.
He massacred African-American prisoners.
I know this grosses out my listeners.
But what's worse, he's been given a day to be honored.
His war crimes are not to be pondered.
7/16/19

Palestinians faced two Israeli teams, what a drag.
One flying an Israeli flag, the other an American flag.
Israel proposes an idea; the U.S. proposes the same one.
Palestine lost before negotiations were begun.
7/17/19
*Inspired by The Israel Lobby and U.S. Foreign Policy
by John J. Mearsheimer and Stephen M. Walt

One-sided accounts about Israel and its founding
Add to the Palestinian denouncing.
AIPAC defends Israel in policy debates.
Israel and America equate –
One of their outrageous claims.
The two countries' values are not the same.
Israel's values put it to shame.
7/17/19
*Inspired by The Israel Lobby and U.S. Foreign Policy
by John J. Mearsheimer and Stephen M. Walt

MSNBC debate-moderators did not ask
About Israel, which was part of their task.
They were afraid of all the e-mails and phone calls
Starting a pro-Israel anti-Israel brawl.
The next debate host will be CNN.
Will questions about Palestine be asked then?
CNN might fear a consumer boycott.
Ask about the Palestinians? Better not.
Besides they're mulling over Jared's proposal,
Which is the Palestinian state disposal.
7/17/19

I don't have a racist bone in my body.
The racism is all in my soft tissue.
My bones are sinless, oddly.
Bigotry inhabits my sinews.
Go back to from where you came.
You are not wanted around here.
Your skin color reveals your blame.
Your departure will bring me cheer.
7/18/19

Even legitimate Israel criticism
Is denounced as "anti-Semitism!"
The free market of ideas
Is not for American ears.
Israel is not to be spoken.
America is not to be woken.
Why is Israel not thought about?
Because it's not talked about.
7/18/19

Sunday, July 14, 2019
Poetry Group Five Hundred Seventeenth Posting 7/14/19

Congresswoman Betty McCollum opposed
An AIPAC bill against its foes.
Hamas won Gaza, so the P.A. must be caned.
The Congresswoman thought this bill insane.
AIPAC said her "support for terrorists will not be tolerated."
She demanded an apology and was exonerated.
All are welcome in her office except
Israel lobby reps.
7/6/19
Inspired by The Israel Lobby and U.S. Foreign Policy
by John J. Mearsheimer and Stephen M. Walt

Voting against Israel is like voting against lumber in Washington State.
Be careful not to stoke the Prime Minister's hate.
Legislators who cross AIPAC are playing with fire.
They won't be re-elected if that is the lobby's desire.
AIPAC inserts itself into the legislative and policy making process.
The lobbyists are the legislators' bosses.
They work on legislation, advise on tactics, draft speeches,
Collect co-sponsors, marshal votes, and perform research.
Uncontrollable legislators get besmirched.
7/7/19
Inspired by The Israel Lobby and U.S. Foreign Policy
by John J. Mearsheimer and Stephen M. Walt

Ten percent of Congressional trips overseas are to Israel.
Aren't any of the other 200 countries critical?
These junkets burnish a legislator's pro-Israel credentials.
They boost fund-raising for the next electoral adventure.
AIEF spent $1 million on visits from January 2000 to mid-2005.
AIPAC's sister organization continues to thrive.
7/7/19
*Inspired by The Israel Lobby and U.S. Foreign Policy
 by John J. Mearsheimer and Stephen M. Walt
AIEF is the American Israel Education Foundation*

Thank God we have AIPAC, like our flag unfurled,
The greatest supporter we have in the world.
If you want to help Israel, help AIPAC.
May the state of Israel never lack.
AIPAC has an almost unchallenged hold on Congress.
The Israel lobby constantly makes progress.
Soon West Bank annexation will be approved.
AIPAC will ensure the reception is smooth.
7/8/19
*Inspired by The Israel Lobby and U.S. Foreign Policy
by John J. Mearsheimer and Stephen M. Walt*

Abusing a prophet is ironic and not wanted.
Howard Dean advised an "even-handed role" in the conflict.
Top Democrats sent him a hate letter.
Yet had we listened to Dean, the Middle East would be better.
Dean told the truth and was castigated.
Students of history will be fascinated.
7/8/19
*Inspired by The Israel Lobby and U.S. Foreign Policy
by John J. Mearsheimer and Stephen M. Walt*

The Knesset will pass laws to shield Bibi from prosecution.
To save himself, he will corrupt Israel's legal institutions.
New laws would nullify the indictment against him.
He will annex the West Bank on a whim.
Palestinians will never have the same rights as Jews.
Embargo is the only way that Israel can lose.
7/10/19
*Inspired by "This Time, the Risk of Re-Electing Bibi is Clear"
 by Thomas L. Friedman NYT OP-ED 7-10-19*

Israel says Palestinians can't use their streets any more,
Not even to get to their own front doors.
Now the place is all abandoned buildings and homes.
Israel likes Palestinians to roam.
When they're gone, "settlers" illegally move in.
Palestinians are not allowed to win.
7/11/19

What's wrong with Israeli surrender?
Israel must be the injustice ender.
The Palestinians have suffered too much.
It's time for Israelis to be just.
The Zionist thieves must leave.
To the land Palestinians cleave.
7/12/19

The wealthy's idea of Yankee Doodleism
Is to take America back to feudalism.
So few lords exploiting so many serfs
And it's up to the lords what a serf is worth.
Evangelicals yearn for feudal times too.
The church will have all power over you.
11/19/10
PG 81st Posting 3/6/11
from Poet Against Israel by Timothy J. Callahan

Mining for gold and sometimes finding some
Sure makes mining hard to walk away from.
There's a mother lode down here maybe.
Perhaps my devotion will repay me.
But I have grown pale toiling in this night.
Someday I'll rest here in skeleton white.
3/8/11
PG 85th Posting 4/3/11
from Poet Against Israel by Timothy J. Callahan

Sunday, July 7, 2019
Poetry Group Five Hundred Sixteenth Posting 7/7/19

I was told what my opinions were to be,
Before they took me aside and grilled me.
They told me exactly what words to use.
I took the money and have no excuse.
I and similarly bought American legislators
Served up Israel's orders like fine waiters.
Israel never had to pay the bill,
Because of Zionist will.
6/30/19
**Inspired by The Israel Lobby and U.S. Foreign Policy*
by John J. Mearsheimer and Stephen M. Walt

U.S. elections have become increasingly expensive to win.
Many candidates commit the sell-out-to-Israel sin.
AIPAC affects the U.S.-Israel relationship,
Which is the U.S. firmly in Israel's grip.
Selling out to Israel bears no risk.
Americans give Palestinians a miss.
7/1/19

Senator Adlai Stevenson offered an amendment to a bill:
Stop building "settlements" or your coffers won't be filled.
Of course the amendment failed in the AIPAC owned Senate.
What's worse, AIPAC labeled Stevenson a menace.
Later in a governor's race he lost
Crossing AIPAC inflicts a cost.
He and his wife were called anti-Semites.
The Israel lobby delights.
7/1/19
*Inspired by The Israel Lobby and U.S. Foreign Policy
by John J. Mearsheimer and Stephen M. Walt*

Senator Percy declined to sign AIPAC's "Letter of 76".
When Percy ran again, AIPAC put in the fix.
He said Arafat was moderate as terrorists go.
Was Percy re-elected? The answer is no.
One donor spent $1.1 million on anti-Percy ads.
There is no point in getting mad.
You don't cross these people or they take you down.
That is how American legislators are bound.
7/2/19
*Inspired by The Israel Lobby and U.S. Foreign Policy
by John J. Mearsheimer and Stephen M. Walt
Line 7 by J.J. Goldberg, former editor of the Forward*

In 1998, Hillary Clinton supported Palestinian statehood.
Palestinian supporters saw her ascending to sainthood.
The next year she embraced Suha Arafat publicly.
The Israel lobby tried to turn this into something ugly.
But Clinton defended Israel when she ran for office herself.
She wanted the lobby to give all possible help.
The contributions were continuous.
She forgot about the indigenous.
7/3/19
*Inspired by The Israel Lobby and U.S. Foreign Policy
by John J. Mearsheimer and Stephen M. Walt*

Senator Jesse Helms opposed substantial aid to Israel,
So AIPAC decided to make him miserable.
During a campaign the lobby funded his rival,
And reminded Helms of Jews in the bible.
He won, but the election was close.
He decided he would strike a new pose.
With a yarmulke on his head, he kissed the Western Wall.
Next campaign he took in a haul.
7/5/19
*Inspired by The Israel Lobby and U.S. Foreign Policy
by John J. Mearsheimer and Stephen M. Walt*

I would give you a kidney,
Give you my heart.
Please don't kid me.
Have you felt Cupid's dart?
2/10/11
PG 78th Posting 2/13/11
from Poet Against Israel by Timothy J. Callahan

Before my fishing trip was accomplished,
I leaned over the side and vomited.
I didn't have any luck after that.
While puking, I lost my lucky hat.
2/14/11
PG 80th Posting 2/27/11
from Poet Against Israel by Timothy J. Callahan

When the prodigal son made his repentant return
His older brother was really burned:
Why does this bum get the fatted calf?
Relax my son, you shall have half.
6/17/10
PG 81st Posting 3/6/11
from Poet Against Israel by Timothy J. Callahan

Sunday, June 30, 2019
Poetry Group Five Hundred Fifteenth Posting 6/30/19

AIPAC money helps candidates generally.
It hurts those deemed Israel unfriendly.
In 2002, Cynthia McKinney was unseated,
By opponents who were AIPAC treated.
Re-elected in 2004, she was defeated in 2006,
By a politician AIPAC made rich.
You could say the Congresswoman has moxie.
She won't bow down to Israel's proxies.
6/23/19
**Inspired by The Israel Lobby and U.S. Foreign Policy*
by John J. Mearsheimer and Stephen M. Walt

The Israel Lobby called Paul Findley an enemy of Israel.
His objectivity made AIPAC miserable.
So they found this guy named Durbin and gave him a hundred thousand bucks.
Another Zionist in Congress really sucks.
Now he's a U.S. senator in Israel's pocket.
He aims at the Palestinians and cocks it.
6/23/19
*Inspired by The Israel Lobby and U.S. Foreign Policy
by John J. Mearsheimer and Stephen M. Walt*

Jepson supported selling Saudi Arabia AWACS.
His promise to Reagan pissed off AIPAC,
Which gave Tom Harkin a hundred grand.
Jepson's re-election was panned.
So we got another Zionist in Congress.
America doesn't make any progress.
6/23/19
*Inspired by The Israel Lobby and U.S. Foreign Policy
by John J. Mearsheimer and Stephen M. Walt*

Who are you not allowed to criticize?
Israel, but this John Cusak defies.
Mistreatment of Palestinians he condemns.
His career he risks for them.
A charge of anti-Semitism is a pillow,
Meant to suffocate and kill you.
Follow the money he said.
Lobbyists and legislators in bed.
6/24/19

The Middle East peace process is not supersonic.
Only a political solution will solve the conflict.
So Kushner comes out with an economic plan,
To buy off the rest of Palestinian land.
The Palestinians want a sovereign state of their own.
They won't let Kushner throw them a bone.
He thinks it's about money, but it's about land.
This was true before baby Jared began.
6/24/19

If a deal was offered that Palestinians found digestible,
Then Kushner could make the territories investable.
But no political solution has been offered.
Jared wants the Palestinians to forfeit.
That Palestinians will sell out is a presumption
That they won't fight back an assumption.
6/26/19

Tony Blair believes in Palestinian aspirations,
But dealing with Israelis is exasperating.
Jared Kushner says no Palestinian state.
He says dealing with Israelis is great.
6/27/19

Israel is largely immune from criticism on Capitol Hill.
There's little debate about an Israel bill.
Funny because Congress is usually contentious.
When Israel is the subject it becomes tendentious.
6/27/19

I walk through the trees
With the greatest of ease.
My head never goes clunk
On a branch or a trunk.
1/16/10
PG 28th Posting 2/28/10
from Poet Against Israel by Timothy J. Callahan

Heaven doesn't have convenience stores,
Or pickup trucks or street whores.
So I've decided to go to hell,
Where it never rains, so I've heard tell.
8/29/09
PG 29th Posting 3/7/10
from Poet Against Israel by Timothy J. Callahan

The jaundiced eye sees what it always sees,
No incongruous evidence please.
The biased mind reaffirms the status quo,
There is simply nothing else to know.
It only uses reason's lantern
To see the same old pattern.
4/16/10
PG 36th Posting 4/25/10
from Poet Against Israel by Timothy J. Callahan

Sunday, June 23, 2019
Poetry Group Five Hundred Fourteenth Posting 6/23/19

If only the Israel lobby had some competition,
But in fact it has no opposition.
Paid off U.S. legislators have nothing to lose:
Support Israel and Palestinian abuse.
If a Congresswoman took a righteous stand,
No one would give her a hand.
American values are not critical,
When it comes to supporting Israel.
5/17/19

I had to subordinate my emotional preferences,
To my perception of the national interests.
I had relatives killed in the Holocaust,
But the President, not the Prime Minister, was my boss.
American and Israeli interests sometimes conflict.
I know whose interests to pick.
6/17/19
*Inspired by The Israel Lobby and U.S. Foreign Policy
by John J. Mearsheimer and Stephen M. Walt
Lines 1-2 by Henry Kissinger*

Dual loyalties were drilled into me by my parents,
My Hebrew school teachers, my grandparents,
My rabbis, and Israeli teen-tour leaders.
When it comes to Israel, I don't teeter.
I was brought up a Jewish nationalist, even a quasi-separatist.
Whatever is good for Israel gets deference.
6/17/19
*Inspired by The Israel Lobby and U.S. Foreign Policy
 by John J. Mearsheimer and Stephen M. Walt
Lines 1-3 by Eric Alterman (Journalist)
Line 5 by Stephen Steinlight (former director of
national affairs at the American Jewish Committee)*

War with Iran is in the offing,
But the targets need softening.
Drop out of the Iran nuclear deal,
Despite how the rest of the world feels.
Any company doing business with Iran gets sanctioned.
Europeans are resentful and anxious.
What else can Americans do
To make Iran feel the turning of the screw?
Call the Islamic Revolutionary Guard terrorists.
The Pentagon added this to the Trump error list.
Let's send over an aircraft carrier.
Iranian defenses will be no barrier.
Nobody buys Iranian oil or steel.
The wrath of Trump they fear.
6/17/19

Moderators should put the candidates in a bind.
Ask what each would do for Palestine.
Who would dare say Justice will prevail?
Who would dare say a Greater Israel will fail?
TV puts the Israeli lobby in the room.
Crossing them leaves quite a wound.
6/19/19

The Israel lobby is no cabal or conspiracy.
It operates openly, proudly, and fearlessly.
The lobby advertises its formidable clout
To teach candidates what contributions are about.
Its indivisible attachment to Israel
Enables the lobby to make Palestinians miserable.
6/22/19
*Inspired by The Israel Lobby and U.S. Foreign Policy
by John J. Mearsheimer and Stephen M. Walt

I feel a shudder of fear
As my lover comes near.
She is at her best
When I don't know what she'll do next.
5/21/10
PG 61st Posting 10/17/10
from Poet Against Israel by Timothy J. Callahan

Israeli "settlers" are squatters,
Father-fuckers like Lott's daughters.
They are full of evil indifference.
In the world body, they are syphilis.
10/14/10
PG 62ⁿᵈ Posting 10/24/10
from Poet Against Israel by Timothy J. Callahan

If my lucky rabbit's foot quits me,
Where will the bullets hit me?
Anywhere above the waist or in the lower part.
If it's any consolation, they aim for the heart.
9/16/10
PG 64ᵗʰ Posting 11/7/10
from Poet Against Israel by Timothy J. Callahan

Sunday, June 16, 2019
Poetry Group Five Hundred Thirteenth Posting 6/16/19

The Fordham professors teach
That students get no free speech.
The Catholic Church is not inclined
To allow a club for Palestine.
The Jesuits have the same disposition
That they had during the Inquisition.
The Palestinians were not God's chosen.
Their human rights remain frozen.
6/9/19

Lew, I have a favor to ask,
And I need it done fast.
You are to approach Jeff Sessions
And impress upon him this lesson:
The investigation must be curtailed.
Heaven help him if he fails.
Investigations should be for future elections only.
Stick a feather in it and call it macaroni.
6/9/19

The war of Ezekiel 38-39
Could break out anytime.
The good watchman never gets bored.
Keep an eye out for the coming of the Lord.
The restoration of Israel was a sign,
That we are in end-times.
The Palestinians are already damned.
Trump calls their grievance a sham.
6/15/19

Dispensationalism does not include a happy ending for the Jews.
They either convert or their lives they lose.
Baptizing Jews is a long term goal.
All will take the Eucharist from the same bowl.
Evangelicals do not like Jews per se.
They like them as characters in their play.
6/15/19
*Inspired by The Israel Lobby and U.S. Foreign Policy
 by John J. Mearsheimer and Stephen M. Walt

Suspend your judgment as you listen
To people's tales of the missing.
The revolution was a violent time.
Killing people was not a crime.
2/8/10
PG 60th Posting 10/10/10
from <u>Poet Against Israel</u> by Timothy J. Callahan

I was intrigued by her,
But he was in league with her.
So I had to arrest them both.
Sometimes I regret my oath.
I need something to take the edge off.
I can't relax after taking the badge off.
I want to be ordinary sometimes,
But I can't stop looking for crimes.
10/1/10
PG 66th Posting 11/21/10
from <u>Poet Against Israel</u> by Timothy J. Callahan

All of creation is God's ideation,
Yet not all of creation is meant for salvation.
Why does God let species go extinct?
Does a species die off whenever God blinks?
He clearly disfavors polar bears.
In a blink of His eyes, they'll be out of there.
Why doesn't God love all His creation?
Why did He make what He meant for destruction?
11/19/10
PG 67th Posting 11/28/10
from <u>Poet Against Israel</u> by Timothy J. Callahan

Sunday, June 9, 2019
Poetry Group Five Hundred Twelfth Posting 6/9/19

The top one percent owns more than the bottom 90 percent.
Bernie will make billionaires repent.
Most Americans live paycheck to paycheck.
They're working the best jobs they can get.
The top 1 percent receive half of all new income.
Low income workers receive none.
Elect someone from the working class,
Who is not afraid to kick some ass.
6/2/19
Inspired by "Helping Americans Make Ends Meet"
by Senator Bernie Sanders, NYT OP-ED 6-3-19

The coming nuclear showdown with Iran is a certainty.
The U.S. and Israel must attack furtively.
Iran must not be able to respond.
God will wave his magic wand.
Total annihilation will be the focus.
God will say hocus-pocus!
Sacred Israel will not be touched,
Or at least not that much.
6/4/19
Inspired by The Israel Lobby and U.S. Foreign Policy
by John J. Mearsheimer and Stephen M. Walt
Line 1 by John Hagee

Gulf Oil had underwritten some pro-Arab activities,
With which the Israel lobby always disagrees.
The ADL gave Gulf a public drubbing.
Its head the corporation was rubbing.
In The Times, Gulf apologized for the sin,
And swore it would never happen again.
6/5/19

The Israel lobby has such a powerful proposition,
Partly because it has no opposition.
There will be no praise
For one who inveighs
Against Israeli conduct.
She will not be wanted.
There will be no bad consequences,
If you have a religion like Pence's.
6/5/19

Israel obviously was a very bad idea.
What's more, we gave up our right to steer.
Now all we can do is stand by helplessly,
While Israel acts brutally and selfishly.
6/7/10
PG 43rd Posting 6/13/10
from <u>Poet Against Israel</u> by Timothy J. Callahan

Listen to the music; forget what the words say.
Your body doesn't want meaning anyway.
Listen to the music; let your body sway.
Music makes it not your body anyway.
3/24/10
PG 44th Posting 6/20/10
from Poet Against Israel by Timothy J. Callahan

What is being told us
Is that Master has sold us.
And here's the real chiller:
He sold us down the river.
12/27/09
PG 45th Posting 6/27/10
from Poet Against Israel by Timothy J. Callahan

Sunday, June 2, 2019
Poetry Group Five Hundred Eleventh Posting 6/2/19

Assange's prosecution will raise First Amendment issues
Investigative journalists are grabbing tissues.
You can hear the teeth chatter
Of those who cover security matters.
Trump's Justice Department has a proclivity
For discouraging journalistic activity.
Trump wants to prosecute reporters,
And put them behind brick and mortar.
5/25/19

Jewish American leaders must be of Zionist quality:
Only Israelis decide Israeli policy.
American Jews should stand publicly united with Israel.
Disputes stay private or you will be miserable.
Thomas L. Friedman was invited to speak at an ADL dinner
But as Jews complained, his welcome got thinner.
He is pro-Israel, but he can be critical,
Of the inhumane policies of Israel.
5/26/19
*Inspired by The Israel Lobby and U.S. Foreign Policy
by John J. Mearsheimer and Stephen M. Walt
ADL is the Anti-Defamation League

We must love our Israel reflexively.
Never criticize her verbally or textually.
After Bush released his "road map" for Middle East peace,
The Israel lobby wrote to Har'aretz: be at ease.
If the Israeli government dislikes Bush's road map,
The Jewish community will call it crap.
And that will be the end of that.
5/26/19
*Inspired by The Israel Lobby and U.S. Foreign Policy
by John J. Mearsheimer and Stephen M. Walt*

About AIPAC's board, let there be no confusion:
Directors are picked by size of contribution.
Members willing to give the largest amount,
Know what a greater Israel is about.
They pretend Israel is vulnerable and beleaguered.
The contributions are never meager.
They say anti-Semitism spreads like wildfire.
Sympathy for Israel is their true desire.
Israel creates anti-Semitism itself.
It doesn't need any help.
5/27/19

Putting me in the closet, she said,
Mommy doesn't love you anymore.
The closet floor became my bed.
That's not what closets are for.
The child will cry itself to sleep.
There's no harm in that.
Better he than you weep,
Holding the newborn you sat.
5/28/19

Though I intervene in the politics of Israel,
No Israelis should be critical.
Bibi, I say this of my own volition:
You will form a great coalition.
We'll make the alliance stronger than ever.
There will be a Palestinian state never.
Iran is just itching to be attacked.
I know Israel will have our back.
5/28/19

Pro-Israel groups move ever rightward to keep the money flowing in.
The majority of Jews are represented by a minority without knowing it.
Hard-line Zionists, Orthodox, and neo-conservatives
Fight for a fascist Israel fervently.
Jewish groups need Israel to legitimate their existence,
Or the contributions fall below subsistence.
5/28/19

Expect a period of tribulation before Christ returns.
I remind all sinners that fire burns.
All these catastrophes are preordained.
Under God, time was trained.
God's miracles occurred in '48 and '67.
It won't be long, we'll be raptured to heaven.
But AmerIsrael must get rid of the Palestinians.
Wish we could massacre them like was done to the Indians.
5/28/19

\

I was built for comfort not for speed.
Keep the meth; pass the weed.
When you are done in,
I'll still be cool running.
8/11/09
PG 52ᵑᵈ Posting 8/15/10
from Poet Against Israel by Timothy J. Callahan

Let me ask you another question,
And I don't want any guessing:
Where do babies really come from,
And how can I get me some?
10/6/09
PG 31ᵗʰ Posting 3/21/10
from Poet Against Israel by Timothy J. Callahan

Do birds and angels have common ancestors?
After all, both have feathers.
Who had man's face first, God or monkeys?
Did God make mules or did horses and donkeys?
2/26/10
PG 31ᵗʰ Posting 3/21/10
from Poet Against Israel by Timothy J. Callahan

Sunday, May 26, 2019
Poetry Group Five Hundred Tenth Posting 5/26/19

America's foreign policy is determined by religious groups.
About the separation of church and state we were duped.
Christ would not support the merciless Israeli state.
The Palestinians would have had a much better fate.
Those same religious groups want to control a woman's body.
Again the separation of church and state is shoddy.
Women are autonomous, equal and free willed.
If the state denies this, with rebellion it will be filled.
5/18/19

The South African anti-apartheid movement inspired B.D.S.
Western nations' embargo aided the Black Africans' quest.
Boycotting apartheid-Israel is deemed anti-Semitic.
Another embargo is needed, but the Israelis checked it.
If you support the Palestinians, you're an anti-Semite.
To deny or refute this label you have no right.
Nothing can be said against the state of Israel.
Anyone who dares will be made miserable.
5/20/19

Withhold aid to Israel until it settles the conflict.
Make Nitwityahoo and the other fascists convicts.
Teach Israelis there is no god to give them the land.
It will be divided in accord with Justice's demand.
Someday Zionism (racism) will die,
As the two states sit side by side.
What was done to whom will be remembered,
But it will happen again never.
5/20/19

The strategic and moral cases for supporting Israel are weak.
The aid is unconditional, unjust, and not cheap.
Israel doesn't have to reciprocate in any way.
About its mistreatment of Palestinians, we have no say.
Israel does nothing but receive its annual billions,
While it makes Palestinians miserable in the millions.
America is Israel's milk cow.
Why did this happen and how?
5/20/19

Kushner has described his plan straight:
There will be no Palestinian state.
He will buy off core Palestinian demands:
No homeland on their ancestral lands.
Palestinian refugees yearn
For implementation of their right of return.
But that and East Jerusalem will be taken.
For money Palestine will be forsaken.
5/21/19

Dozens of pro-Israel PACs allocate
Money to the right candidates.
In the 2006 midterm election,
Three dozen PACs made their selections.
Three million dollars was spent.
To Congress the bought candidates went.
5/21/19
*Inspired by The Israel Lobby and U.S. Foreign Policy
by John J. Mearsheimer and Stephen M. Walt

For a Jew to criticize Israeli hate
Is worse than marrying out of faith.
For Jews not to donate what's in their wallets
Is worse than not going to college.
If Israel doesn't like our government's views,
They will be changed by American Jews.
Jews support the government of Israel,
Although its human rights record is miserable.
5/21/19

Having a Tel Aviv, Israel Eurovision
Was an immoral political decision.
But the song competition was boycotted.
Eighty thousand fewer seats were allocated.
But why did Madonna sing
At an apartheid country's fling?
Is she ignorant of the Palestinian plight?
Does she not know that Israel is a sepulcher white?
5/22/19

Hollywood, please no more Nazi movies.
Fairness is one of your sacred duties.
Now shine your cinematic light
On the Palestinian plight.
2/11/10
PG 27th Posting 2/21/10
from Poet Against Israel by Timothy J. Callahan

I will prove my worth is greater than my sin.
I will bring you the water of Gungadin.
Beautiful poetry I shall produce
By the grace of my beloved muse.
She rewards my fidelity
And compares me to Penelope.
She holds me closest of all men.
She holds me like Jacob held Ben.
09/16/09
PG 35th Posting 4/18/10
from Poet Against Israel by Timothy J. Callahan

Drive away shadow;
Dry up moisture.
Come back tomorrow,
The more to loiter.
I miss you tonight,
You giver of light.
Each and every star
Looks very, very far.
At last it is dawn;
The East is lightning.
Night is gone;
The day is brightening.
Thank you, almighty sun
For the cheer you bring everyone.
11/3/09
PG 38th Posting 5/9/10
from Poet Against Israel by Timothy J. Callahan

Sunday, May 19, 2019
Poetry Group Five Hundred Ninth Posting 5/19/19

Camp David left little to build a nation upon:
The West Bank divided into two or three cantons.
A continuous Palestine was not meant.
Camp David offered 81% of 22%.
Israel planned to keep control of the Jordan River Valley
That Camp David was good for the Palestinians is a fallacy.
To go on talking, the Palestinians were able,
But the Israelis walked away from the table.
5/12/19
Inspired by The Israel Lobby and U.S. Foreign Policy
by John J. Mearsheimer and Stephen M. Walt

In the seven years after the Oslo peace process began,
The Israelis confiscated 40,000 acres of Palestinian land.
They built 30 "settlements" and doubled the number of "settlers."
On the West Bank, Israel is the klepto-intermeddler.
Frustration with the checkpoints showed
The Palestinians were ready to explode.
Ariel Sharon brought the explosion about,
When he took a police battalion to the Holy Mount.
5/12/19
Inspired by The Israel Lobby and U.S. Foreign Policy
by John J. Mearsheimer and Stephen M. Walt

The bible directs U.S. foreign policy.
Armageddon will be rollicking,
But it won't happen without a greater Israel.
Annex the West Bank and make sinners miserable.
Christian Zionisits support the powerful Jewish state.
For Judgment Day we won't have long to wait.
5/13/19

Trumpublicans took Tlaib's words out of context.
What representative would not be vexed?
House Speaker Nancy Pelosi lost her patience.
"Apologize for your gross misrepresentation."
Senator Bernie Sanders had Tlaib's back.
He chided the president for his ugly attacks.
Trumpublican rhetoric lacks verity.
Trump will fail miserably.
5/14/19

The Second Intifada erupted out of Palestinian rage.
The Occupied Territory was their cage.
The Palestinians were held by their Jewish jailers.
The Oslo peace process was a colossal failure.
The Palestinians were denied dignity and well-being.
None of this were Americans seeing.
Sharon and his police were the precipitating factor.
The Americans were home awaiting the rapture.
5/15/19
*Inspired by The Israel Lobby and U.S. Foreign Policy
by John J. Mearsheimer and Stephen M. Walt*

Eurovision is a chance for Israel to rebrand itself.
But dozens of LGBT boycotts are no help.
Hatari used the spotlight to criticize Israel
Only Tel Aviv accommodates secular liberals.
There'd be no Eurovision if it were up to the ultra-Orthodox.
They view the world from within the bible box.
5/15/19

It is a matter of course
That a knight has a horse.
It goes without saying
There's a lady he's laying.
Nobody knows about it
Until later a witch shouts it.
But first the knight must go on a quest.
The lady lets him know how much he'll be missed.
Later, on the dark road, subject to chance,
He sniffs his lady's underpants.
7/2/09
PG 59th Posting 10/3/10
from Poet Against Israel by Timothy J. Callahan

In heaven you won't feel sorry for your loved ones in hell.
You'll know they are there, but you won't care, oh well.
God wants you happy while you praise Him.
Christ is your savior but God had to raise him.
7/3/10
PG 59th Posting 10/3/10
from Poet Against Israel by Timothy J. Callahan

A torpedo hit her hull.
The effects were practically null.
A cannonball hit the mainmast.
The ball fell and the mast held fast.
The Captain said, I have not yet begun to fight!
The first mate said, Yes, sir, but do you think you might?
9/14/10
PG 64th Posting 11/7/10
from Poet Against Israel by Timothy J. Callahan

After Sharon let the Phalangists into the camps,
The ground turned red and damp.
An Israeli commission with jurisdiction and ability
Found Sharon to bear "personal responsibility."
But the Defense Minister was not condemned.
The Israelis voted him in as PM.
5/4/19
Inspired by The Israel Lobby and U.S. Foreign Policy
by John J. Mearsheimer and Stephen M. Walt

If the Israelis were under Arab occupation,
They would give in to the resistance temptation.
Jews take pride in the Warsaw uprising against the Germans.
That brave act is celebrated in Rabbis' sermons.
So why are Israelis surprised,
When Palestinians arise?
5/4/19

God gave your gun a trigger – pull it.
Give the other people your bullets.
Always have plenty to fire,
If mass killing is your desire.
Don't fear a headshot from the police.
You will live on on TV.
5/5/19

Shamir did not regret his terrorist past.
His bombs killed civilians fast.
Zionists invented bus bombing.
The Jewish soldiers were zombies.
Zionists killed the U.N. mediator in 1948.
He proposed a compromise, which sealed his fate.
Jews showed Arabs the value of bombs,
As they confiscated their homes and farms.
5/5/19
*Inspired by The Israel Lobby and U.S. Foreign Policy
by John J. Mearsheimer and Stephen M. Walt*

Israel imposes an air, land, and sea blockade.
Patience in Gaza is very frayed.
Israel has little or no ambition
To correct dire humanitarian conditions.
Frustration erupts in rockets and gunfire,
Just the provocation Israel desires.
It can attack from air, land, or sea.
Nothing Palestinian can be.
5/6/19

I don't chastise the press, I threaten it.
Soon I'll sue; you can bet on it.
Twitter is treading on dangerous territory.
More tweets should tell a positive story.
Facebook and Google should also be careful.
Their corporate futures look baleful.
An unavenged attack is lunacy.
No critic gets impunity.
5/6/19
*Inspired by "Defending the Free Press"
by Charles M. Blow NYT OP-ED 5-6-19*

At least 22 Palestinians were killed in Gaza this weekend.
In Israel, there were four dead.
Extend the fishing zone off the Gaza coast.
Palestinians need help the most.
Let Gaza workers get paid.
The local economy fades.
Lift the siege or the truce will fail.
Israel chases its own tail.
5/7/19

Trump and Nitwityahoo are co-conspirators.
That's what hand picked attorney generals are for.
Separately and together they commit crimes.
However they can help each other they try.
Like Trump trashing the Iran deal,
Even though it was for real.
Nitwityahoo calls Trump's Jewish donors.
Their money clones Trump voters.
5/10/19

He on the cross bleeding from his wounds
Knows what's happening on each of Neptune's moons.
He knows how many scales on each and every cod.
He looks bad right now, but he is Almighty God.
7/7/09
*PG 3rd Posting 9/6/09 from
Poet Against Israel by Timothy J. Callahan

Saint Francis licked the sores of lepers.
I like pizza with sausage and peppers.
He had the courage to be a saint.
I hang drywall and paint.
12/8/09
*PG 39th Posting 5/16/10 from
Poet Against Israel by Timothy J. Callahan

You are to be excommunicated; the Pope won't bend
Yes, but do I have to attend?
No, they can excommunicate you from there.
When it happens, will I be aware?
6/6/10
*PG 56th Posting 9/12/10 from
Poet Against Israel by Timothy J. Callahan*

Sunday, May 5, 2019
Poetry Group Five Hundred Seventh Posting 5/5/19

We met them with the utmost effrontery.
We came here and stole their country.
Their resentment is just.
In them we can put no trust
And they cannot trust us.
To them we've been unjust.
4/27/19

The IDF killed hundreds of Egyptian prisoners of war,
In '56 and '67, and they would have killed more.
The war crime did not phase Israel.
It was making millions miserable.
Israel killed thousands of Arabs looking for employment.
When the bodies were returned, the scene was poignant.
"Infiltrators" these Arab workers were called.
Their grieving families were galled.
4/28/19

*Inspired by The Israel Lobby and U.S. Foreign Policy
by John J. Mearsheimer and Stephen M. Walt*

The IDF used truncheons in protest zones.
Thousands of children sustained broken bones.
This was during the First Intifada.
This is what the Israelis wanted.
Thousands of children hit by gun fire.
This is what Israel desired.
The IDF turned into a killing machine,
Like the world has seldom seen.
4/28/19

*Inspired by The Israel Lobby and U.S. Foreign Policy
by John J. Mearsheimer and Stephen M. Walt*

The Second Intifada came with a higher cost,
Israel killed 3.4 Palestinians for every Israeli lost.
An American was crushed by an Israeli bulldozer.
American media barely showed her.
The perpetrator was never punished.
The Israeli people are Hunnish.
4/28/19

*Inspired by The Israel Lobby and U.S. Foreign Policy
by John J. Mearsheimer and Stephen M. Walt*

Bret Stephens is upset over a cartoon in The Times.
(What doesn't bother him are Israeli war crimes.)
Nitwityahoo is a guide dog leading Trump along.
Trump wears dark glasses and a yarmulke, which isn't wrong.
Stephens never discussed the cartoon's rich meaning.
About a false charge of anti-Semitism he was preening.
AIPAC givers and takers gave us 9/11.
What made it sadder is there is no heaven.
4/29/19
*Inspired by "A Despicable Cartoon in The Times"
by Bret Stephens NYT OP-ED 4-29-19*

The Republicans' favorite pitch
Is we will cut taxes for the rich.
To make up for the hit on the national debt,
We will dismantle the social safety net.
Republicans stick to an argument no matter how discredited.
Climate change is not man-made – take a sedative.
To combat climate change we are loathe.
Think what that would do to economic growth.
4/29/19
*Inspired by "The Zombie Style in U.S. Politics"
by Paul Krugman NYT OP-ED 4-30-19*

Criticizing Israel is not anti-Semitism.
Those who say it give me aneurisms.
Criticisms of Israel must be put to effect.
Get the Israeli boot off the Arab's neck.
The war crime "settlements" will be evacuated,
Which is a move calculated
To satisfy the right of return,
When each refugee family learns
That it will get a home in a once Jewish "settlement."
Something evil will be turned for benefit.
5/1/19

Sunday, April 28, 2019
Poetry Group Five Hundred Sixth Posting 4/28/19

Ever since the Palestinians were vanquished,
Jews denigrate them and rarely get sanctioned.
"Palestinians are beasts walking on two legs,"
Menachem Begin once said.
IDF chief Eitan called them "drugged roaches in a bottle,"
To be tolerated but never coddled.
"A good Arab is a dead Arab," Eitan also said.
He wanted all Palestinians dead.
Trump's Hispanic immigrant castigation
Has included "infestation."
Where do you think he got the idea for a wall?
On a Nitwityahoo call.
4/20/19

*Inspired by The Israel Lobby and U.S. Foreign Policy
by John J. Mearsheimer and Stephen M. Walt*

I have one of the greatest memories of all time.
Not using it keeps me free of crime.
Of all the world's memories, mine is the greatest,
Unless my lawyers give me a subjects to evade list.
Funny how my recollection waned
When they asked about my campaign.
Thirty plus times I didn't recall what they were asking.
"I do not remember" is my way of knowledge masking.
No one cross-examined or refreshed my recollection.
I will skate through the next election.
4/21/19
*Inspired by "'Greatest Memory' Lapsed in Response to
Mueller's Queries" by Peter Baker NYT
National section 4-21-19*

They have waited for the U.S.-led peace process to give them a state.
By failing, we have sealed their second class fate.
Nitwityahoo plans to extend Israeli sovereignty
Over the West Bank in a grand theft larceny.
Black South Africans fought against apartheid.
Whites told them where and where not to reside.
America joined a boycott of that racist nation.
Apartheid died to the people's elation.
Will America join an embargo of Israel,
An apartheid nation making millions miserable?
4/22/19

Trumpublicans with Donald at the top,
Are sure in 2020 to flop.
There is no point in impeaching him now.
Let the voters decide fair from foul.
Democrats have a once in a lifetime opportunity
To debunk Trumpublican lunacy,
And to set up a progressive government
That the voters might make permanent.
4/23/19
*Inspired by "A Bigger Prize Than Impeachment"
by Joe Lockhart NYT OP-ED 4-23-19*

Harm them without mercy, women and children included.
Let the voice of horror be muted.
There is a need now for strong and brutal reaction.
In history our bloody deeds will be redacted.
There is no need to distinguish between guilty and not guilty.
All the indigenous are foul and filthy.
Let our Jewish soldiers commit atrocities.
Arabs will feel our bullets' velocity.
4/24/19
*Inspired by The Israel Lobby and U.S. Foreign Policy
by John J. Mearsheimer and Stephen M. Walt;
Lines 1,3,5 by David Ben-Gurion*

In their hate filled dystopia,
Nothing motivates like Islamophobia.
Their current object is a congresswoman, Muslim and Black,
Who's not afraid to give Israel flack.
If we had more leaders like her in the past
9/11 would not have come to pass.
4/26/19

Sunday, April 21, 2019
Poetry Group Five Hundred Fifth Posting 4/21/19

The myth of Israel as a victim
Is easily refuted as a false dictum.
In '67, the Arabs did not want war,
But Israel is a landgrabber to the core.
Israel claims it attacked preemptively.
Israel's propagandists spoke inventively.
Comparisons to David are Israel's favorite,
But Israel is Goliath, not David.
4/13/19
*Inspired by The Israel Lobby and U.S. Foreign Policy
 by John J. Mearsheimer and Stephen M. Walt*

To slander someone, Trump tweeted the burning Trade Towers.
All kinds of dirty tricks are within his powers.
Omar had spoken about Muslims and civil rights,
Which Trump believes should only be for whites.
She won't back down from Trump's racism and hate.
Unconditional support for Israel determined our fate.
AIPAC legislators brought 9/11 down on us.
The scales of justice frown on us.
4/13/19

Arabs already dwelt in the land Jews wanted for their state.
Jews treated the Arabs with greed, brutality and hate.
The Jews committed significant crimes against local residents.
To kill Palestinians, the Jews are not hesitant.
Why can't the Palestinians keep 20% of Palestine?
Why on all the land must Jews dine?
4/14/19

When your sister is attacked in an unfair fight,
You can't wait to get the politics right.
Ninety minutes after the offensive video appeared,
Senator Sanders criticized it and jeered.
The video is disgusting and dangerous, Bernie berated.
It's filled with racism and hatred.
Later, other Democrats spoke out.
Solidarity this is all about.
Except for one presidential candidate.
She gave credence to the president's hate.
Senator Omar did not minimize 9/11 pain.
Senator Gillibrand lied as she was paid.
Ironically, it was other AIPAC legislators,
Who inspired the 9/11 haters.
Congress gave Israel everything for nothing in return.
There will be another 9/11 if we don't learn.
4/15/19
*Lines 1-2 by Jennifer Epps-Addison, co-executive director
of the Center for Popular Democracy*

Zionism defenders are now insecure.
Their motives have never been pure.
They barred Barghouti from the United States.
He is someone they're afraid to debate.
B.D.S. makes Israel pay a price
For treating Palestinians not nice.
Anti-Zionism won't stop being true,
Though Trump kept one activist from getting through.
4/16/19
*Inspired by "Anti-Zionists Deserve Free speech"
by Michelle Goldberg NYT OP-ED 4/16/19*

Israel takes more and more
Of what belonged to Palestinians before.
Nitwityahoo will unilaterally annex parts of the West Bank.
For the quick recognition, he'll tell Trump thanks.
Trump will persecute Muslims all the more.
The U.S. has become an Israel metaphor.
4/16/19

Sunday, April 14, 2019
Poetry Group Five Hundred Fourth Posting 4/14/19

America subsidizes Israel no matter what its policies are.
That willingness has given us 9/11 so far.
Slobbering over Israel creates anti-American extremists.
We support Israel even at its meanest.
Our allies doubt our wisdom
And damn our Zionist vision.
America is slave to the Israel lobby.
It will be the death of us probably.
4/6/19

To make their Jewish state fabulous
They ethnically cleansed the native inhabitants.
The Palestinians resisted.
The Jewish response was twisted.
Palestinians are even more miserable
As Israel seeks a Greater Israel.
4/6/19

The Democratic Party would be better off without
People who view the two-state solution with doubt.
Zionist Democrats are out of place.
They belong in Trump's base.
Justice is coming to Palestine-Israel
Brought to you by Democratic Liberals.
4/6/19

Israelis, give me a fourth consecutive term,
And I will make the Palestinians squirm.
I will extend sovereignty over the West Bank.
The "settler" movement will have me to thank.
International law is not for Israel to obey.
There will be no penalty to pay,
Especially with Mr. Trump on our side.
He too wants an Israel wide.
4/7/19

AIPAC says anti-Zionists want to "delegitimize the Jewish state."
That is a falsehood I would like to negate.
Anti-Zionists want Zionism rolled back.
We want the West Bank to be a "settlementlesss" tract.
The Palestinians themselves recognize Israel.
It's the vicious country that makes them miserable.
The Occupation is illegitimate.
We oppose that with diligence.
*Inspired by "Making the Case for AIPAC"
by Mark Horowitz NYT OpEd 3/23/19*

Ocasio-Cortez did not sit taciturn.
She called the Palestinian deaths a massacre.
Rashida Tlaib wants to cut Israel's military aid,
But the many AIPAC legislators are well paid.
Ilhan Omar called Israel an apartheid state.
Like Apartheid South Africa, Israel will meet the same fate.
McCollum said bigotry, racism, and segregation
Lead to Palestinian degradation.
These women confront Israel without getting weak in the knees.
We need more representatives like these.
4/8/19
Inspired by "The Battle Over BDS"
by Nathan Thrall NYT Magazine 3/31/19

Sunday, April 7, 2019
Poetry Group Five Hundred Third Posting 4/7/19

Israel and America are thought to be good mates.
But Israel spies on the United States.
It has the second most active foreign spies here.
Yet Israel is such an ally dear.
The "special relationship" makes it easier for Israel to steal.
If the spies are caught, they do not squeal.
3/30/19
Inspired by The Israel Lobby and U.S. Foreign Policy
by John J. Mearsheimer and Stephen M. Walt

The Israelis refused to tell what Pollard gave them.
They believe spies like Pollard will save them.
Sometimes spies are convicted; in prison they languish.
To corporate victims, Israel pays damages.
Why does Israel bite the hand that feeds it?
America thinks Israel needs it.
3/30/19
*Inspired by The Israel Lobby and U.S. Foreign Policy
 by John J. Mearsheimer and Stephen M. Walt*

Snipers with Palestinians in their sights
Pulled the triggers with all their might.
Forty-six were wounded by gunshots, three died.
Israel should be praised, the press lied.
What restraint those Israelis showed!
Their rate of fire sure has slowed.
3/31/19

In the new Democratic Party platform,
New language will be born unlike the norm.
There will be a pro-Palestinian plank.
The voting public will say thanks.
Aid to Israel will be conditioned
On fulfilling the Palestinian vision.
No more unconditional support.
This is our last resort.
4/1/19
*Inspired by "The Battle Over B.D.S."
by Nathan Thrall NYT Magazine 3/31/19*

More than 900 towns in Israel contain no Arab families.
Each town secure under the military panoply.
School funding the Israelis will take,
If the Nakba a school commemorates.
If a Jew and a Palestinian find wedded bliss
The Palestinian will be denied citizenship.
What Israel values, we reject.
The country is run by a greedy sect.
4/1/19
*Inspired by "The Battle Over B.D.S."
by Nathan Thrall NYT Magazine 3/31/19*

Smug Israelis are hunky-dory,
Occupying Palestinian territory.
They believe they are unmovable
And the Palestinian grievance unsoothable.
The "settlers" are not the least bit anxious
About Boycott, Divestment, Sanctions.
They believe they are in God's will
And God lets them steal and kill.
The U.S. provides $3.3 billion in military financing.
That for the rest of the world far surpassing.
The United States funds the occupation.
America is an everything-for-the-Jews nation.
4/1/19

Israel is another Rhodesia.
About crimes, it has amnesia.
Millions are ruled by racists.
The army promotes the basest.
Apartheid Rhodesia eventually fell.
Apartheid Israel will go to hell.
4/1/19

Begin led the Irgun paramilitary group.
Many Palestinians did they shoot.
Begin blew up the King David Hotel.
Ninety innocent people fell.
As Prime Minister, he used bulldozers and tanks
To vastly expand "settlements" on the West Bank.
He wanted a Greater Israel to be sure.
Palestinian dreams he interred.
4/3/19
*Inspired by The Israel Lobby and U.S. Foreign Policy
 by John J. Mearsheimer and Stephen M. Walt

Charges of anti-Semitism based solely on Israel criticism
Are examples of Zionist cynicism.
Support the Palestinians, and AIPAC will indict:
You, sir, are an anti-Semite.
If you tell them you're anti-Zionist,
They will call you a Holocaust denialist.
4/3/19

Sunday, March 31, 2019
Poetry Group Five Hundred Second Posting 3/31/19

Democrats distance themselves from AIPAC.
It stabs Palestinians in the back.
People skipped the conference and were not embarrassed
Like Sanders, Warren, O'Rourke, Castro and Harris.
Young Jews hate Israel's human rights abuses.
For the Israel lobby they have no uses.
AIPAC is not bipartisan anymore.
It is far right to the core.
3/24/19

Israel sold Iran military supplies,
While U.S. hostages were Iran's prize.
In war, Israel was Iran's military supplier.
Iran was a reliable cash buyer.
Israel sold American technology to the Chinese,
And to any other third country it pleased.
Of all our allies, Israel is not the best
Foremost to Israel is its own interest.
3/25/19
*Inspired by The Israel Lobby and U.S. Foreign Policy
by John J. Mearsheimer and Stephen M. Walt*

America won't solve the Arab-Israeli conflict.
Its Israel-biased officiating is not wanted.
America wants Israel to decide
Where the Palestinians will abide (if at all).
America gives Israel a big allowance
To kill civilians with IDF cowards.
America should impose a Palestine.
If Israelis don't like it, that's fine.
3/26/19

Even as the Golan Heights are digested,
What territory will AmerIsrael next hit?
If you answered, the West Bank,
Then you get a raise in rank.
AmerIsrael delegitimizes the United Nations.
It wants international law invalidation.
It wants to take all of the other people's land.
This is what AmerIsrael always planned.
3/27/19

Trump's attitude toward Israel is anything goes.
Take the Golan Heights, Trump crows.
I will give you the West Bank soon.
The Palestinians will dance to your tune.
What do I get out of all this?
My rich Jewish donors give me a kiss.
And I will long be remembered in Israel,
For making the Palestinians much more miserable.
3/27/19
*Inspired by "America Risks Loving Israel to Death"
by Thomas L. Friedman NYT OP-ED 3/27/19*

Sunday, March 24, 2019
Poetry Group Five Hundred First Posting 3/24/19

Unconditional support for Israel makes winning the war on terror more difficult.
From the "special relationship" informed people will revolt.
To betray justice like this, we never did
Arab public opinion of us is negative.
Backing Israel makes terror fighting harder.
Stop unconditional support for Israel as a starter.
3/16/19

Gaza is a bitter abode.
The people burn tires and block roads.
Life there is full of hardships.
Israel has the place in its grip.
A big demonstration will occur on March 30.
You can bet the Israelis will fight dirty.
They have shot hundreds dead here,
Along the Gaza Frontier.
3/18/19

Fox News had to suspend Jeanine Pirro
For slandering Representative Omar, my hero.
Jeanine said Ilhan was not loyal to the United States,
Because of the Congresswoman's Muslim faith.
President Trump told Fox to fight back.
He said Omar should be the one sacked.
Pirro assuaged Trump's base.
He said suspending Jeanine was a disgrace.
3/18/19

White-nationalist violence is on the rise.
President Trump isn't the least bit surprised.
(My base will be violent if they don't get their way.)
Anything to foment violence, Trump will say.
Like Second Amendment people will prevent
Liberal judges to court being sent.
Trump normalizes political violence
But his critics have not chosen silence.
3/18/19
*Inspired by "Trump Encourages Violence"
 by David Leonhardt NYT OP-Ed 3/18/19

U.S. support for Israel's cruel policies
Resembles a king of Israel idolatry.
Israel is more of a liability than an asset.
U.S. support for war crimes is tacit.
Israel's strategic value has declined since the Cold War.
Israel is not any help anymore.
To the world we look hypocritical and callous.
The White House is a dictator's palace.
3/18/19

Each candidate should say one state or two.
If two states, what are you going to do,
To make that come about?
Will you throw the "settlements" out?
Or will you be another of the Jewish state's tools,
Another in a long line of fools.
3/18/19

March 30 marks the one year anniversary
Of border protests; may Israel have mercy.
This past year it killed 189.
Those snipers were really trying.
They wounded. 6,000 or more,
None of whom was outfitted for war,
Some of whom can't walk today.
Gun shots can cause big change.
The U.N. doesn't want this repeated.
Sniper-fire murder is not needed.
3/19/19

Trump gave the Israelis the Golan Heights,
Which was against international law and rights,
And undid decades of American policy.
Nitwityahoo exclaimed, golly gee!
Because he is in a close election.
Trump made clear his selection.
Next he will recognize Putin's land grab.
The U.S. President wants to re-draw maps.
The Arab League condemned the decision.
They don't share Trump's Zionist vision.
3/23/19

Poetry Group Five Hundredth Posting 3/17/19

AIPAC says it doesn't raise money for candidates.
The truth and that denial do not equate.
AIPAC's members raise the cash
That to the right candidates they pass.
Political action committees work independently of AIPAC
But their missions and membership align with AIPAC's.
At policy conferences, members gather in side rooms
To raise money and distribute it too.
3/10/19

Seventy-five percent of Americans favor higher taxes on the rich.
Republicans will not grant the people's wish.
Paid maternity leave enjoys 67 percent support.
On social issues, Republicans come up short.
Ninety-two percent want Medicare to negotiate lower drug prices,
Supporting Big Pharma is one of the Republicans' vices.
Two-thirds of the people should usually get what they want.
Republicans say maybe, just for a taunt.
3/10/19
Inspired by "What the Public Wants, It doesn't Get"
by Tim Wu, NYT OP-ED 3/6/19
Lines 1, 3, 5 and 7 by Mr. Wu

Trump is more admired in Israel than at home.
That popularity will keep Nitwityahoo on the throne.
Trump has provided politically useful gems,
Like moving the Embassy to Jerusalem.
Aid to Palestinians he repeatedly cut,
All the while improving his putt.
He says Palestinian refugees are no longer refugees,
And that Israelis may seize as much as they please.
3/11/19

Support for Israel helped inspire the 9/11 attacks.
Bin Laden and al Qaeda wanted to hit back.
They used the Palestinian plight as a recruiting tool.
Unconditional support for Israel makes America a fool.
Israel is a liability in the war on terror.
Slavery to Israel is America's error.
Israel creates anti-Americanism.
There needs to be a schism.
3/12/19
*Inspired by The Israel Lobby and U.S. Foreign Policy
 by John J. Mearsheimer and Stephen M. Walt

Of all his themes, payback for injustices suffered
By the Palestinians, whom AmerIsrael smothered,
Is the most recurring notion in bin Laden's speeches,
Which went out to the world's farthest reaches.
Unconditional support for Israel imposes secondary costs,
Like the thousands on 9/11 lost.
3/12/19
*Inspired by The Israel Lobby and U.S. Foreign Policy
 by John J. Mearsheimer and Stephen M. Walt

Support for Israel is inconsistent with America's professed values.
American unfairness influences Muslim world views.
America applies justice at home but not abroad.
The more Israel kills and steals, the more Republicans applaud.
Muslims see the killings on Al Jazeerah and the Internet.
The weapons are U.S. made and the killing done with U.S. consent.
American enabled carnage Muslims see with their own eyes.
It's all because America is Israel's prize.
3/12/19
*Inspired by The Israel Lobby and U.S. Foreign Policy
by John J. Mearsheimer and Stephen M. Walt*

Sunday, March 10, 2019
Poetry Group Four Hundred Ninety-Ninth Posting 3/10/19

It can be gotten through and you will get through it.
Beseech the world to help you do it.
Palestinians, the Democrats are coming.
Nitwityahoo is fumbling.
You will make a Palestinian state.
Endure, resist, wait.
Justice will prevail.
Good will not fail.
3/3/19

The U.N. Human Rights Council looked into
Israeli war crimes true.
Israeli snipers are vicious haters.
They killed 189 demonstrators,
And wounded 9,000 more,
Some of whom are still sore.
Israel commits crimes against humanity,
But escapes punishment uncannily.
It kills innocents from hundreds of yards away,
Whom Israel had no need or right to slay.
3/3/19

Nitwityahoo will be tried for bribery, breach of trust, and fraud.
Most of the rest of the world will applaud.
If world support for Palestinians wasn't so vague,
Nitwityahoo would be tried at The Hague
For crimes against humanity and war crimes.
In the Israeli trial, will justice be blind?
3/4/19

From a lower middle class family in Brooklyn,
To lead our nation Bernie is looking.
His policies are for the people but not the richest.
(Republicans burn Socialists as witches.)
Tuition-free college and a $15 minimum wage
Those and other ideas make Sanders sage.
He will win with grass roots funding
And live to be a hundred.
3/4/19

Here is how I learned my lesson.
I ask Rabin to make concessions.
So he says to me all mild and meek,
I can't make concessions because Israel is weak.
So I give him more arms
But this is no charm:
I need not make concessions because Israel is strong.
Next year we will sing the same song.
3/4/19
*Inspired by The Israel Lobby and U.S. Foreign Policy
 by John J. Mearsheimer and Stephen M. Walt
and: lines 2,4,5,7, by Henry Kissinger*

AIPAC so warped the Israel policy debate,
That dissenters are told to sit quietly and wait.
But AIPAC pushes for allegiance to a foreign country.
Representative Ilhan Omar says so bluntly.
AIPAC's money has an outsized influence.
The congresswoman says this with exuberance.
An anti-Semite she has been branded.
She is a patriot to be candid.
3/5/19

They accuse Omar of using historical anti-Semitic tropes.
She doesn't use old tropes; her critics are dopes.
Anti-Semitism before Israel in 1948
Has nothing to do with criticism of the Jewish state.
American Zionists have dual loyalty.
That has become the new normalcy.
American Zionists won't deny it.
They want all Americans to try it.
3/9/19

Sanders would advance progressivism beyond our shores,
Against authoritarianism and more.
Nitwityahoo is among the top five culprits,
But evangelicals praise him from the pulpits.
What do Putin and Nitwityahoo have in common?
They both promote civilian bombing.
How do Putin and Nitwityahoo function?
They function by corruption.
The global rise in illberalism
Explains the rise of illIsraelism.
2/24/19

A racist anti-Arab party joined the coalition.
Otzma Yehudit passed the audition.
Their views align with Nitwityahoo's.
If you can kill a Palestinian, do.
They want the West Bank annexed.
Expel the Palestinians, check.
Shoot to kill stone throwers.
Be ultimate war sowers.
2/25/19

Consider the child care proposal from Elizabeth Warren.
She is already the tax-the-rich-crowd's darling.
Families who need it should have subsidized child care.
The expense of which the rich will bear.
The children could play and learn.
Their parents could work and earn.
Millions of lives would be improved.
A family headache would be soothed.
2/26/19
*Inspired by "Democrats For Family Values"
 by Paul Krugman in NYT Opinion Page 2/22/19*

Kushner will reveal his long-promised peace initiative.
A Palestinian state I wish it will give,
With East Jerusalem as its capital.
Nitwityahoo must be adaptable.
Israel can't take all of Palestine.
With 80% they should be fine.
Zionism should have ended in 1948.
A Palestinian state the world awaits.
2/27/19

Terrorism is not a movement but a tactic.
Photos of terror strikes are graphic.
But not all terrorists are alike.
The same countries they don't strike.
Hamas does not attack the U.S.
Though the U.S. helps Israel oppress.
Al Qaeda does not strike Israel
Though Israel makes millions miserable.
2/27/19

Nixon gave Israel another $2 billion not for peace,
And started the oil embargo and production decrease.
The military assistance came during the October War.
Israel didn't need anymore.
So the Arabs did what they had to do,
Which hurt the American economy too.
Support for Israel imposes additional costs.
Why does America let Israel be boss?
2/27/19
*Inspired by The Israel Lobby and U.S. Foreign Policy
by John J. Mearsheimer and Stephen M. Walt*

Sunday, February 24, 2019
Poetry Group Four Hundred Ninety-Seventh Posting 2/24/19

The wall is very, very on the way.
I called a national emergency today!
I'll claw back money from the military budget.
They say it's unconstitutional, but fuck it.
This will go through the courts for a while.
But at least my base will see I tried.
2/17/19

Chancellor Merkel got a standing ovation.
She said nations should cooperate with nations.
Vice President Pence met with silence.
He wanted to do the Iran deal violence.
He told the Europeans to withdraw,
So the U.S. and Israel can start a war.
2/17/19

Ford and Kissinger grew sick of Israeli intransigence.
They threatened to curtail Israel's numerous advantages.
So 76 senators signed a letter sponsored by AIPAC,
And all of Israel's aid was back on track.
Presidents learn they can only use the carrot not the stick.
The "special relationship" with Israel is sick.
2/18/19
*Inspired by The Israel Lobby and U.S. Foreign Policy
 by John J. Mearsheimer and Stephen M. Walt*

America's willingness to take Israel's side
Increases significantly over time.
For Israel, there is nothing we won't do
Including ban the Palestinian point of view.
The U.S. vetoed 42 U.N. Security Council resolutions
Critical of Israel (they were the solution).
That's half the U.S. vetoes cast between '72 and '06.
The U.S. ensures the problem never gets fixed.
2/18/19
*Inspired by The Israel Lobby and U.S. Foreign Policy
 by John J. Mearsheimer and Stephen M. Walt*

Nixon pledged to consult Israel before any peace proposal.
He put American power down the garbage disposal.
He gave Israel a quasi veto
Over what we wanted to do.
Abba Eban called this the golden age in U.S. arms supplies.
The cost was not for the public's eyes.
2/18/19
*Inspired by The Israel Lobby and U.S. Foreign Policy
 by John J. Mearsheimer and Stephen M. Walt*

Here in North Carolina's Ninth Congressional District,
Republicans steal elections right quick.
For fraud, they have a talent:
They forged over one thousand ballots.
They blame non-citizens for election fraud.
That accusation is way overbroad.
White Republicans carried this out.
Usurping democracy it was all about.
2/20/19

The U.S. and Israel want war with Iran yesterday.
Pence believes it is foreordained destiny.
But the signing members of the nuclear deal
To Trump's imploring will not yield.
These foreign leaders have their big kid pants on
But war with Iran, baby Trump ran on.
2/20/19

Treat Israel like a normal country.
$38 billion should not be perfunctory.
Condition aid on an end to the occupation.
Palestinians deserve their own nation.
Make Israel conform its policies to U.S. interests.
Make it have an American values system.
2/21/19

Israelis made U.S. negotiators fools.
Take for example "the no-surprise rule."
No new idea could the Americans advance,
Without telling the Israelis beforehand.
The U.S. adopted the position of the Israeli Prime Minister.
Purporting to be neutral, America was sinister.
We argued Israel's brief
Leaving the Palestinians in grief.
Israel never revealed its bottom line.
The status quo was fine.
2/21/19
*Inspired by The Israel Lobby and U.S. Foreign Policy
by John J. Mearsheimer and Stephen M. Walt*

Sunday, February 17, 2019
Poetry Group Four Hundred Ninety-Sixth Posting 2/17/19

Will we rise to the great moral challenge of our time,
The 70 year old crisis in Israel-Palestine?
The Israel lobby weighs Congress down.
Due to fear, Congress will not rebound.
It will take journalists, and there are only a few,
Who, about Israel, tell the truth.
Michelle Alexander is one such writer.
She makes the light around truth brighter.
2/11/19
*Inspired by "Time to Break the Silence on Palestine"
by Michelle Alexander, NYT Sunday Review 1/19/19*

Society's lax gun control enforcement
Gives murderers an endorsement.
Everybody has guns. So why not me?
I will shoot the next person I see.
My how the bodies do pile up.
They should not have riled me up.
The consequences of this may be hard.
I'll show the cops my NRA card.
2/11/19
*Inspired by "Surprise! It's Not the Gun, It's the . . ."
by Gail Collins NYT OP-ED 2/9/19

Over Trumpublicans, the people will vault.
Go as far left as the people want.
Tax the top 1% commensurate with their wealth.
Make sure all can take care of their health.
Expand Social Security and Medicare.
It's time for the rich to be fair,
And pay their fair share.
2/11/19

The Times says AIPAC doesn't contribute to campaigns.
But it once did, which could have been ascertained.
AIPAC told The Times the truth maybe,
But I think it's done with Benjamins, baby.
Omar was not offending Jewish Americans as a whole.
Criticizing AIPAC takes its toll.
But she will not be bullied away,
From the honest dialogue we need today.
2/12/19

Older Democrats tow the Israeli line.
The younger ones want a new Palestine.
They hate Israel's human rights abuses,
And its cover-ups and excuses.
They want all of America to know,
That Israel causes Palestinian woe.
They want all Americans to see,
The Palestinian plight on TV.
It's not anti-Semitic to criticize Israel,
Which makes millions miserable.
2/12/19

Neither Congress nor Mexico will pay for Trump's wall.
Humpty-Dumpty had a great fall.
He wants to finish what was never started.
He sits in the White House broken hearted.
Trump wants Representative Omar to resign
For remarks about AIPAC, which were fine.
Stating legitimate criticism of Israel
Will make any free speaker miserable.
So many apologies are owed to her.
If AIPAC isn't paying, they once were.
2/13/19

In supporting Israel, America's guiding principle
Is that all aid be unconditional!
No matter how many "settlements" Israel builds,
Or how many Palestinians it kills
Aid to Israel will continue to incline.
Money and material arrive on time.
2/2/19
*Inspired by The Israel Lobby and U.S. Foreign Policy
 by John J. Mearsheimer and Stephen M. Walt*

Stand against injustice and oppression,
Which occur in Israel without question.
Accuse Israel of human rights abuses.
Reject its Zionist excuses.
Demand movement toward a Palestinian state.
Republicans are Manchurian candidates.
Israel is the apple of their eyes.
America is Israel's prize.
2/4/19

Silence in the face of tyranny is betrayal.
Indifferences to evil can be fatal.
So can standing up to evil many times
Like for those who fight for Palestine.
They often face condemnation.
Being blacklisted is a bad sensation.
Michelle Alexander risks losing her career,
Because she will write more about Palestinians this year.
Her conscience leaves her no choice.
Listen for her remarkable voice.
2/6/19
*Inspired by "Time to Break the Silence on Palestine"
by Michelle Alexander, NYT Sunday Review 1/19/19*

The senate passed an anti-B.D.S. bill,
Which gives the First Amendment a chill.
Private companies will be punished
(This legislation is rubbish)
For boycotting the Jewish state.
Free speech the senate abates.
Because the senate is bought and sold
With Israel lobby gold.
2/6/19

Sunday, February 3, 2019
Poetry Group Four Hundred Ninety-Fourth Posting 2/3/19

The U.S. takes on economic burdens for Israel's benefit,
To the American taxpayers' detriment.
We maintain a strategic oil reserve,
For Israel whom we serve.
Several hundred million is the cost.
Oil to Israel will never pause.
1/27/19
*Inspired by <u>The Israel Lobby and U.S. Foreign Policy</u>
by John J. Mearsheimer and Stephen M. Walt*

Israeli contracts for less than half a mil
Get no prior U.S. review, nil.
The head of Israeli Air Force procurement
Had an embezzler's endurance
And diverted millions in U.S. aid.
This Brigadier General did not make the grade.
The Defense Department called the program miserable.
But we want no turbulence in our relationship with Israel.
1/27/19
*Inspired by The Israel Lobby and U.S. Foreign Policy
by John J. Mearsheimer and Stephen M. Walt*

U.S. money helps Israel's defense industry.
Subsidize Israeli companies, why must we?
These funds should support U.S. high-tech.
Tear up that Israeli aid check.
Israel sold American technology to the Chinese.
Israel afflicts America like a disease.
1/28/19

Israel repeatedly denied it had a nuclear program.
Ben-Gurion told Presidents this is no sham.
In the late '60's the CIA found out.
But nothing was done about it.
Why do you think Iran wants a bomb?
Israel is erratic and has a long arm.
1/28/19
*Inspired by The Israel Lobby and U.S. Foreign Policy
by John J. Mearsheimer and Stephen M. Walt*

Maybe Jews can no longer be Democrats.
Democratic values they scraped.
They strongly support and fully own,
The most right wing Israeli government ever known.
In Israel racism is codified.
American Jews have been modified.
1/29/19

Republicans accuse of anti-Semitism any critics of Israel.
Lovers of free speech are miserable.
Is the world playing "The Emperor's New Clothes"?
Falsehood is what Republicans chose.
Anti-Semitism is their charge
Against those who make truth large.
1/29/19

Israel is the oppressor of a marginalized group.
Those who don't believe so are duped.
Israel killed 200 protestors in six months time,
And even now continues the crime.
Granholm buries her head in the sand,
And shouts, Israel is grand!
She chooses Israel over America.
She is a stupid and uninformed character.
1/29/19

Obama was for the two-state solution.
He passed legislation against pollution.
Trump believes in one state,
Ruled by racism and hate.
Trump tears up vital regulations.
He fosters planet degradation.
If only we could have Obama back.
That great man is colored black.
1/30/19

Raise taxes on the rich to increase revenue;
Limit the concentration of wealth, too.
That's what Senator Warren wants to do.
She'll need votes from people like you.
Tax the oligarchic dynasties.
Leave them their wealth and finery.
Do not make rich people poor,
But tax them much more.
1/30/19
*Inspired by "Elizabeth Warren does Teddy Roosevelt"
by Paul Krugman NYT Opinion Page 1/29/19

Sunday, January 27, 2019
Poetry Group Four Hundred Ninety-Third Posting 1/27/19

The Israel lobby maintains this fact:
The "special relationship" will remain intact.
But its strategic and moral grounds are weak.
Some other means it had to seek
Like stifling critics of Israel.
And making the honest miserable
1/20/19
*Inspired by The Israel Lobby and U.S. Foreign Policy
by John J. Mearsheimer and Stephen M. Walt*

The U.S. is a pluralist democracy where freedom of speech is guaranteed.
A perfect place for AIPAC to succeed.
Because America accommodates,
AIPAC dominates.
We need open discussion of this matter.
The iron lobby must be shattered.
America is led by the nose
To wherever Israel goes.
1/21/19
*Inspired by The Israel Lobby and U.S. Foreign Policy
by John J. Mearsheimer and Stephen M. Walt*

The costs of backing Israel have risen.
It's an ever more costly mission.
Yet the benefits of backing Israel decline.
That this goes on is a sign
That AIPAC controls Congress.
Cutting aid to Israel would be progress.
1/21/19
*Inspired by The Israel Lobby and U.S. Foreign Policy
by John J. Mearsheimer and Stephen M. Walt*

Israel's Second Lebanon War would be foolish and wrong.
American officials knew this all along.
They couldn't warn their Israeli counterparts,
Because that would break the lobby's heart.
The lobby pushed a policy that tarnished America's image,
And strengthened Hezbollah, which is not timid.
1/22/19
*Inspired by The Israel Lobby and U.S. Foreign Policy
by John J. Mearsheimer and Stephen M. Walt*

Ben-Gurion said he would keep the Sinai he seized.
President Eisenhower was none too pleased.
He threatened to cut all public and private aid.
Full restitution Ben-Gurion made.
Why can't presidents today threaten Israel?
Because the Israel lobby would make them miserable.
The "special relationship" is a straightjacket,
Or we're standing in concrete and can't crack it.
1/23/19
*Inspired by The Israel Lobby and U.S. Foreign Policy
by John J. Mearsheimer and Stephen M. Walt*

Israel does not have to say how the aid was spent.
It does not use the money for what it was meant.
The aid is not to be used on the West Bank.
Israel builds "settlements" with it and never says thanks.
Why does modern Israel need our money?
They have so much wealth it isn't funny.
Donations to Israeli charities are tax deductible
Thanks to Congress which is corruptible.
1/23/19
*Inspired by The Israel Lobby and U.S. Foreign Policy
by John J. Mearsheimer and Stephen M. Walt*

Let's not trump to conclusions.
A certain person doesn't like losing.
Who says the rot starts at the head?
How close will Mueller get?
That could have serious implications.
Is this a Sopranos imitation?
Will the President get, you know . . .?
Will he seek sanctuary in Moscow?
1/26/19

Sunday, January 20, 2019
Poetry Group Four Hundred Ninety-Second Posting 1/20/19

Israel gets massive U.S. support,
Thanks to the Israel lobby, of course.
Nothing else can explain
Israel's huge financial gain.
None of this can be spoken,
America is not to be woken.
Justice is not applicable here.
Israel is very dear.
1/15/19
Inspired by The Israel Lobby and U.S. Foreign Policy
by John J. Mearsheimer and Stephen M. Walt

The U.S. does harm when its policies are misguided.
It satisfies Israeli greed and hides it.
Americans don't know why the rest of the world hates us.
The world is disgusted at how Israel takes us.
A new relationship between the U.S. and Israel would benefit both.
Israel no longer the parasite, and we no longer the host.
1/15/19
Inspired by The Israel Lobby and U.S. Foreign Policy
by John J. Mearsheimer and Stephen M. Walt

A strong moral case for Israel's existence exists.
But why must the land taking persist?
Morally, the Palestinians have the better case.
But America kicks sand in their faces.
Toward the Palestinians we should lean.
When Israel attacks, we should intervene.
1/16/19

The U.S. favors Israel far above the rest,
Far beyond what national interests would suggest.
America's largess is no mystery,
The situation has no equal in history.
Diplomatic cover the U.S. provides,
Behind which Israel hides.
America does not say no,
As the "settlements" grow.
1/18/19
*Inspired by <u>The Israel Lobby and U.S. Foreign Policy</u>
by John J. Mearsheimer and Stephen M. Walt

Melting ice causes polar vortex breakdowns.
That's when arctic wind leaves snow in mounds.
The arctic warms twice as fast as the average rate.
Big storms now come in mid winter and late.
The wind bands that hold back polar air
Fall apart and make us care.
Climate change affects us.
Chilling cold gets us.
1/19/19
*Inspired by "Icy Invasions from the Arctic, and You're
Going to Have to Get Used to Them"
by Kendra Pierre-Louis NYT 1/19/19

Sunday, January 13, 2019
Poetry Group Four Hundred Ninety-First Posting 1/13/19

A "settlement" at the heart of the Gaza Strip,
Gush Qatif was not hip.
The army had trouble protecting it.
There was no land bridge connecting it.
The mother country decided to evict it.
That's when the "settlers" became wicked.
1/7/19
*Inspired by Israel by Ilan Pappe

One colonist state survived the twentieth century.
Bloody Israel did not do so gently.
The colonies multiply and expand,
On Palestinian land.
The indigenous are oppressed
With help from the West.
No other colonies exist,
But Jewish "settlements" persist.
1/8/19

Israelis think the one state solution is better than the two.
But they don't think through what one state would do.
Israel would irrefutably be an apartheid state.
For pariahood it would not have long to wait.
Israel will not be absolved of its sins
In oppressing the Palestinians.
The world united against apartheid before
And will do so once more.
Israel is religious and militaristic.
The country's run by bloody mystics.
1/8/19
*Inspired by Israel by Ilan Pappe

Nitwityahoo booked prime time out of fear.
The coming indictment threatens his career.
He bribed a TV station for positive coverage.
Nitwityahoo calls this good governance.
Hundreds of millions of dollars are involved,
Yet Nitwit thinks he should be absolved.
Nit's hysteria escalates
As the attorney general waits,
Whose motives Nit impugns.
The law lies in ruins.
1/8/19

The religious "settlers" stoned a woman to death.
Now five of them are under arrest.
She was with her family in a car,
When her head was fatally marred.
She was killed for her ethnicity.
The five religious boys are fidgety.
1/8/19

The powerful Israel lobby
Affects U.S. foreign policy.
The Israel/U.S. synthesis
Is not in America's interest.
The Jewish lobbyists are not modest.
They increase attacks from Jihadists.
They affect relationships with our allies.
Most Americans don't realize.
1/12/19
*Inspired by <u>The Israel Lobby and U.S. Foreign Policy</u>
by John J. Mearsheimer and Stephen M. Walt*

Neither strategic nor moral grounds explain
The level of support, which is insane.
Something else must account
For the enormous amount.
That something else is the Israel lobby.
Subverting America is its full time hobby.
We're giving them $38 billion over ten years.
They have a higher standard of living than we have here.
1/12/19
*Inspired by The Israel Lobby and U.S. Foreign Policy
by John J. Mearsheimer and Stephen M. Walt

Sunday, January 6, 2019
Poetry Group Four Hundred Ninetieth Posting 1/6/19

The diplomats were detached from reality on the ground.
More Jewish "settlers" were West Bank bound.
Even as the talk was about removing colonies,
Israel increased their quality and quantity.
Its international image deteriorated.
Good will toward Israel faded.
But by trade Israel is normalized.
A boycott must be formalized.
12/31/18
*Inspired by Israel by Ilan Pappe

With Israeli attacks, a naval blockade, and the siege,
Liberation is hard to believe.
Will Gazans ever be free?
The UN predicts a catastrophe.
That would be too bad, Israel says.
America chimes in, Yes.
12/31/18
Inspired by Israel by Ilan Pappe

The EU sanctions goods from Jewish colonies,
And says to the world, follow me.
Israelis call this anti-Semitic.
They pretend they don't get it.
Colonialism is bad.
Stealing their land makes people mad.
BDS is here to stay.
Boycott something Israeli today.
12/31/18
Inspired by Israel by Ilan Pappe

Israel invests millions to improve its image.
When concocting propaganda, Israel isn't timid.
But lies don't blunt the world's accusation,
That Israel runs a cruel occupation,
Which undermines its international standing.
(The U.S. provides a gentle landing.)
Israel is materially secure,
But known for its lopsided wars.
America sends military power,
To make civilians cower.
1/2/19

Palestinians decrease in quantity,
Due to Israel's "settlement" policies.
Ethnic cleansing is a cruel
Anti-personnel tool.
Palestine is more and more Judaized.
Palestinian resentment is no surprise.
America takes the side of injustice
Though justice was to be her sustenance.
12/26/18

Israel's image improved under Oslo in 1993.
International investors heartily agreed.
There was mutual recognition between Israel and the PLO
From the peace process, good feelings flowed.
Then came the assassination of Prime Minister Rabin.
Since then, Israeli good faith is seldom seen.
12/26/18

After 9/11 and the "Islamic Terror,"
Many Americans made this error:
They associated Palestinians with
Al-Queda fundamentalists.
These same Americans today
Make an intentional mistake.
Anti-Zionism and anti-Semitism they confound.
Anything for Israel, they propound.
12/26/18

Israelis no longer envision a Palestinian state.
They tell the Palestinians don't bother to wait.
Israelis don't see their cynicism as a threat.
They don't see American aid as a debt.
Only a Palestinian state
Could make terrorism abate.
The Palestinians have a just grievance.
Rectifying it would be an achievement.
12/27/18

Sunday, December 23, 2018
Poetry Group Four Hundred Eighty-Eighth Posting 12/23/18

Trump promised justices who'd dump Roe v. Wade.
Two such justices he has already made.
Conservatives are the majority of the court.
There may soon be no right to abort.
Will the justices follow precedent,
Or the will of the President?
Now in place for near half a century,
Roe will not go down gently.
12/17/18
*Inspired by "Reading the Tea Leaves on Abortion"
by Louise Melling NYT OP-ED 12/17/18*

There had been Arab revolutions before.
Israel claimed Jordan would make one more.
On this pretext, Israel wanted to attack the West Bank.
America said no; Jordan said thanks.
This was the Middle East crisis of 1958.
Another nine years Israel had to wait.
12/17/18
Inspired by Israel by Ilan Pappe

Israel said it used nonlethal bombs for roof-knocking,
But the world Israel was mocking.
Antipersonnel missiles Israel uses.
Humanitarian law it abuses.
Two Gaza teens were killed by such a "warning" shot,
Which put their families in a mourning spot.
Israel has a legal obligation.
To spare the civilian population,
Israel's war crimes
Will stand for all time.
12/18/18
Inspired by Israel by Ilan Pappe

AIPAC bribes politicians at the start of their terms.
Unconditional support for Israel they learn.
If they refuse AIPAC's money and demands,
AIPAC puts the money in their adversaries' hands.
This way AIPAC owns most of Congress.
Members take the money and make the promise.
12/19/ 2018

Presidents and candidates must attend
AIPAC's conference or their careers end.
The skip by Senator Bernie Sanders
Shows one man's bold candor.
More people should stand up to AIPAC.
Its power we should take back.
12/19/18

Israel's invasion of Lebanon in 1982,
Showed again that Israeli greed is true.
A U.N. report found Israeli war crimes,
But the U.S. buried that report in no time.
No one paid a fine or went to jail.
Every attempt at justice failed.
12/19/18
Inspired by Israel by Ilan Pappe

Sunday, December 16, 2018
Poetry Group Four Hundred Eighty-Seventh Posting 12/16/18

The President awoke from his stormy reverie,
And directed Cohen to commit a felony:
That transaction Trump later denied.
About this his minions also lied.
Trump defrauded American voters,
That's why they elected this joker.
Breaking campaign finance law is a federal crime.
Someday Trump will do time.
12/10/18
Inspired by "Surviving a Criminal Presidency"
by Charles M. Blow NYT OP-ED 12/10/18

Lame duck Republicans pass legislation
Meant to cause an executive power confiscation.
For governor, the people want Democrats,
Whose powers are undermined by dirty rats.
The powers of each branch should be as equal as can be.
The constitution Republicans fail to see.
Only their ideology do they prize.
With each dirty trick, the Republic slowly dies.
12/10/18
*Inspired by NYT editorial "The Price of
Shattering Civic Norms" 12/10/18*

Apartheid South Africa, Israel praised,
And the two did trade and exchange.
In the late 1980s, Apartheid died.
Israel stayed up late and cried.
All the African states supported a Resolution
That Zionism is racism, no illusions.
The ANC took the Palestinian side.
Israel cannot hide its own Apartheid.
12/11/18
Inspired by Israel by Ilan Pappe
UN Resolution 3379, November 1975

Point out its diminishing international image,
And Israel will respond with a grimace.
Fortunately, economic ties aren't affected.
And the far right always gets elected.
World trade feeds us.
The world needs us.
Fear no international embargo.
They're hooked on our cargo.
12/11/18

Israel supports archaeological discovery,
And ancient artifact recovery.
But the state's less interested in the Arab past,
No matter how vast.
Hebrew sites of ancient date,
Strengthen the Jewish state.
They get the most attention.
They're the only sites mentioned.
12/12/18
Inspired by Israel by Ilan Pappe

There was a time when America had some clout,
Over what Israel was about.
America made Israel withdraw from the Sinai
During the Suez Canal crisis
When the right of return Israel would not debate
The U.S. imposed sanctions on the Jewish state.
Today America worships Israel,
Which is allowed to make millions miserable.
12/12/18
Inspired by Israel by Ilan Pappe

Sunday, December 9, 2018
Poetry Group Four Hundred Eighty-Sixth Posting 12/9/18

I am critical of Israel,
Because I am an American liberal.
Injustice anywhere is abhorrent.
Serve Nitwityahoo with a warrant.
His bloody war crimes are legion.
He is the mad dog in the region.
Don't just fight for civil rights at home.
Let your sense of justice roam.
12/3/18

Thrice this year the police urged criminal prosecution,
For Nitwityahoo and his criminal contributions.
Bribery, fraud and other corruption cases,
Will serve as the indictment's basis.
But justice here might not be tenable.
Nitwityahoo picked the attorney general.
Nitwit would destroy law enforcement
To get the right people's endorsement.
12/3/18

Trump has many Russian associates
For a Moscow hotel he negotiates.
He says he has absolutely no connection:
We haven't even built one section!
I have no Russia deals whatsoever,
(But a Trump Tower Moscow would be a worthy endeavor.)
Thusly, Trump lied to America.
He is a mendacious character.
12/3/18
*Inspired by "What Would Happen If . . ."
by Charles M. Blow, NYT OP-ED 12/3/18

If you come up with an alibi, please send it.
I do not want to be a criminal defendant.
The key for me is re-election.
I will be the people's selection.
Who could indict me then?
I am Bibi, short for Ben.
12/4/18

Anti-carbon measures do not function,
Because of Republican corruption.
Conspiracy theorizing on the right,
Hurts the war on carbon fight.
Willful ignorance plays a role.
Never finding out is the goal.
Politicians are threatened.
Intimidation gets them.
12/4/18
*Inspired by "Climate Denial As the Crucible
For Trumpism" by Paul Krugman, NYT OP-ED 12/4/18*

Reality can be interpreted in a non-Zionist way.
Those West Bank "settlements" don't need to stay.
Pluralism would improve Israel's cultural identity.
Israel could be better in the 21st century.
Inspired by Israel by Ilan Pappe

Zionism is rigid, racist, and extreme.
Demonizing Palestinians is the theme.
For its cruelty, Israel pays a price:
The world knows Israel is not nice.
12/5/18
Inspired by Israel by Ilan Pappe

Liberal media has no impact on Israeli society,
Which ever moves toward messianic piety,
And away from everything liberal.
That's 21st century Israel.
11/26/18
Inspired by Israel by Ilan Pappe

Climate change will knock 10% off GDP by century's end.
The vendors will have less to vend.
Trump says planet trashing will bring about a boom.
But his policies are economic doom.
We should work to mitigate global warming.
Mother Nature has given her warnings.
The future will not resemble the past,
Unless we reduce carbon emissions fast.
11/26/18

A brave new world is aborning.
Republicans deny global warming.
They try to confuse America.
They are depraved characters.
Civilization itself may be at stake.
Republicans say science is fake.
They are well paid by big oil,
To whom they are ever loyal.
11/27/18
Inspired by "The Depravity of Climate-Change Denial"
by Paul Krugman NYT Opinion Page 11/27/18

For science, President Trump has no reverence,
Including for unequivocal scientific evidence.
Trump rolls back helpful Obama policies.
His claims about "clean coal" are fallacy.
Trump will add carbon in the millions of tons,
To help trap the heat from the sun.
Trump will be remembered as the carbon president.
To cut regulations, he is not hesitant.
11/27/18

Israel's pretension to be a democracy
Is a good example of hypocrisy.
It can't be a democracy and a Jewish state,
For non-Jews Israel berates.
Their minority votes will never be enough.
To get them full citizenship and stuff.
11/27/18

Sunday, November 25, 2018
Poetry Group Four Hundred Eighty-Fourth Posting 11/25/18

Nitwityahoo accepted a cease fire in the Gaza fight.
He saved lives, which is always right.
But some Israelis, including the defense minister,
Saw in this cease fire something sinister:
Not nearly enough Palestinians had died.
Lieberman quit and went home and cried.
11/19/18

Their land Palestinians have been denied.
Every "settlement" is illegal and a war crime.
Airbnb's listings will no longer contain "settlements."
About 200 will be dropped for justice's benefit.
No more bed-and-breakfast on stolen land.
Airbnb refused Zionism's command.
11/20/18

Jewish Home threatened to leave the government without a majority.
But the ministers changed their minds heartily.
They realized they were not prone
To ruin the most right wing government ever known.
What if Trump wants the two state solution?
What if he's not convicted of collusion?
Then the religious right must unite.
No time for internecine fights.
11/20/18

Israel is no journalistic oasis.
Freedom of the press has no legal basis.
A self-appointed committee guides the press.
Anything printed must be blessed.
Israeli journalists learn this lesson:
The government's version is never questioned.
Much censorship is self-imposed.
Before it begins, the investigation is closed.
11/24/18
Inspired by Israel by Ilan Pappe

Sunday, November 18, 2018
Poetry Group Four Hundred Eighty-Third Posting 11/18/18

For months, Israel has tried to quell Gaza's borders by force.
But now Israel is taking a different course:
Partially easing its longstanding blockade
To let in fuel and financial aide.
Could this show that Israel wants peace?
Imagine if the stealing and killing ceased.
Israel is heading off another Gaza war.
Its aims seem humane, and I'd like to see more.
11/11/18

A group once about outdoor sports
Is now a far-right group of sorts.
Its magazines tell members who to vote for
In the anti-gun control war.
The Second Amendment is a curse.
The NRA makes it worse.
11/11/18

The talks showed progress in recent days.
Israeli cooperation was praised.
So what does Israel do after that?
It acts like a dirty rat,
And sends commandos into the Gaza strip,
Which made Hamas and others flip.
Now munitions fly in and out of Israel,
Which can't help itself from making people miserable.
11/13/18

I am the President, so I must alert you:
Partisanship now defines truth and virtue.
Democrats and their "objective facts,"
Are nothing but do-gooder hacks.
Any news against me is fake.
Don't believe it for Jesus's sake.
Miriam Adelson gets the Medal of Freedom.
She's another one that knows how to cheat 'em.
11/13/18
*Inspired by "Truth and Virtue in the Age of Trump"
by Paul Krugman. Opinion Page NYT 11/13/18*

Israel wants quiet on Gaza's borders,
But won't give the necessary orders
To allow Palestinians to work in Israel.
It would rather keep them miserable.
Israel sabotaged the cease fire.
Killing Palestinians is its true desire.
Israel makes homeless longtime residents.
Israel's war crimes are self-evident.
11/14/18

The world should ask the question:
Why can't Israel control its aggression?
And why must Israel have all the land?
Is Zionism some kind of trance,
That can never be broken?
Think how many wasted words have been spoken.
11/14/18

The revival of Hebrew was part of the project.
Yiddish did not fit Zionist logic.
It was the language of exile,
Seen by some "settlers" as vile.
Hebrew is spoken down the line,
Just like in biblical times.
Hebrew was much expanded,
To be candid.
11/14/18
Inspired by Israel by Ilan Pappe

Sunday, November 11, 2018
Poetry Group Four Hundred Eighty-Second Posting 11/11/18

Gaza did not exist as a separate region in the past.
Its long prosperity and stability did not last.
The strip was created near the end of the war.
Israel shoved in hundreds of thousands or more.
Gaza became a giant refugee camp,
With the lid tightly tamped.
11/5/18
Inspired by Israel by Ilan Pappe

Do you want a congress of Trump puppets?
Give Republicans their comeuppance.
For Trump they lie and cheat.
Vote them out on the street.
They are the President's flunkies
Real power junkies.
Even the best of them acquiesce
To Trump's nationalist B.S.
11/5/18
Inspired by "Vote, Vote, Vote!" by Charles M. Blow
NYT OP-ED 11/5/18

Three Palestinian boys were killed by an Israeli airstrike.
Their dying instant was very bright.
Israelis claimed they were planting an explosive device,
But lying to the press is Israel's delight.
No explosive device was found.
Wadi al-Salqa was their home town.
11/6/18

Protective Edge took place in 2014.
The IDF made Gaza scream.
2,200 Palestinians lost existence
From munitions thrown at them from a distance.
When the army tried to fight guerrillas face to face,
It found itself in another kind of disgrace.
Sixty-six Israeli soldiers became ghosts.
Israeli soldiers can't fight up close.
11/7/18
*Inspired by Israel by Ilan Pappe

Israel has the widest gap between rich and poor in the OECD.
Part of the long-term solution is peace.
Israel also heads the poverty indexes
With Palestinians it needs a better nexus.
It has the lowest level of reported well being and welfare.
About Palestinians Israel doesn't care
11/7/18
*Inspired by Israel by Ilan Pappe
* The OECD is the Organization for Economic
Cooperation and Development

I need a favor, President Trump began,
Speaking to the Prime Minister of Japan.
They were at Mar-a-Lago, where deals are struck.
President Trump believes he has all the luck:
My friend needs a casino license for Yokohama.
He didn't want to ask Obama.
He donated heavily to my campaign.
So I want to further his gain.
10/29/18

In 1994 a "settler" opened fire in the Ibrahimi Mosque.
29 dead and 125 wounded was the cost.
The consequent suicide bombers killed dozens,
Including Jewish children and mothers.
Nitwityahoo blamed the Oslo Accords.
The real cause of the terror he ignored.
Nitwit was there when the rabbis gave their verdict:
Prime Minister Rabin may be murdered.
10/29/18

Zionism should be reversed.
Ethnic cleansing is the worst.
Israel should leave the West Bank.
The world would have Israel to thank.
Israel doesn't care to please the world,
Only its mythical Lord.
Which tells it to take all
Then put up a wall.
10/31/18

Stephanie Ruhle proved herself cruel.
She implied that college students aren't cool.
She inferred they are anti-Semitic.
She doesn't give them any credit
For their anti-Zionist views,
 Which Stephanie abused.
She's afraid to say Palestinians on air.
About them she doesn't want to care.
She could never criticize Israel,
Though it makes millions miserable.
10/31/18

I update my doctor about my delusion:
The plot winds toward the grandiose conclusion.
For now I am a legend in my own mind,
But someday I will be one in time.
The muse has left her mark on these pages.
Some of my poems belong to the ages.
11/4/18

Sunday, October 28, 2018
Poetry Group Four Hundred Eightieth Posting 10/28/18

Jordan wants full sovereignty over all its land,
But Israel isn't sure Jordan can.
Israel has been leasing two tracts from Jordan,
On which it has been making a fortune.
Al-Baqura and Al-Ghamr are ours,
King Abdullah said within his powers.
But at stealing land, Israel is deft.
Soon Jordan will be bereft.
10/22/18

Gaza was cordoned off by a barbed wire in 1994.
And the Israelis did more.
Checkpoints were as numerous as grains of sand.
Israel expropriated other people's land.
Most of the water in the Gaza Strip
Was in the Jewish colonists' grip.
In the occupied sector
Israel remained tax collector.
10/27/18
Inspired by Israel by Ilan Pappe

A terrorist attack in Netanya in 2002
Gave the IDF their cue.
To use planes to bomb Palestinian camps and towns
Anything to bring the population down.
This was the first time they used bomber jets,
A handful of terrorists to catch.
The army had to throw the public red meat,
To bury the shame of the Lebanon defeat.
10/27/18
Inspired by Israel by Ilan Pappe

The second Lebanon war
Was because in Israel's withdrawal
From the first Lebanon war
It took a little more.
Israel couldn't help annexing,
(While exiting)
A piece of Lebanon, no matter how vexing.
10/28/18
Inspired by Israel by Ilan Pappe

In late 2008 Israel launched operation Cast Lead.
By the end, fifteen hundred Palestinians lay dead.
Hospitals, schools, and mosques were not spared.
All the people were dead or scared.
In 2012 the next round came.
Returning Echo was the operation's name.
200 Palestinians were killed this time.
2014 would bring a bigger crime.
10/28/18
Inspired by Israel by Ilan Pappe

Sunday, October 21, 2018
Poetry Group Four Hundred Seventy-Ninth Posting 10/21/18

America promised its Arab allies against Iraq,
That it would help the Palestinians after the attack.
The first war led to the Madrid conference,
But the Israeli PM treated it like nonsense.
Shamir had no wish to help the Americans find a solution.
He would not lead Israel in a peace revolution.
He wanted to maintain the status quo
For a hundred years or so.
10/13/18

Right wing nationalists charted Israel's path.
Israeli hate became Israeli wrath.
They have less interest in people's human rights
And more interest in lopsided fights.
They killed 200 Palestinians in six months time,
Many of them were shot from behind,
Because they were shot as they ran away.
Give us our rights the dead bodies say.
There were no injuries on the Israeli side.
That's what happens when troops and protestors collide.
10/15/18

I would never say I was wrong to folks,
But climate change is not a Chinese hoax.
Something is happening, but it will go back,
No matter if mitigation lacks.
Maybe there's a difference, but it's not manmade.
If you're too damn hot, stay in the shade.
10/16/18

Ever since Rabin supported the Oslo Accords,
He was demonized by right wing hordes,
Out of which came the religious one,
Who asked his rabbi to bless his gun.
Then he did as God had said:
At a peace rally, he shot Rabin dead.
10/16/18

Hezbollah fought a successful war against the IDF,
Which left Lebanon after so much death,
Like the bombardment of the refugee camp near al-Qana,
Where there was much death and panic.
If there was an endless supply of civilians,
The IDF would kill them by the millions.
10/17/18

Sunday, October 14, 2018
Poetry Group Four Hundred Seventy-Eighth Posting 10/14/18

If you care about social justice issues,
The Israeli occupation cannot miss you.
Palestinians live under foreign occupying forces,
Which American aid to Israel endorses.
Criticizing Israel's apartheid regime
Is not hatred of Jews though they make it seem.
10/8/18

Begin proposed a Palestinian autonomy on the West Bank.
(For that we had Jimmy Carter to thank.)
But later in talks he had no intention to get anywhere.
Zionism was about to go on another tear.
The government emphasized the "settlement" project.
Theft of Palestinian land was the object.
So the "Autonomy Plan" was forever shelved.
Israel would take all the land for itself.
10/9/18

Sharon met secretly with the leaders of the Phalangists,
Maronites who follow fascism and St. Francis.
They would get the government when Israel took Beirut.
Then the Maronites could skin every Muslim they shoot.
Many Israeli officers and soldiers refused to serve.
Heavy losses turned public opinion averse.
Then came the massacre of Palestinian refugees.
Israelis cried, We've done enough, let us leave!
Hundreds of Israeli soldiers died in vain;
The wounded suffered unnecessary pain.
10/10/18
Inspired by Israel by Ilan Pappe

Hate the sin, but not the sinner.
You can even be a beginner.
Apartheid must be despised,
Though you and Jews abide.
Jewish achievements should be praised.
Likewise, Gaza's siege must be raised.
Despite false charges in endless repetition,
Criticism of Israel is not anti-Semitism.
10/10/18

Occupying millions of people against their will,
Israel is not afraid to steal and kill.
Palestinians arrested without trial
Stay in jail a long while.
When a house is marked for demolition,
The owner can do nothing of his own volition.
Arab lands are always confiscated.
Israel will never be sated.
10/10/18

Sunday, October 7, 2018
Poetry Group Four Hundred Seventy-Seventh Posting 10/7/18

The privilege of being a white man isn't what it used to be.
The #Me Too movement is getting through to me.
It's wrong to hold your hand over a girl's mouth,
When you're on top of her on a couch.
And you shouldn't throw ice cubes in a bar.
That could be pushing privilege too far.
A Supreme Court Justice I will become.
Kind to all and fair to some.
10/2/18
Inspired by "The Angry White Male Caucus"
by Paul Krugman NYT Opinion Page 10/2/18
Line 1 by Mr. Krugman

Israelis should learn common decency,
And show Palestinians leniency.
Israel imposed harsh military might.
Palestinians lost civil and human rights.
Judaisation occurred in dense Arab areas.
Then the Jews put up barriers.
The policy was as anti-Arab as possible.
The rise of resentment was probable.
10/3/18

The "settlers" think they are divinely sanctioned.
"God" is their pillar; they are not anxious.
The native population must move or die.
Resistance is futile, but they will try.
Israel has complete impunity
To persecute the Palestinian community.
Some thought they were citizens of a democracy,
But Israel is a cruel theocracy.
10/3/18

I can't write a poem,
Unless I am home.
I can't perform the synthesis,
Unless I am self-intimate.
Writing stuff down is a wager
Made to get something down on paper.
Sometimes I win, sometimes I lose.
I win if there's something I can use.
10/5/18

It is no sacrifice to return what is not yours,
For example, Israel, land you took by force.
Return what you stole and expect no pity.
Your human rights record is pretty shitty.
For once, make some atonement.
You make the whole world your opponent.
10/6/18

Sunday, September 30, 2018
Poetry Group Four Hundred Seventy-Sixth Posting 9/30/18

America is bought and paid for,
A mercenary in Israel's war.
For centuries to come people will die
For the redemption of Palestine.
The world will bleed due to Israel's greed.
This warning no one will heed.
The injustice of Israel is too great
Not to affect human fate.
9/22/18

American viewers would watch with revulsion
The massacres, demolitions, and expulsions.
But TV doesn't show these things,
And the misery that they bring.
Israel calls these acts "self-defense."
That's what passes as common sense,
In the aggressive Jewish state.
Justice will be welcome, though it come late.
9/22/18

G.O.P. policies hurt more people than they help.
A vote for G.O.P. is a vote against yourself.
Tax cuts were for rich corporations and individuals.
Middle class resentment is residual.
Republicans want to destroy Obamacare.
With Democrats the people will better fare.
Take from ordinary families and give to the rich.
That is the Republican's age old pitch to the rich.
9/25/18
*Inspired by "The Party of No Ideas" by Paul Krugman
NYT Opinion Page 9/25/18*

Israeli Palestinian citizens are barred from the military.
Israeli Jews are biliary.
If the sign says, we only want people who served in the army,
A Palestinian doesn't get the job or apartment.
9/25/18

Mossad paid Egyptian Jews to set off explosives,
And rise to the top like Joseph.
But the plot was discovered,
By the Egyptians who governed,
Who executed the Egyptian Jews,
Which made the Tel Aviv news.
What were the targets of this vipers' nest?
Buildings with Western interests.
The Israelis called it "the Affair."
About Western interest, they don't care.
The Plan was to divide Egypt from the West,
But Mossad made a big mess.
9/25/18
*Inspired by Israel by Ilan Pappe

Nitwityahoo is a sorehead
With hundreds of nuclear warheads.
There's no telling what he'd do,
If Iran built something new.
Why does Israel have nukes but Iran does not?
Because Nitwityahoo is a chauvinist snot.
9/25/18

Fusing nationalism to religion undermines the democratic regime.
Making Palestinians second class is the general theme.
Even Mizrahi Jews are discriminated against.
To technological schools they are sent
With less opportunity for job or career.
The Ashkenazi sneer.
The Kibbutzim or collectives,
Were also very selective.
Jews who came from Arab lands
Were seen as less than Jewish man.
9/26/18
Inspired by Israel by Ilan Pappe

France enabled Israel to develop nuclear capacity.
The world regrets France's audacity.
Vanunu told about the nuclear fission,
For which he spent a long time in prison.
Israel wants to be unique -
The only Mideast nuclear freak.
If Iran tries to build a bomb,
All of Iran will be gone.
9/26/18

Israel believed it was a fatal historical mistake,
Not to have taken the West Bank in '48.
But in '67, Israel remedied that
With a dastardly surprise attack.
It also took Gaza, the Sinai, and the Golan Heights.
Millions more Palestinians lost their rights.
9/26/18

Sunday, September 23, 2018
Poetry Group Four Hundred Seventy-Fifth Posting 9/23/18

Americans don't know the Palestinian point of view.
The Palestinian story is kept off TV by the Jews.
Americans are taught to focus on Israel.
They don't know about the Palestinians miserable.
Journalists fancy themselves reporter-heroes.
But every one of them is a cowardly zero.
They should tell the Palestinian point of view,
Even though they are not allowed to.
 9/16/18

What news source will break the story,
Of the occupied Palestinian territory?
What do you think most Americans will say,
When they see that Palestinians have a better claim?
9/17/18

Mueller builds cases against those in Trump's train,
Then he pressures them to cooperate up the chain.
To date, Manafort is Mueller's biggest fish.
A reduced sentence is his fervent wish.
Should President Trump be worried?
Mueller will not be hurried.
9/17/18
*Inspired by "Manafort Folded: Now What?" by Noah Bookbinder,
Barry Berke, and Norman Eisen NYT Op-Ed 9/17/18*

Republicans protect Trump's lawlessness,
But their efforts are not flawlessness.
They can't stop Trump from tweeting,
Which is often self-defeating.
They can't stop Trump's cronies from testifying.
Trump will tweet they all are lying.
9/17/18

When Israel was but nascent,
It perpetrated a displacement
Of 800,000 Palestinians
Forced off like American Indians.
Arabs have a legitimate national claim to the land,
But Israel is America's favorite brand.
9/17/18

Punishing Palestinians is the work of a sophist.
Trump closed the PLO's Washington office.
He thinks he's teaching them a lesson
And extracting mucho concessions.
But Palestinians have been punished before.
Trump's punishment they will ignore.
Resolution of the conflict Trump bungles.
Hang on PLO; Trump's days are numbered.
9/18/18

The Republican policy of cutting taxes on the rich
While slashing social programs is a bitch,
So Republicans obscure their true intentions,
And cutting Medicare they barely mention.
They lie about helping those with preexisting conditions.
Destroying Obamacare is their mission.
Voting for Trump his voters dare
Only to lose their healthcare.
9/18/18
*Inspired by "Kavanaugh and the Politics of Bad Faith"
by Paul Krugman NYT Opinion Page 9/18/18*

The Palestinian state must be contiguous.
Palestine must not be ambiguous.
Arabs won't accept disconnected cantons,
Though Nitwityahoo throw a tantrum.
Arab East Jerusalem deserves self-rule.
Israeli rule is not cool.
9/19/18

Sunday, September 16, 2018
Poetry Group Four Hundred Seventy-Fourth Posting 9/16/18

Israel's legitimacy is still questioned.
Israel's democracy is but a gesture.
Look at the circumstances of its birth,
To see what Israel's "legitimacy" is worth.
Israelis thought they had the final word.
The voice of the Palestinians was not heard.
But in the 1980s, Palestinian scholarship
Put history in the people's grip.
9/10/18
Inspired by Israel by Ilan Pappe

The discriminative structure of the Israeli government
Is an apartheid, not a democratic, covenant.
Israel is a hypocrisy not a democracy,
Because Israel is a klepto-ethnocracy.
Israel is not the only democracy in the Middle East.
It is a racist, ethnocentric beast.
Full citizenship depends on having the right religion.
Whoever says Israel is a democracy is a pigeon.
9/10/18
*Inspired by BDS: Boycott, Divestment, Sanctions
by Omar Barghouti*

Republicans run on white identity politics.
At the poor they throw bricks.
Obamacare is in their sights,
Though that system is running right.
They won't protect those with preexisting conditions.
Policies won't pay for hospital admissions.
Killing Obamacare Republicans will dare.
Millions more people will be without healthcare.
9/11/18

Nitwityahoo puts no faith in the diplomatic process.
His party controls his Israeli congress.
He pushes the "settlement" of occupied land.
He is a brutal, greedy, racist man.
He says the Palestinians left by their own free will,
And how they're only good to rob and kill.
9/11/18
Inspired by Israel by Ilan Pappe

The native population was the main obstacle.
So ethnic cleansing became topical.
But expulsion did not reach totality.
The world came to a higher morality.
So Israel runs an apartheid regime.
The military enforcers are mean.
9/11/18
Inspired by Israel by Ilan Pappe

He catered to big coal, the bastard.
He delivered by lowering pollution standards.
Increasing the deficit while the economy is growing,
Is wasteful (without Trump caring or even knowing).
Faced with so much increasing debt,
Trump will turn Social Security on its head.
But the rich will get more tax cuts.
Trump says, no ifs, ands, or buts.
9/12/18
Inspired by "Anonymous Is Hiding In Plain Sight"
By Thomas L. Friedman, NYT OpEd 9/12/18

Evangelicals are superstitious liars:
Israel means the second coming of the Messiah,
And the resurrection of the dead.
Christ and His Church will wed.
This myth determines the U.S. point of view.
To a Zionist Christian nothing exceeds a Zionist Jew.
The ethnic cleansing is a religious imperative,
Disregarding the Palestinians' long heritage.
9/12/18

Sunday, September 9, 2018
Poetry Group Four Hundred Seventy-Third Posting 9/9/18

Kushner got the funding cut he wanted.
Five million Palestinians he taunted,
Who will lose education and health care.
Protests against Israel they'll dare.
Vaccines and prenatal care will disappear.
Sneering Kushner will be in good cheer.
9/2/18

UNRWA's mandate is to help refugees,
Until a permanent solution can be reached.
U.S. funding cuts could end services.
In Israel there is nervousness.
The U.S. forfeited its role in negotiating peace.
Trump's hate for Palestinians will never cease.
Trump warned he would totally take Israel's side,
With his Jewish son-in-law as his guide.
9/2/18
Unrwa is the U.N. Relief and Works Agency
for Palestine Refugees in the Near East

Trump thinks he will get more concessions
By increasing Middle East tensions.
Trump wants to kill the right of return
For which millions of refugees yearn.
He thinks that by suffering starvation,
Palestinians will join the conversation.
He supports the Israeli religious right.
His friends can never be too white.
9/2/18

Israeli academia is complicit in the denial of rights.
Its scholars resemble those of the Third Reich.
They justify war crimes, racism, and rights violations.
They are every bit a part of the Zionist nation.
Suspend Israel from international forums.
Zionist participants lack decorum.
9/4/18

All their land Palestinians must lose,
Simply because they are non-Jews.
But a Jew from anywhere who's never been there
Can go to Israel as King David's heir.
Israel obscures its apartheid reality.
Nitwityahoo is excused his venality.
Oppressed and oppressor are not equally to blame.
Colonizers and colonized are not the same.
9/4/18

Trump moved our embassy to Jerusalem from Tel Aviv.
The Palestinians got nothing, though aggrieved.
If our President was really a great dealmaker,
Israel would be a giver not a taker.
Kushner makes Palestinians suffer.
Less aid makes their lives tougher.
Still they will not give up their birthright.
They want a nation, and they know the site.
Less aid will close the secular schools.
Trump and his son-in-law are fools.
The religious schools will double in size.
All the young aspirants will be taught to despise.
9/5/18

Two Trumpublicans were recently indicted.
Trump wishes Sessions would fight it.
One misappropriated funds for personal use.
The other faces insider trading abuse.
Trump does not care about their corruption.
He said so in a twitter eruption.
These two were Trump devotees.
Wounded loyalists are all he sees.
9/5/18

Sunday, September 2, 2018
Poetry Group Four Hundred Seventy-Second Posting 9/2/18

Projects with Israel give the false impression of normalcy.
Meanwhile racist oppression continues formally.
Apartheid will not lead to peaceful coexistence.
If you were Palestinian, you would support the resistance.
8/28/18
Inspired by BDS: Boycott, Divestment, Sanctions
by Omar Barghouti

When Israel's oppression is met by substantial resistance,
The demand for rights will have world insistence.
Many Jews will no longer support the occupation.
Palestinian patience will have led to elation.
Europe must shoulder the moral responsibility
To give Palestinians a national identity.
To have a homeland on their own land,
Europe must lend a hand.
8/28/18

Racial resentment, not economic distress, drove Trump voters.
Republicans are go-for-the-throaters.
In Georgia, they closed many polling places.
Republicans are white nationalist racists.
Their power they want to entrench.
Democratic principles do not make them flinch.
They replaced an entire state supreme court
With a loyal, obsequious sort.
8/29/18
*Inspired by Why it Can Happen Here"
by Paul Krugman, NYT Opinion Page 8/28/18*

In accordance with the Zionist plan,
Jews ethnically cleansed the land.
Many Palestinians are refugees today,
Because of the Jews' Zionist ways.
Displaced persons are protected by international law,
Which Israel has long ignored.
Occupation and colonization are legally banned,
But Jews "settle" someone else's land.
8/30/18

Refrain from cooperation with Israeli institutions,
Until Israel makes restitution.
Boycott Israel at every level.
Cooperation with Israel is a pact with the devil.
Support Palestinians at the U.N.
Don't let Nikki betray us again.
Israel is what greed has wrought.
It is evil and must be fought.
8/30/18

The Israeli academy chose the hegemonic establishment.
Ethnic cleansing is slow banishment.
Academics support the status quo.
They perpetuate Palestinian woe,
And should be welcome nowhere.
When it's too late, America will care.
Israel dominates the American government,
Despite our founders' covenant.
8/30/18
*Inspired by BDS: Boycott, Divestment, Sanctions
by Omar Barghouti*

Trump wants objective reality and Republican propaganda treated equally.
He wants the truth distributed meagerly.
Right-wing media make many false claims,
But mainstream media must treat them the same.
The political pressure will be effective:
Half the news will be defective.
8/31/18
*Inspired by "Trump's Assault On Google"
by Michelle Goldberg, NYT OpEd 8/31/18*

"Israel must be like a mad dog, too dangerous to bother."
Those words were said by one of Israel's fathers.
But Israel is too menacing and lawless to ignore.
Nevertheless, Europe still snores.
8/19/18
Inspired by BDS: Boycott, Divestment, Sanctions
by Omar Barghouti, Line 1 by Moshe Dayan

Trump's onetime chief strategist,
Who knows his Republican catechism,
Is in Europe trying to unite the far right,
But Europe's far right doesn't want to unite:
We reject any supranational entity.
I am not speaking tentatively.
We reject the American model
And its president Donald.
8/20/18
Inspired by "Steve Bannon's New Best Friend"
by Ivan Krastev, NYT OP-Ed 8/20/18

Some people especially hate those they've mistreated.
That's why lock-her-up Hillary is still needed.
Trumpublicans depend on the ignorance of the base.
Trump speaks of "deep state" with a straight face:
Trumpublicans, believe me.
Climate change is a conspiracy,
Involving scientists worldwide.
The truth they hide.
8/22/18
Inspired by "The G.O.P.'s Climate of Paranoia"
By Paul Krugman, NYT Opinion Page 8/21/18
Line 1 by Mr. Krugman

Too bad the German police got you,
For putting up a Nazi statute.
Our Nazis were the Confederates,
Slave beaters inveterate,
Whose monuments are coming down.
Only empty pedestals can be found.
Democrats are the nemesis
Of white supremacists.
8/22/18
*Inspired by "Broken Tributes to a Morally Bankrupt Cause"
by Blain Roberts and Ethan J. Kytle, NYT OpEd 8/22/18*

One can't attack a ship and then claim self-defense if the people resist.
The Gaza bound humanitarians had a right to be pissed.
Israel attacked them in international waters.
The IDFs are always ready to slaughter.
8/23/18
*Inspired by BDS: Boycott, Divestment, Sanctions
by Omar Barghouti*

Convince Israel of its moral degradation,
Like its Palestinian segregation.
Show Israel its ethical isolation.
Stealing and killing are its vocation.
Have nothing to do with the outlaw state.
Until it changes, wait.
8/23/18

Liberals worldwide disdain Israel,
Which will never itself be liberal.
It values the building of "settlements,"
To hurt the Arabs for its benefit.
"Equality" doesn't appear in the nation-state bill.
Israel torments Palestinians to break their will.
Ironic that the Jews became fascists.
About this the world needs more passion.
8/12/18

Our capitalism makes socialism more appealing.
The wealthy's wealth is through the ceiling.
The people get no raise in wages.
Their President puts children in cages.
Changes are needed around here.
Trump promotes hate and fear.
8/12/18

The Jewish Diaspora faces a generational divide.
Legalized racism young people despise.
They know about the Palestinian plight,
And that Jews do not treat Arabs right.
Young Jews raise doubts their elders never raised.
They don't like Israel's cruel, racist ways.
They do not take their identity
From an apartheid entity.
8/14/18
*Inspired by "Israel, This Is Not Who We Are"
by Ronald S. Lauder NYT Op-Ed 8/14/18*

The Democratic Socialists should be Socialist Democrats.
Capitalism's end? The people don't want that.
They want social programs saved.
That will take a blue wave.
The blood red Republicans are in a hurry
To cut Medicare and Social Security.
They say the rich need more tax cuts
But right now they lack the guts.
8/15/18

The denial of Palestinian rights
Includes the use of military might.
A Palestinian's right to free speech
Ends with a missile's screech.
A right you never see in germination
Is the Palestinians' right of self-determination.
Israel chose to be a colonial society,
Which ignores international treaties.
8/15/18
*Inspired by BDS: Boycott, Divestment, Sanctions
by Omar Barghouti

Having killed 2,200 Gazans in air and ground attacks,
The IDF now bury the facts,
And exonerate themselves of any wrong
In the 2014 war, which was 50 days long.
The civilians killed had presented no threat,
Yet they made up most of the dead.
So Israel stands self-cleared.
World opinion it never feared.
8/16/18

Picture four boys playing on a beach.
But a Zionist drone is in reach.
The next thing you know, these boys are dead.
We thought they were Hamas, Israel said.
8/16/18

Israel enjoys entrenched impunity
Which gives it free opportunity
To act like an uncontrollable mad dog
That consumes everything like a hog.
8/17/18

Sunday, August 12, 2018
Poetry Group Four Hundred Sixty-Ninth Posting 8/12/18

800,000 people were forcibly displaced.
In the years following, their villages were erased.
This was operation "cleaning the landscape."
Vestiges of Palestinians were scraped.
8/7/18

Palestinians have too long waited
For Gaza to be unblockaded,
And for Israel to stop bombing
The civilians of isolated Gaza.
The Air Force sends waves of attacks.
Bombs Israel does not lack.
A pregnant woman and her child died yesterday.
Killing civilians is the Israeli way.
8/9/18

Trump is king of the crony elites,
Some of whom are stock market cheats.
Don't let the right say the left are elites.
The real elite demands tax cut treats.
Trumpublican politicians provide.
Jesus is somehow their guide.
8/9/18

Pack the court with rightist ideologues,
To pass the loot to the money hogs
And stamp out all the labor unions.
Ignore the economically wounded.
8/9/18

What has once gone by is not ours,
For example hours, flowers, and powers.
What is present we can share,
But soon it won't be there.
Not even God can change the past.
And He cannot make the present last.
But over the future He has control.
He knows what will happen to each and every soul.
8/10/18
*Line 1 by Marcus Aurelius
Line 5 by Agathon

Zionism is greed.
On other people's land it feeds.
Zionists claim racial superiority.
They treat Palestinians horridly.
Give back the land, Israel – make haste.
Force alone cannot make you safe.
You will be embargoed soon.
Israel will be like the man in the moon.
8/10/18

Sunday, August 5, 2018
Poetry Group Four Hundred Sixty-Eighth Posting 8/5/18

Knowledge is the strongest weapon for a struggler.
Like the knowledge of a Gaza smuggler.
Or that of an international lawyer.
Ahed will be a different kind of warrior.
At 16 she dared kick an Israeli soldier,
Few Palestinians are bolder.
She did eight months in an Israeli jail,
Which was like the lifting of a veil.
7/30/18
Line 1 by Ahed Tamimi

Here comes a $100 billion tax cut for the rich.
That $1.5 trillion one did not do the trick.
86% of benefits go to the top one percent.
Government revenues will suffer a dent.
Republicans give the rich tax boondoggles.
Why people support them is mind boggling.
7/31/18

Judaism is the only national expression permitted by law.
Non-Jewish citizens are nationally flawed,
And roundly discriminated against.
To Israelis, racism makes sense.
Gradual ethnic cleansing Judaizes the place
So Palestinians have less space.
7/31/18
*Inspired by BDS: Boycott, Divestment, Sanctions
by Omar Barghouti*

Israel subjects an entire human community
To life threatening conditions of cruelty.
Israel used concentrated sonic booms for weeks on end.
Gazan children's symptoms were hard to mend.
Chronic malnutrition leads to low birth weights.
Stunted growth comes from empty plates.
7/31/18
*Inspired by BDS: Boycott, Divestment, Sanctions
by Omar Barghouti*

The Druse helped the Zionists kill,
And could never get their fill.
The Jews told the Druse, "we're brothers"
And that the Druse were above the others.
But now Israel is the nation state of the Jews.
The Druse and other non-Jews lose.
The betrayal of the Druse is fitting.
I guess the army they'll be quitting.
8/1/18

When he's summoned to court, he'll need luck.
His conduct has been meant to obstruct.
Trump's tweets are central to the ruse.
He tweeted that Sessions should unrecuse.
He has attacked Mueller, the media, and the courts.
Trump is an autocratic sort.
No one should be able to investigate me.
I'm the President, don't you see?
8/2/18

Israel's war crimes refute its self-defense claim.
Gazans are attacked and take the blame.
In the 12/27/08 military offensive,
Israeli soldiers were not sensitive.
They killed over 1,400 Palestinians.
Genocide, like against American Indians.
Israel will reduce Gaza to abject destitution.
Boycotting Israel is the only solution.
8/2/18
*Inspired by BDS: Boycott, Divestment, Sanctions
by Omar Barghouti

You can share your racism in public.
President Donald Trump does it.
Trump's white nationalism pleases his base,
Who want the country segregated by race.
We've come too far to return to that.
Be sure to vote for Democrats.
8/3/18

Stealing land contravenes the laws of occupation.
Israeli "settlements" are abominations.
What kind of people could take all and share none?
Thanks to America, those people won.
7/24/18

The ultra-Orthodox wield significant influence.
Their persecution of gays shows sinfulness.
Some gay men want to be fathers.
Nitwityahoo isn't bothered.
Gay men pay taxes and perform military service.
But the ultra-Orthodox make Nitwit nervous.
Israel is run by the religious right.
Hence, the Palestinian plight.
7/24/18

The U.S. is giving Israel $38 billion
But can only give Palestinians $60 million.
The schools may open late or not al all.
I guess the parents will have to call.
Half a million kids will be on the street
Confronting the Israeli heat.
7/27/18

Happiness is not a possessions surplus,
But devotion to a worthy purpose,
Like the birth of modern Palestine.
Working for which, I feel fine
7/29/18

You see it coming but there's nothing you can do.
A truck pulled out in front of you.
You're too scared now to be annoyed.
You just hope the airbag deploys.
7/29/18

I want to save you as much as you want to save me.
You want to use Jesus; I want to use glee.
You could leave Him and stay on with me.
I promise days and nights of gaiety.
Nay, I shan't leave my Lord
Though he keeps me frigid and bored.
7/29/18

Sunday, July 22, 2018
Poetry Group Four Hundred Sixty-Sixth Posting 7/22/18

Trump praised Putin without reservation.
Republicans will hurt for generations.
What does Putin have over him?
The answer is still dim.
Trump denigrated our intel community.
His behavior is lunacy.
7/16/18

We want peace based on justice and human rights.
That kind of peace Israel fights.
Israel will not concede on inalienable, UN-sanctioned rights.
They would rather take war to new heights.
7/17/18

Israel won't respect Palestinian rights unless compelled to.
A higher standard it must be held to.
But America gives Israel carte blanche.
Soon war against Iran Israel will launch.
Indiscriminate killing and land confiscation
Will continue in the apartheid nation.
Trump loves Nitwityahoo and Putin.
Both men instigate shooting.
7/17/18

America perpetuates an unjust social order:
Palestinians with Israel as their warden.
Expect no help from the U.S. controlled U.N.
The Palestinians are betrayed again.
7/18/18

The "settlements" are war crimes under the Geneva Convention.
Repressive occupation measures are Israeli inventions.
The wall is illegal according to the ICJ at The Hague.
The world won't stop it for the Palestinians' sake.
Indiscriminate killings are chilling.
The IDF find them thrilling.
These and other measures are designed
To make the Arab population decline.
7/18/18
*Inspired by BDS: Boycott, Divestment, Sanctions
by Omar Barghouti*

Colonial settler regimes don't give up voluntarily.
The indigenous people need solidarity.
Palestinians also need world powers
To make the Israelis cower.
Apartheid South Africa was ostracized.
The nations against it were worldly wise.
We need an anti-apartheid choir
To make Israel a pariah.
7/19/18
*Inspired by BDS: Boycott, Divestment, Sanctions
by Omar Barghouti*

Israel's colonial and apartheid regime
To Palestinians is very mean.
Israel destroys Palestinian homes
And so should live alone.
The Star of David phantom
Kills people at random.
7/20/18

Annexation of the West Bank creeps on.
Persecution of innocents keeps on.
Palestinians don't get access to the Supreme Court.
For land disputes they have no resort.
Gay couples can't have children through surrogacy.
They are told to live in purgatory.
Only the Jews get self-determination.
Palestinians get sniper fire penetration.
7/21/18

Israel is a sepulcher white.
It denies refugees rights.
Israel is a South African simulation,
With legalized racial discrimination.
7/9/18

All universities in Israel are state funded,
So is it any wonder,
That academics further state policy?
They contribute to the military solidly.
Propaganda flourishes at universities.
No professors are worse than these.
They conceived and designed the wall.
They put it on Palestinian land, the gall.
7/9/18
Inspired by BDS: Boycott, Divestment, Sanctions
by Omar Barghouti

Israeli academics serve as occupying troops,
Where justice has been denied truth.
They return to academia much enriched,
Especially if they made a kill.
7/9/18
Inspired by BDS: Boycott, Divestment, Sanctions
by Omar Barghouti

Unless the price for its apartheid is raised,
Negotiating with Israel will be a waste.
The conflicting parties are not equivalent.
The weak versus the strong is not ambivalent.
The fact is the weak are righteous.
Knowledge of this is denied us.
We have made the strong stronger
And drawn out the conflict longer.
7/12/18

As the South African anti-apartheid struggle showed,
Boycott, divestment, sanctions are the right road.
Unless the price of Israel's apartheid is raised,
The cruel Zionists will not be fazed.
7/13/18

Sunday, July 8, 2018
Poetry Group Four Hundred Sixty-Fourth Posting 7/8/18

President Racist hates people black and brown.
Motherless children make a harrowing sound.
He tries to weaken our faith in the truth.
His insults to our allies are uncouth.
He attacks our respect for the rule of law.
He wants to join Israel in an Iran war.
He pins the needle on the gauge
When he injects fear and rage.
7/3/18
*Inspired by "Trump's Rage Junkies"
by Charles M. Blow NYT OP-ED 7/2/18*

Based on the Fourth Geneva Convention,
The U.N. has often mentioned,
That Israel's "settlements" (colonies) are unlawful,
And that the military occupation is awful.
Europeans don't like their companies complicit
In Israeli rail projects illicit,
Which connect "settlements" on occupied land.
Such companies in Europe are often banned.
One wanted to run the Stockholm subway.
The Swedes organized and said no way.
The Swedish pension fund stopped investing in another.
Zionist companies are not Sweden's brothers.
7/5/18
*Inspired by BDS; Boycott, Divestment, Sanctions
by Omar Barghouti*

Almost all the land is off limits to non-Jews.
93% of it is exclusively for Jews to use.
South African whites kept 87%.
Apartheid South Africa went.
Israel's case is worse.
The non-Jews are cursed.
Racism is legalized.
The IDF have eagle eyes.
7/5/18
*Inspired by BDS; Boycott, Divestment, Sanctions
by Omar Barghouti*

Israel satisfies the U.N. conditions for apartheid.
In the West Bank two races separately reside.
Separate roads, separate housing, separate everything.
Palestinians are peasants, Israel King.
Apartheid dwells inside Israel as well.
These things American TV does not tell.
7/6/18
Inspired by BDS; Boycott, Divestment, Sanctions
by Omar Barghouti

Sunday, July 1, 2018
Poetry Group Four Hundred Sixty-Third Posting 7/1/18

The U.S. withdrew from the top human rights body.
The move was biased and stupid more than cocky.
Before the only outcasts were North Korea, Eritrea, and Iran.
Our leverage against human rights abusers is gone.
The U.N. Human Rights Council passed five resolutions
Against Israel as part of the solution.
Trump cannot see Israel's abuses.
For his own, he makes excuses.
6/24/18

Israel will clear the West Bank of Bedouins,
To make room for more Jewish "settlements".
Israel's drip-drip campaign to make life miserable
Causes Palestinians to hate Israel.
Bedouins will no longer be allowed to raise sheep.
Their villages will be rendered heaps.
Bedouins were a place saver for an eventual state,
For which the world ever waits.
6/25/18

Kushner's plan doesn't call for a Palestinian state.
Trump says a state is not their fate.
Kushner says West Bank "settlements" will stay.
Maybe Arabs will have a capital someday.
Al Aqsa mosque will remain in Israel's hands
As would all that used to be Palestinian lands.
Kushner expects to dictate
For the malicious Jewish state.
He expects that Palestinians will sacrifice.
As if they haven't already, Christ!
6/25/18

Trump cut aid to Palestinian refugees.
The loss will cause instability.
Supplies of emergency food aid
Will begin to fade.
Broken minds need to mend.
Psychosocial help will end.
Palestinians will know who to thank,
When job programs end in the West Bank.
6/26/18

Trump is no honest Mideast broker.
He's a egomaniac and a gloater.
Palestinians want refugees in, "settlers" out.
Borders are what peace is about.
Palestinians won't give up their heritage.
Landlessness will not end the narrative.
They deserve a homeland on their own land.
They suffer in the occupied zone land.
6/27/18

Nikki says the U.N. picks on Israel,
A state which makes Palestinians miserable.
U.N. resolutions against Israel are deserved.
Israel gets on the world's nerves.
Nikki, the world is against you.
It has a true view.
Israel's war crimes are real,
Products of Zionist zeal.
6/27/18

Sunday, June 24, 2018
Poetry Group Four Hundred Sixty-Second Posting 6/24/18

President Trump makes false assertions:
It's the Democrats' fault in his version,
That families are separated at the border.
He could stop this with one order.
He wants his horror to serve as a deterrent
To the northbound human current.
He can't empathize with a terrified child.
His malevolence toward the poor is vile.
6/17/18

None of the Trumps have guilty feelings
About their charity's self dealings.
The New York AG is suing,
But the Trumps won't stop what they're doing:
Paying off legal claims and political backers.
This is okay with Trump's base of crackers.
That "non-profit" was meant for the poor,
But Trump saw it as another score.
6/17/18

Israel and America have a world-excluding unity.
Israel violates human rights with impunity.
It practices occupation, colonization, and apartheid,
But in America's heart, will always abide.
For trading with Israel, we have a history,
Which is one of egregious complicity.
Israel's genocide in Gaza is highly lethal.
Israel's military kills the most people.
6/18/18

Zionists who say Israel is the best,
Betray the defense of the oppressed.
Trump is one such Zionist pig.
Israel is his favorite gig.
His audiences are better there.
About fascism they don't care.
6/18/18

Trading with Israel in any field
Is complicity for real.
Israel is an apartheid state
Filled with racism and hate.
Even its academics approve
Of its fascist, apartheid moves.
Do not trade with Israel.
Zionism makes the indigenous miserable.
7/19/18

Israel is the last surviving colonial bastion,
Which rules in a cruel and brutal fashion.
Relations flourish only after oppression's end.
That will happen, Israel pretends.
It clings to racial discrimination
And seeks Palestinian elimination.
It enforces the occupation.
Israel is an apartheid nation.
6/19/18

Coexistence can't be achieved with Zionist oppression.
Palestinians suffer from dispossession.
Israelis call ethnic cleansing "transfer."
To Palestinians, it's a cancer.
Their right to self-determination is inalienable.
The state of Palestine is inevitable.
6/19/18

Sunday, June 17, 2018
Poetry Group Four Hundred Sixty-First Posting 6/17/18

Bullets do not pierce gently.
Gun deaths happen frequently.
The Second Amendment is a curse.
The NRA makes it worse.
The gun cult should not rule.
Let them form a circle and duel.
Let us rid the country of guns,
Except for the military and law enforcement ones.
6/11/18

There is no time to lose, Francis said.
Act before the planet is dead.
We need actual energy transition.
Then we can all make an act of contrition.
6/11/18

Blatant ego-stroking is how Trump likes to be handled.
The whole time the Nobel Peace Prize Kim dangled.
Little Rocketman was the object of Trump's charm.
He promised not to do any nuclear harm.
Trump promised no more South Korean war games.
The U.S. alliance with the south wanes.
Will Kim Jong-un keep his promise?
Trump looked like the novice.
6/13/18

Human impact alters how the planet functions.
Saving ourselves should become a compulsion.
Mankind should do itself a favor.
And cease its worst behavior.
Someday Earth will abide without us.
To forestall that, I doubt us.
Someday our species will not succeed,
Earth will be covered with weeds.
6/13/18
*Inspired by "Earth Will Survive. We May Not"
by Adam Frank NYT Op-Ed 6/13/18*

Israel oppresses its non-Jewish citizens.
American morality quit again.
Nikki blames the Palestinians for their losses.
Every shot was fired by their Israeli bosses.
America keeps Israel above the law.
Israel's cold heart will never thaw.
6/15/18

Sunday, June 10, 2018
Poetry Group Four Hundred Sixtieth Posting 6/10/18

Pence's religious beliefs are a complex delusion,
Saying so warrants my exclusion.
Barr called a black woman an ape.
Presidential condemnation she escaped.
Anglo evangelical churches remain silent.
Christian critics of Trump are silent.
6/4/18

Congressmen have shielded and protected him.
They excused and accepted him.
And so the Trumpublican party was born.
Morality, ethics, propriety forlorn.
Trumpublicans worship their fearless leader,
Though he is a liar, a racist, a cheater.
The majority of white women will vote for him again.
They believe certain liberties are owed to men.
6/4/18
*Inspired by "Where Trump Succeeded"
by Charles M. Blow NYT OP-ED 6/4/18
The first two lines are by Mr. Blow*

The Republican race is in devolution.
It denies the theory of evolution.
Climate science is also denied.
The bible was their only guide.
But Republicans no longer follow Christ.
Children are ripped from parents by ICE.
Programs for the poor will be no more,
Say Republicans hardcore.
6/5/18

Nikki wonders why America keeps losing at the U.N.
It's the rest of the world against us again.
Nikki can't see what the rest of the world sees:
That Israel is a deadly disease.
America is infected.
There was a resolution, our veto wrecked it.
6/5/18

Don't think your poet pays no price
For giving you this advice:
Israel is pernicious.
Toward Arabs, it's vicious.
Zionists try to lose me my job.
My livelihood they want to rob.
They vandalize my car.
Zionism's tentacles travel far.
6/5/18

Israeli soldiers just don't get it.
They killed an unarmed Palestinian medic.
She was only 20, but rendered aid.
A Palestinian martyr the Israelis made.
She was the 119th person shot dead.
From multiple holes she bled.
6/6/18

Detention is never in the children's best interests,
Nor is seeing handcuffs on their parents' wrists.
Cruelty is the manner in which Trump governs.
He takes crying babies from crying mothers.
Stop deeming entry a criminal offence.
What happened to the Christianity of Pence?
6/6/18

The U.N. Human Rights Council voted
To censor Israel full throated,
For disproportional use of force.
Israeli soldiers are coarse.
They killed an unarmed medic.
They frankly admit it.
She was a boon to the wounded.
Who supported her death? You did.
6/8/18

The Republican party is a cult of personality.
The most backwards party in the galaxy.
Republicans are very hesitant
To criticize the President,
So his popularity rises
No matter what the crisis.
His base then solidifies
The truth they can't visualize.
6/8/18

Sunday, June 3, 2018
Poetry Group Four Hundred Fifty-Ninth Posting 6/3/18

Mr. President, do not congratulate Putin.
After his sham election, it wouldn't be suiting.
Mr. President, why do you hate the press?
The press I don't hate, I detest.
I discredit the press,
So no one will believe this mess.
Freedom of the press we're going to take.
Bad news about me is always fake.
5/28/18

The following fact I send ya:
Obama was born in Kenya,
Which means he was never president.
Spread that, and don't be hesitant.
I don't take history, I make history.
The latest involves a "deep state" mystery,
Which attached a spy to my campaign.
That's how Democrats slander my fame.
5/28/18

Israel killed 120 Palestinians since March 30.
Israeli snipers fight dirty.
They killed 60 Palestinians in one day,
But the resistance will stay.
Bombing for bombing and blood for blood.
Israel chose the path of the gun.
Rather than extend a hand,
Israel steals all the land.
5/30/18

To criticize Israel is not anti-Semitism.
Trump's answer to the conflict is nepotism.
Israel is bad from a fact based perspective.
To see its war crimes doesn't take a detective.
5/30/18

On Israel, America dotes,
And was again the sole no vote,
To condemn Israel and protect Palestinians,
At the U.N. the U.S. is the silly one.
Israel killed 120 protesters behind a fence.
Its use of lethal force makes no sense.
Only Israel is above the law.
Only the U.S. says take more.
6/3/18

Pastor Bob Jeffress has warned you:
You can't be saved being a Jew.
He supports the Israeli land grab,
And that Palestinians should be nabbed.
But someday there'll be a holy heist:
Israel will belong to Jesus Christ.
Only the saved will He save.
God deems Israelis depraved.
They can't say amen to our prayer
Because Jesus Christ is there.
5/21/18

Nitwityahoo does not appease liberal Jews.
He has more evangelicals than he can use.
The views of the Diaspora are moot.
Evangelicals have given them the boot.
Reformers of conversion and the Western Wall
Hear from Nitwityahoo not at all.
For ethnic cleansing he is filled with zeal
But not about a land for peace deal.
5/21/18

Nitwityahoo proves illiberalism can prevail.
Greed, racism, and brutality never fail.
He takes his victories for granted.
Springtime is enchanted.
With Trump as his devoted squire,
Nitwityahoo gets what he desires.
5/21/18

Putin interfered in the 2016 election.
Donald Trump was his selection.
The FBI tried to warn the campaign,
Which treated the warning with disdain.
Some say the Trump presidency
Will end in a penitentiary.
Many have Russia ties.
Putin really tries.
5/22/18

Here comes the shooter down the hall.
Kids' brains stick to the wall.
Blood is slippery, then it gets sticky.
That last shot went right through Ricky.
TV viewers should see a child bleed out.
Then there would be gun control, no doubt.
TV hides the strongest incentive.
Piercing bullets are inventive.
5/22/18

Israeli leaders are frightened
That they might be indicted
For killing unarmed protesters.
Those snipers are go getters.
Let justice ring
For Palestinians.
Now is the time
For a free Palestine.
5/23/18

Israel implants "settlers" in Palestinian areas,
And puts up separation barriers.
Israel is content to be an apartheid state
For change, the world will forever wait.
But we struck a blow against Israeli enmity.
No Democrat went to the new embassy.
5/23/18

Sunday, May 20, 2018
Poetry Group Four Hundred Fifty-Seventh Posting 5/20/18

The consular services of the U.S. Consulate General
Will house a branch of the Embassy venerable.
The Ambassador will work between Jerusalem and Tel Aviv.
What did opening a sister embassy achieve?
5/14/18

The shot woman had not been acting in a menacing way.
Get off our land was all she had to say.
Gazans taunt the hyper-snipers,
Who strike as quick as vipers.
Palestinians fight for rights by peaceful insistence.
If the rights aren't given, they switch to resistance.
5/14/18

Many more whites than blacks receive food stamps.
Instead all will receive Christian work camps.
Trump will snatch food from the desperate.
Evangelicals won't call that irreverent.
Life shouldn't be too pleasant for the poor.
They shall get food stamps no more.
Trump's rhetoric will be inventive.
Less food gives the hungry incentive.
5/15/18
*Inspired by "Let Them Eat Trump Steaks"
by Paul Krugman NYT OP-Ed 5/11/18

Moving the embassy is devastating.
Christians think it's Revelations.
Palestinians say the city should be shared.
The Israeli usurpers don't care.
The embassy is a step away from peace.
Kushner's plan is a tease.
Israel has no conscience
Like a man named Pontius.
Israel is inhumane.
It metes out pain.
5/16/18

Israel needs boot-in-the-ass assistance:
End the occupation to end the resistance.
Give back the other people's land,
Or peace will slip through your hands.
Israel, loosen the blockade.
Liberation for oppression trade.
Palestinians deserve human rights.
Make free movement a common sight.
5/20/18

Sunday, May 13, 2018
Poetry Group Four Hundred Fifty-Sixth Posting 5/13/18

Nothing and nowhere are out of sight
Like on a cloudy, moonless night.
This nothing above me
Cannot love me.
5/6/18

Palestinians downed two Israeli drones,
With slingshots, nerve and stones.
They burned 400 acres of wheat.
Israeli farmers felt the heat.
By the most primitive of means,
Palestinians defeat Israeli machines.
But the Israelis shot 45 dead.
Hundreds of wounded also bled.
5/7/18

Trump aides hired an Israeli Intel firm
To try to make Rhodes and Kahl squirm,
Who worked on the Iran nuclear deal,
The fate of which is sealed.
The Intel firm couldn't find any dirt.
No former Obama people were hurt.
The Trump team employed foreign spies
To hurt people and undo a deal of the wise.
5/8/18
*Inspired by "Why did a Creepy Israeli Intel Firm Spy on Obama Alums?"
by Michelle Goldberg, NYT Opinion Page 5/8/18*

Republicans sabotage healthcare,
Which for many will not be there.
Premiums will rise and coverage fall.
The people won't know who's to blame at all.
Trump will say Obamacare is failing.
Not that Republicans deserve jailing.
He'll say it's all Obama's fault
That Obamacare must halt.
5/8/18
*Inspired by "Gnawing Away at Health Care"
by Paul Krugman, NYT OP-Ed 5/8/18*

Israel violates the Fourth Geneva Convention of 1949,
But Israelis don't mind.
They build "settlements" on occupied territory.
That's a serial crime story.
They deny Palestinians civil rights.
Snipers get them in their sights.
5/8/18

To his base, the President hollers,
"The deal gave Iran billions of dollars!"
So his base thinks Americans paid;
It wants America to invade.
Trump's followers will never know
The money was Iranian all along.
It was frozen Iranian assets.
As to truth Trump remains tacit.
5/9/18

Israel prepares its public for war.
America's entry will bring more war.
Trump gives Israel the opportunity
To use American infantry.
American pilots will be at risk.
Surface-to-Air missiles are quick.
Americans will die for Israel again.
Only Nitwityahoo knows when.
5/9/18

The Iranians are compliant
But President Trump is defiant:
No more Iran nuclear deal.
My European critics should kneel.
My heart belongs to Nitwityahoo.
Whatever he says, my military will do.
Israeli values, not European ones,
Inspire me to unleash the guns.
5/9/18

Sunday, May 6, 2018
Poetry Group Four Hundred Fifty-Fifth Posting 5/6/18

Deprivation and desperation
Bred Gazans without hesitation.
Anyone there could be shot anytime.
Unarmed protesting is a capital crime.
Hurling stones with a sling
Can be a self-destructive thing.
Cutting Israeli barbed wire,
Behind the smoke of burning tires,
Could manifest a death desire.
Israel drove these people to despair.
It takes and does not share.
Israel pens these people in
And wonders why protests begin.
4/30/18

Nitwityahoo's show was not elegant.
He wasn't even relevant.
Iran stopped trying in 2009.
In 2015 the deal was signed.
So his documents were too old.
But I bet Trump was sold.
The U.S. and Israel make quite a force.
A force for ill, of course.
5/2/18

To a nuclear weapon, Iran never got close.
Yet Israel hates Iran the most.
The dangers are in Nitwit's head.
Nitwit wants Iranians dead.
Iran never breached the nuclear deal,
Which does not affect how Trump feels.
He respects Israel over Europe.
An Iran war he will serve up.
5/2/18

When and why did you decide to fire Comey?
That guy's a rat, and you can quote me.
Did you secretly promise to pardon Flynn?
I will do anything in order to win.
Did you expect cover from AG Sessions?
I am not prone to confessions.
5/2/18

Sunday, April 29, 2018
Poetry Group Four Hundred Fifty-Fourth Posting 4/29/18

Right through the head, the sniper said.
That Palestinian boy is dead.
The sniper fired his blast
When the kid ran from tear gas,
And had nothing in his hands.
He dies for Palestinian lands.
The military expressed no regret.
He deserved it, the sniper said.
But not for the misery Israel inflicts,
Palestinians would not take such risks.
4/23/18

Had we enforced UN Resolution 181,
Two states would already be done.
But we enabled Israeli greed.
Israel's bloody orders we heed.
Israel's crimes are American crimes.
They will stain for all time.
4/23/18

She was not the first to make this resolution:
The actress refused to go to Jerusalem.
She did not want to endorse Nitwityahoo.
Her heart for Palestinians is true.
4/23/18

This goes without mention:
We have the best intentions.
We are extinguishing regulations.
States can skimp on education.
We are tax cutting heroes.
The school budget is zero.
4/25/18

The wounds of the protestors were horrid.
When people got shot, others moved forward.
They fear neither death nor martyrdom.
A hand grenade wounded some.
This week people reached the second barrier.
They had to be carried out.
The world is watching this.
Israel botches it.
4/28/18

They went to the nonviolent protest,
And found eternal rest.
The soldiers shot to harm or kill.
That is their order still.
Hundreds of Palestinians have been shot.
The Israelis say that's not a lot.
Unarmed Palestinians are ready to sacrifice.
Shoot to kill was bad advice.
Once again the world takes notice:
Israel kills unarmed people at protests.
4/15/18

God did not hand out pardons,
In that once unfallen garden.
But in the now debased White House,
Pardons the President will shout out:
Manafort, Kushner, and Cohen!
Trump pardoned Libby but didn't know him.
He can't help targets of state investigations.
Sing Sing might be their destination.
4/15/18

This was the Palestinians' last resort,
Death brought international support.
Palestinians in the hundreds were shot.
Some died on the spot.
More Palestinians came next week.
World recognition they seek.
They are ready to die,
To catch an American eye.
4/17/18

Justice is the durable foundation of peace.
Vacate the West Bank; end Gaza's siege.
Alas, Israel will do neither of these.
Palestinian land it will decrease.
Internationally boycott Israel.
Make it miserable.
So Israelis will see the light.
It will be right over might.
4/22/18

Sunday, April 15, 2018
Poetry Group Four Hundred Fifty-Second Posting 4/15/18

Israelis snipe at people from hundreds of feet away.
Nitwityahoo says we were born to slay.
Snipers shoot the unarmed
To kill or do harm.
Protesters pay with their lives
To show Palestinian pride.
4/1/18

The Israeli soldiers used lethal force,
Which should only be used as a last resort.
The soldiers were not threatened by death,
Yet they took protesters' breath.
4/8/18

Israel killed 30 Palestinians in two weeks.
Annihilation Israel seeks.
Disproportionate force
Israel employs, of course.
The Palestinian burden
Is that Israelis push murder.
Before one shoots, he sneers,
Then his comrades shout cheers.
4/11/18

Two hundred twenty-three of the wounded had been shot.
But give up they will not.
Palestinians dare to endanger themselves.
Sincerity and devotion sell.
But Americans are not allowed to see
The two hundred twenty three.
They are not allowed to understand,
Why Palestinians make this stand.
4/15/18

The protester was a few meters from the fence,
So the sniper shot in self-defense.
The victim had no weapon to drop.
His body just flopped.
The sniper's comrades cheered in glee,
The dead Palestinian to see.
4/15/18

Sunday, April 8, 2018
Poetry Group Four Hundred Fifty-First Posting 4/8/18

Israelis shot unarmed protesters,
Calling them trouble fomenters.
Arabs sought to raise world consciousness,
When met with Israeli wantonness.
One woman waved a Palestinian flag.
She found herself in a body bag.
One man was shot standing up from prayer.
In Israel such shootings are not rare.
4/2/18

Pence wants to hasten Armageddon.
He's always doing holy vengeance.
He'll be ready when the natives are gone,
And Israel pure enough to have God's war upon.
In those days, Christians will baptize Jews,
Ignoring the Jews' views.
Christ will defeat Satan's forces,
And set free the Four Horses.
To napalm fire like in Viet Nam,
You will be forever dammed.
4/3/18

Nitwityahoo quickly reneged
On the U.N. deal he made,
To settle migrants in the Jewish state.
Their skin color determined their fate.
Long having been bigoted haters,
Israelis call migrants infiltrators,
Who must inevitably be expelled.
That's how migrant problems are quelled.
4/3/18

Twenty Palestinians died at the protest.
How many innocents will be shot next?
A thousand Palestinians were injured,
All done in accord with God's Word.
Lethal suppression of demonstrations
Continue that people's attenuation.
Pent up frustrations will show,
Ending in Palestinian woe.
4/5/18

Israeli soldiers fire live ammunition,
Never feeling the least contrition.
Unarmed protestors fall to the ground.
The dead ones don't make a sound.
Soldiers fired into the Gaza Strip.
The snipers scored perfect hits.
They are illegal and immoral,
And on the wrong side of the quarrel.
4/6/18

Trump tries to discredit the free press:
"They're all fake news," Trump says,
"Because journalists uncover
Things that make me suffer.
They spy on my administration.
I am growing impatient.
Some news sources will be closed.
They are platforms for my foes.
4/6/18

Sunday, April 1, 2018
Poetry Group Four Hundred Fiftieth Posting 4/1/18

Trump's desperation grows.
He knows Meuller knows:
Why was Russia ever born?
Soon Meuller will have me sworn.
Why did I traffic in Russian money?
Putin and his friends are cunning.
I may have to lift a sanction or two,
To show Putin I am still true.
3/26/18

Iran undergoes rigorous monitoring,
The nuclear deal ensuring.
The Iranians have been compliant.
Trump has always been biased
Against peace when war can be had.
That's why the hiring of Bolton is sad.
But Israel is happy
That we are so sappy.
3/26/18

Too much power the NRA wields.
The Second Amendment should be repealed.
Make schoolchildren safer;
Turn gun owners to Quakers.
We don't need a well regulated militia,
Nor the NRA to grow richer.
Take the guns from their cold, dead hands.
America is not NRA land.
3/28/18

Anxiety makes distractions
When I do my subtractions.
Teacher wonders why I take so long,
And get so many wrong.
That is what I was worried about.
That impaired my ability to count.
Fear led to my self-doubt.
3/29/18

Each of Israel's apologists,
The truth demolishes:
"Occupation is not antithetical to
Freedom, rights, or truth.
Let the Palestinians eat cake.
Our soldiers make them quake.
Palestine is not their land,
Though they were here a long span."
3/30/18

Israel once closed Palestinian schools for years.
Instruction was replaced by mothers' tears.
Underground education was a crime.
Students were made to lose a lot of time.
And if students demonstrate,
They could be shot in the face.
The IDF shoots to harm.
TV raises no alarm.
3/30/18
*Inspired by BDS: Boycott, Divestment, Sanctions
by Omar Barghouti

Non-Jews have a lesser status than Jews.
Palestinians generally lose.
Deprived of individual and national rights,
Palestinians will win when the world fights.
Israelis support colonial oppression.
Evangelicals consider this a blessing,
That will lead to Almighty Armageddon
When Christ and the Church have their wedding.
3/18/18

Thirteen million live between the Jordan and the Med.
Almost half of them Palestinians, God said.
Where's their homeland on their own land?
Israel, this is a reprimand.
I want to see the two state solution,
Before I grant you absolution.
You must give back land and admit your blame,
Or I will not uphold your name.
3/19/18

We want to frighten the occupation,
With half our population,
Sitting near Israel's border fence,
And camping out in tents.
We will gather at the border
Despite Israeli orders.
The massive crowds
Will be loud.
The world will see
We should be free.
3/20/18

Jews depend on secular, pluralistic states.
Yet in Israel, non-Jews don't rate.
Jews are generally liberal,
But not about Israel.
Jews are generally sane,
But not about their house of pain.
3/21/18

Israel and its lobby groups affiliate,
America to humiliate.
The U.S. said expand the "settlement" freeze,
But Israel would not appease,
The country that bankrolls it,
Which is a slave and doesn't know it.
Our foreign policy is Israelized.
Israel will never be liberalized.
3/22/18

Sunday, March 18, 2018
Poetry Group Four Hundred Forty-Eighth Posting 3/18/18

Apartheid is part of the colonial project to dispossess.
Land is stolen in the colonial conquest.
The judicial system in Israel is liberal and cool.
The one in the Occupied Territories is cruel.
Palestinians get no democracy.
Israelis fear demography.
3/12/18
*Inspired by BDS: Boycott, Divestment, Sanctions
by Omar Barghouti

America wants to liquidate the national Palestinian project.
AmerIsrael does not want racial progress.
Palestinians will reject Kushner's peace plan,
Which will grant them too little land.
Nitwityahoo will make no concessions.
His criminal charges? Don't ask any questions.
3/12/18

Excluded from the very definition of the Jewish State,
Palestinians and those black South Africans equate.
Apartheid is a crime against humanity.
Enabling Israel is insanity.
It sends terrorists new recruits.
Israel's inception is terrorism's roots.
3/13/18

Israel limits democracy to a privileged class.
The rest live behind walls they cannot pass.
Mixed marriages are not legal there.
A mixed couple wouldn't dare.
It is an intolerant, faith-driven ethno state.
Its ideals are racism and hate.
3/14/18
*Inspired by BDS: Boycott, Divestment, Sanctions
by Omar Barghouti

Sunday, March 11, 2018
Poetry Group Four Hundred Forty-Seventh Posting 3/11/18

The moral superiority of the Palestinian quest,
Pricks the consciences of sympathizers in the West.
Palestine is a case of right over might.
Israel is handicapped in that fight.
Palestinians have moral clarity.
In Israel there's a scarcity.
3/4/18
*Inspired by BDS: Boycott, Divestment, Sanctions
by Omar Barghouti

Remember where you once went?
A Utah National monument.
Trump shrank it by 85%.
Oil drilling is the consequence.
Are there reserves beneath Bears Ears?
We'll know in less than a year.
3/5/18

People showed Trump climate science.
He quit the Paris Accords in defiance.
People told him recognition would hinder peace.
Since he did it, peace talks have ceased.
People told Trump that no one wins a trade war.
But belligerence is at his core.
People tell him that Iran abides by the pact.
Trump and Nitwityahoo will nonetheless attack.
Two fraudsters cooking up an offensive.
The bombing of Tehran will be intensive.
3/6/18

Israel is more than an irritation:
Ethnic cleansing, siege, prolonged occupation.
Apartheid is a crime against humanity.
Killing Palestinians has become banality.
Israel's legalized system of racial discrimination
Is one of the poison fruits of the invasion.
3/7/18

A menace to peace and security,
Israel must be stopped urgently.
Growing ever more powerful and fanatic,
The Israeli people are satanic.
Palestinians they despise.
Sharpshooters aim for children's eyes.
If Americans could see the gaping wounds,
They would stop Israel soon.
3/7/17
*Inspired by BDS: Boycott, Divestment, Sanctions
by Omar Barghouti

Sunday, March 4, 2018
Poetry Group Four Hundred Forty-Sixth Posting 3/4/18

Decades of Israeli bad faith peace talks
Turned most Israelis into hawks,
Who want peace devoid of justice and rights.
To them Palestinian lives are trite.
More people will die for Palestine.
Expect terrorism for all time.
Israel is the Mother of Terror.
Enabling Israel was error.
2/24/18

Israel is exclusivist and ethnocentric.
Drop liberalism at Zionism's entrance.
Israel won't follow international law.
It commits war crimes all the more.
This the world reviles.
America is all smiles.
2/24/18

The NRA-backed Dickey Amendment,
Should be legislatively rent dead.
It chokes off funding for gun death research,
Yet gun control the people urge.
Republicans won't use science to stop an epidemic.
Instead, the NRA they mimic.
The people want relief.
Republicans give them grief.
2/26/18
*Inspired by "America Is the Gun" by Charles M. Blow
NYT OP-ED 2/26/18

Evangelicals want an American theocracy,
Yet they cling to the King of Hypocrisy.
Even when Trump admits to grabbing pussy,
Evangelicals deny it and get all mushy.
The President is a confirmed liar,
But Evangelicals are deniers.
The President is an obvious racist,
But Evangelicals are gracious.
2/28/18

The International Court of Justice condemns
Israel's wall and "settlements."
But the West doesn't hold Israel to account.
America will keep sending money no doubt.
The road to the US Congress passes through Tel Aviv.
Spend money there, and D.C. affection you'll receive.
Israel profits from its colonies.
It offers no apologies.
2/28/18
*Inspired by BDS: Boycott, Divestment, Sanctions
by Omar Barghouti*

Sunday, February 25, 2018
Poetry Group Four Hundred Forty-Fifth Posting 2/25/18

A party built around bad faith
Does not have any great traits.
Further enrich the powerful plutocrats;
That's the job of Republican rats.
They say they love the people, but they don't.
They could change, but they won't.
2/20/18
*Inspired by "The Content of the G.O.P.'s Character"
by Paul Krugman, NYT Opinion Page 2/20/18*

The police want him charged with fraud and breach of trust.
Nitwityahoo, this is a bust.
You tried to bribe your wife's judge.
Sara stole money, so the judge wouldn't budge.
For favorable news, he bribed a telecom giant.
Against that giant, his government would stay quiet.
The prosecution has a state's witness
To testify to Nitwit's unfitness.
2/21/18

We need public action for the public good.
Republicans don't believe it, but they should.
They fear their freedom they will lose,
If the public good they choose.
They hate Social Security and Medicare,
Because in those things people share.
2/23/18
*Inspired by "Nasty, Brutish and Trump" by Paul Krugman
NYT OP-ED 2/23/18

Israel is greedy to take all the land.
Israeli greed can be seen in one man.
His past fraud and graft
Are investigated facts.
State's witnesses former aides turn.
Nitwityahoo is burned.
2/22/18

The Second Amendment is a suicide pact.
There is much to retract.
Guns kill an average of 96 per day
Even in the merry month of May.
The gun lobby likes blood on its hands.
Assault rifles bloody the land.
They should be collected and melted down.
That would bring some joy to the folks of Newtown.
2/22/18

The NRA holds the GOP in thrall.
AR-15's make any man tall.
Republicans can't vote for the sensible.
NRA bribes are reprehensible.
Now a gun is worth more than a child.
America is still wild.
2/22/18

The Occupation led to colonization.
Apartheid makes for Jewish satisfaction.
Palestinians live where they are told.
Israelis are fascists cold.
Trading with Israel supports its crimes,
And its ever expanding borderlines.
The world must end apartheid.
Palestinians should no longer be denied.
2/23/18

God talks to Pence and tells him what to do.
Without God, Pence would be through.
In his mind, Palestinians are Philistines.
They will die in God's good time.
Ancient Israel must be restored.
So says the Almighty Lord.
Pence has a direct line
To God's mind.
2/12/18

Israel handed us the apple and we bit.
Righteous Palestinians we quit.
The two-state solution we dumped,
Thanks to tricky dick Trump,
Who says, Putin is not my rival.
He is my political survival.
2/14/18

The basic story is that of settlers and natives.
Palestine was invaded by those who hated.
Seen as less than human, not deserving rights,
Palestinians fight for a homeland site,
Which the settlers refuse to give.
They won't let Palestinians live.
2/18/18

The U.S. failed to hold Israel accountable.
Its human rights violations are bountiful.
Israel kills and steals with impunity.
It does so at every opportunity.
2/4/18

America makes the world's efforts difficult.
The world from America should revolt.
Make Israel give back land
Or face a boycott reprimand.
2/4/18

Israeli wars of aggression
Should teach America a lesson:
That Israel is bent on genocide.
Its sucking maw is open wide.
People, factories, houses, and stores
Are the targets in Israeli wars.
Israel says a big war is coming
When Palestinians will get a pummeling.
2/5/18

Israeli pilots drop their bombs,
Without any moral qualms.
Palestinians have no value whatsoever.
Each Israeli soldier is a treasure.
Consider terrorists everyone in the city.
Never show one shred of pity.
Women and children are fair game.
You will never be blamed.
2/6/18

Trump took credit for a rising stock market.
On his back, Fortune saw a target.
Trump never knew that pride goeth before a fall.
Investors no longer heed his call.
His tax cut deficit gives Ryan an excuse.
To commit social program abuse.
A secretary gets an extra buck fifty per week.
Trump's reelection she seeks.
2/7/18

Our fearless leader is disturbed.
He doesn't get the credit he deserves.
So he compliments himself lavishly,
And berates the non-clappers savagely,
Whom he accuses of treason.
To Our Leader this is reason.
Only traitors don't love him.
There is no one else above him.
2/7/18

Sunday, February 4, 2018
Poetry Group Four Hundred Forty-Second Posting 2/4/18

Israel's fascism is showing.
We're not watching where we're going.
Israel gives terrorists righteous cries.
Restoring Palestine would be wise.
Israel is the target on our back.
Freedom from Israel we lack.
The world suffers, indeed,
Because of Israeli greed.
1/28/18

When religious objections are given top priority
Medical care is not top quality.
Women needing abortions
Are put through contortions.
The provider's religious beliefs
Outweigh the patient's needs.
1/29/18

Climate change deniers don't have much data
But they don't think that matters:
It's getting too cold all over the place.
Global warming should be erased.
I believe in good cleanliness in all.
America's pollution is small.
1/30/18

Trump made false and misleading statements.
His lexicon of lies needs maintenance:
Can I keep my lies consistent?
I'd like to blame my assistants.
Trump showed corrupt intent
When Comey went.
Obstruction of justice is the charge.
Trump's case is large.
1/30/18

Fidelity to the Constitution is not foremost.
"My well-being" is Trump's boast.
Republicans grovel at his feet.
They hang on his every tweet.
1/30/18

Trump was to sanction Russia for cyber attacks,
But he disbelieves the Putin meddling facts.
Not one new sanction was imposed.
The President's mind is closed.
The intelligence community knows what Russians did,
Everything in their power to help Donald win.
But he proclaims he got no Russian help,
And that he did it by himself.
1/31/18

Sunday, January 28, 2018
Poetry Group Four Hundred Forty-First Posting 1/28/18

Israel believes in its unquestionable right,
To be a racist state in plain sight.
As an apartheid, exclusivist state,
Israel runs on racism and hate.
Palestinians merit self-determination.
Israeli fascism, termination.
1/21/18

America used to see a duality,
Where now it applies no neutrality.
Republicans are pro-Israel.
Off-putting for a Jewish liberal.
The further right pro-Israel gets,
The more Jews will rejoice and fret.
1/22/18

Those who know the truth must serve it.
Palestinian liberation is urgent.
Don't be afraid to buck the mainstream.
Pro-Palestinian is the right team.
Palestinians will realize their rights,
But not without a fight.
A racist state has no right to exist.
Get pissed.
1/23/18

Pence was playing to the thumpers back home.
The Israelis liked his Zionist tone:
"America and Israel are one!
We'll nuke Iran before we're done.
Palestinians will not slow Israel's progress.
I will redeliver this speech in Congress.
The more Palestinian land Israel takes,
The sooner in heaven we'll all awake."
1/24/18

His speech received standing ovations.
Pence is a Zionist sensation.
"The bible says Jews should be here.
We'll have the embassy done in two years."
Palestinians shun him.
Europeans make fun of him.
1/24/18

President Trump never learns
To avoid racist terms,
Like "shithole countries,"
Where some are hungry.
Trump finds tolerance
Too bothersome
And equality
Just for the polity.
1/16/18

Nikki kicks with her high heels.
The Palestinians have no shield.
To the Israelis, Palestinians must listen,
Or she'll kick out their D.C. mission.
She threatened countries who found null and void,
Trump's Jerusalem hemorrhoid.
1/16/18

One ethnic group rules over another.
They are not sisters and brothers.
Palestinians will be "Residents of the Autonomy,"
With limited access to the economy.
On little pockets of land,
Palestinians will make their stand,
The victims of apartheid
Their homeland denied.
1/16/18

Trump cuts funding for Palestinian refugees,
Who will suffer more if you please.
Some have been refugees for 70 years.
The war Israel desires is almost here.
America supports the winning side,
Which is also the sinning side.
1/17/18

Here is something of great significance.
Fascism threatens Israel's existence.
Palestinians are ruled with discrimination,
And brutal intimidation.
Jews check their liberalism at Zionism's door.
Of Palestinian land, they always want more,
Israeli fascism now and in the past,
Will cause an American backlash.
1/17/18
*Inspired by BDS: Boycott, Divestment, Sanctions
by Omar Barghouti*

Goods made in Israeli colonies,
No matter their innate qualities,
Don't get preferred customs treatment:
Europe wants a fair agreement.
Boycott Israel to end its impunity.
To do otherwise would be lunacy.
Why would we want to trade,
With a fascist apartheid state?
1/20/18

Sunday, January 14, 2018
Poetry Group Four Hundred Thirty-Ninth Posting 1/14/18

Step back and see the forest, not just the trees.
A drone can give you views like these.
Fly above the detailed distortion.
See the trees in proportion.
1/8/18

Israel tries to portray itself as democratic and liberal.
All but Zionists see a fascist Israel
Which blacklists leaders of peace groups,
And rules Palestinians with troops.
Israel suppresses freedom of speech.
Intellectual freedom is out of reach.
1/8/18

Republicans praise Trump to steady him,
As do his aides to ready him.
To question his erratic behavior,
Is to thrust a spear into Our Savior.
1/8/18

President Trump decided to strut:
"The bill provides $5.5 trillion in cuts.
You are so happy you voted for me.
Let the poor hang from the trees.
The rich will be enriched by this bill.
You will get what the rich spill.
And if I miscounted my trillions
It's because I'm used to my billions."
1/9/18

We have a shithole president.
To insult Africa, he is not hesitant.
Haitians he cannot abide.
Nazis he lets slide.
He is no traitor to his class.
To the top the riches pass.
Republicans entirely approve:
Immigrants must move.
1/13/18

Vain Israel looks in the mirror
And sees the South African apartheid era.
They still think they can get away with it.
American leaders still visit.
Only Sweden has the conscience
To boycott the obnoxious.
1/13/18

Israel cynically exploits the Holocaust
To be Washington, D.C.'s boss.
It is an almost invincible shield.
Criticism of Israel must yield.
That's why Nazi movies abound.
Critics of Israel hardly make a sound.
All that Americans hear
Is that Israel is dear.
1/13/18

Sunday, January 7, 2018
Poetry Group Four Hundred Thirty-Eighth Posting 1/7/18

Climate changes lead to extreme conditions.
Trump's denial is an act of sedition.
Manmade warming raises ocean temps.
Republican denial makes no sense.
Storms produce more precipitation.
Trump denies this without equivocation.
1/1/18

Ditch the two-state solution to the conflict.
The path to apartheid Israel instead picked.
The "settlers" will have democracy's tools.
Palestinians will remain under military rule.
Trump doesn't want a just and lasting peace.
Until justice, the killing will not cease.
Israelis fear not foreign intercession.
Jerusalem's recognition tautht them that lesson.
1/2/18

Israel creates obstacles to a land-for-peace deal.
How does that make Palestinians feel?
Trump says Jerusalem is the capital.
Palestinian anger is palpable.
The AmerIsrael entity
Denies Palestinian identity.
Trump will cut off Palestinian aid,
To force a peace talk charade.
1/3/18

The Russians did not hesitate.
They elected Trump president.
Trump did money laundering there.
He and the Russians each got a share.
Mueller is looking into that.
Putin's knowledge of this is a bat,
With which to intimidate Trump
Who fears a Russian thump.
1/3/18

She did not miss him
During his time in prison,
And she wrote him
That she loathed him.
When he got out, he tried to buy a gun.
No one told her this had been done.
So she was less than wary.
About what he carried.
1/4/18

Sunday, December 31, 2017
Poetry Group Four Hundred Thirty-Seventh Posting 12/31/17

Christians and Muslims lived together 1,400 years.
American evangelicals are one of their fears.
Evangelicals believe in bible prophesy,
Which is supernaturalism and sophistry.
They want to make room for the Jews.
Local Christians and Muslims lose.
But prophecies must be fulfilled,
And human rights chilled.
12/25/17

A lopsided majority of U.N. members
Humiliated the U.S. this December,
By denouncing its Jerusalem recognition,
Which it did against U.N. restrictions.
Trump's threats and blackmail
In the General Assembly did not prevail.
Only 9 little countries voted no.
Their dependence on U.S. aid showed.
The U.S. lost 128 to 9 with 35 abstentions,
And managed to increase Mideast tensions.
12/26/17

It's dangerous to keep a gun in the home.
A higher risk of suicide is well known.
Guns are far more lethal than other means,
Especially when no one intervenes.
Half of all suicides are by firearms,
Which cause grotesque harm:
The NRA warns keep it loaded.
That's how gun owners are goaded.
12/27/17
*Inspired by "The Gun Lobby v. Suicide Prevention"
by Erin Dunkerly, NYT, OP-ED 12/27/17

The South African moment has arrived.
Israel's racism is not contrived.
Palestinians resist the colonization of their minds,
In which the lust for freedom resides.
Withdraw support for the apartheid regime.
Nations that love justice must intervene.
12/28/17
*Inspired by BDS Boycott Divestment Sanctions
by Omar Barghouti

The rich are already rich,
Which makes me wonder which
Group of people should get
The tax law's benefit.
The middle class would spend
Any tax cut the government sends.
The government should want to be
The stimulator of the economy.
12/31/17

We see the past more clearly than the present,
Which is filled with uncertainties incessant.
The past has been cooked to perfection.
How much will feed the next election?
Will the people remember
The wealthy's tax cuts in December?
Will the voters have forgotten
That Trump's motives are rotten?
12/31/17

Sunday, December 24, 2017
Poetry Group Four Hundred Thirty-Sixth Posting 12/24/17

To Nazi troops, the Israelis were similar.
They knowingly sealed the perimeter,
Around Shabra and Santila.
Then they let in the killers,
Lebanese who were Israel's friends,
Killed 2,000 Palestinians.
This was an Israeli war crime,
Yet no one was ever confined.
12/19/17

The CDC can no longer say "science based."
Science is nothing compared to God's Grace.
The GOP wages war on expertise.
American scholarship will cease.
No expert endorses this tax bill.
The rich can never get their fill.
Republicans are making a selfish mistake.
Yet Jesus died for their sake.
12/19/17
Inspired by "Passing Through to Corruption"
By Paul Krugman, Opinion page NYT 12/19/17

Maximize benefits for the rich at the expense
-- of almost everybody else.
The tax bill will increase Trump's fortune.
The national debt will balloon.
A greedy senator is Bob Corker.
He loves to raise taxes on New Yorkers.
His real estate business will prosper
Because of tax cuts improper.
12/19/17

Federal workers can't say "reduce greenhouse gases."
The English language Trump thrashes.
He takes out science words with precision.
Even "climate change" will be forbidden.
New language reflects new leadership.
I'm informing my readership.
12/19/17

American and Israeli interests diverge.
Of all allies, Israel is the worst.
The Palestinian plight harms U.S. Security,
But more important is Zionist purity,
Which does not permit peace.
It wants to return land the least.
12/20/17

You cannot buy Turkey's democratic will
With all your moneybags filled.
Recognition of Jerusalem is null and void.
Our flag your Zionism soiled.
It is the world against America and Israel.
That pariah duo makes me ill.
12/24/17
*Line 1 by Turkey's President Recep Tayyip Erdogan

Sunday, December 17, 2017
Poetry Group Four Hundred Thirty-Fifth Posting 12/17/17

The Arab claim to Jerusalem was not acknowledged.
Palestinian dreams were not salvaged.
Trump said he would move the embassy.
He has a Zionist tendency.
Fifty years Israel tried to drive them out.
We're still here, Palestinians shout.
Israel's right fought the Oslo Accords.
Israel behaves like a fascist horde.
Trump makes America unreliable.
Trump knows Israelis are not pliable.
12/11/17

Earthlings can't rely on the United States.
Environmental science Trump berates.
The Paris climate agreement lacks only us,
Yet we produce the most sludge.
Jerusalem's status was to come at the end.
The Palestinians have been betrayed again.
America is no impartial peace broker.
The U.S. President is a joker.
12/11/17

Some delusion is good if you could.
It helps you believe the world is good.
Too much delusion is dangerous.
You're manic when you should be languorous.
Unresponsive to opposing views,
You proceed to light the fuse.
12/11/17
Inspired by A First-Rate Madness by Nassir Ghaemi

"The tax cuts will pay for themselves,"
Says Mnuchin, who needs math help.
He made unrealistic assumptions
About high growth resumption.
The budget projections have nothing behind them.
"Irresponsible" describes Republican men,
Who want everything to go to the top,
Where there are only rich slobs.
12/12/17

If Trump is innocent, what's the worry?
Republicans should not want Mueller to hurry.
Just how long has Trump been preparing
To lift sanctions on a foreign adversary?
A Russian conspiracy helped Trump win.
The question is, was he in?
Fox News wants Mueller in cuffs.
The Special Prosecutor must stay tough.
12/13/17

I want to meet you in the text.
You are fulfilling my request.
Together we will range.
The black words on the page
The text is deliberate.
It is not gibberish.
I am with you indeed
When you begin to read.
12/13/17

One can't fake not having psychosis.
That is a very visible diagnosis.
Mania is difficult to hide.
I don't know any manics who've tried.
Depression cannot be consciously masked.
Minimizing all symptoms is an impossible task.
Mental illness is stigmatizing.
It can't be concealed by lying.
12/13/17
Inspired by A First-Rate Madness by Nassir Ghaemi

The Organization of Islamic Cooperation,
Made a unanimous observation:
Jerusalem is Palestine's occupied capital.
Trump's pretentiousness is laughable.
12/16/17

Sunday, December 10, 2017
Poetry Group Four Hundred Thirty-Fourth Posting 12/10/17

Israel starved Palestinians under the siege,
Who were aggrieved but not believed.
Israel allowed the minimum calorie intake needed.
Many Palestinian children were anemic,
And were not allowed crayons, clothing and shoes.
There was plenty of everything for the Jews.
Gazans live in a prison by the sea.
Israel won't let them be.
12/4/17

Crown Prince made an offer they could not accept:
Only noncontiguous parts could be kept.
Palestinians will reject this in full.
What Zionist move will the Prince next pull?
12/4/17

The money goes to the top few percent.
Exactly what the Republicans meant.
Cuts add $1 trillion to the national debt
Because the rich don't have enough money yet.
The working poor don't make enough to get by.
They will see Social Security die.
The rich get richer
Without lifting a finger.
12/5/17

Why lie if they have nothing to hide?
Trump wants Mueller to let them slide.
Trump's men undermined US foreign policy.
Trump adheres to Putin idolatry.
The Russians interfered with the election.
They successfully got their selection.
Trump says the Russia thing is made up.
When will Putin make Trump pay up?
12/5/17

Israel wants more and more,
So Trump gave away the store.
Like Adam taking a bite of the apple,
Trump proclaimed Jerusalem the capital.
The Palestinians got nothing.
East Jerusalem would have been something.
The Palestinians lost a paradise too.
Today is a day everyone will rue.
12/6/17

Trump claimed to be the best deal maker.
Recognizing Jerusalem proved he's a faker.
What did the Palestinians get in return?
None of the land for which they yearn.
Trump conceded something before bargaining.
That's not smart, the world is arguing.
He weakened America's resolution
That there be a two-state solution.
12/8/17

The U.S. is at war with Islam.
The Muslim world is not calm.
Trump gave Jerusalem to the Jews.
The Palestinians have the blues.
Trump denies the Arab perspective.
His Zionist heart is selective.
Trump does not understand the dispute.
He sends terrorists new recruits.
12/9/17

Sunday, December 3, 2017
Poetry Group Four Hundred Thirty-Third Posting 12/3/17

Religious cabinet ministers are traps.
Resignations can make governments collapse.
That's the danger Nitwityahoo is in
With the resignation of Mr. Litzman.
If another ultra-Orthodox minister resigns,
A new election day will be assigned.
Israel might elect a peace leader
Instead of a someone else's land eater.
And why did Minister Litzman resign?
Because trains are fixed on Sabbath time.
11/27/17

Under the plan, middle class tax increases
Help pay for rich people's decreases.
This bill doesn't reward the voters.
It's designed to repay the donors.
The bill is unpopular, so the senators rush.
They lie about it in public much.
The bill will blow a hole in the deficit.
But don't worry, the "job creators" will benefit.
The bill is filled with Republican hate.
It will end the individual mandate.
Millions will lose health coverage.
That is not good governance.
11/27/17

Israel could be the most admired nation,
But giving back would cause an ego abrasion.
Imagine if Israel gave the West Bank back.
Peace there would never lack.
Two police forces would combine
To suppress violent crime.
Two nations side by side
Where everyone could take pride.
11/27/17

Rush the tax bill to the Senate floor.
Hearings and study are no more.
The class warfare nature of the plan
Will hurt the common woman and man.
Let's get this thing voted on.
Because the wealthy must be doted on.
Their goodwill must not be loosened,
If we want more campaign contributions.
11/28/17

Read the tax bill and judge it,
How will we ever balance a budget?
Moguls would pay taxes on less of their earnings.
Are the millions of Trump voters learning?
The middle class will lose money and healthcare.
The top one percent don't have to share.
Republicans care only for the rich.
Trump voters should switch.
11/29/17

If you do not bear the Zionist gene,
Withdraw your support for the apartheid regime.
When governments refuse, people take the lead.
The West Bank Israel must cede.
At Israel's cruel behest,
Palestinians are dispossessed.
They are told under the Occupation,
You will never have your own nation.
11/29/17

Israel delights
In denying human rights.
It puts Palestinians down,
While it takes their ground.
Ignoring International Law,
It is the most fascist place of all.
Why does America court it?
Why do we mindlessly support it?
11/29/17

America is complicit in the Gaza siege.
About Israel, Americans are naïve.
Palestinians struggle under oppression
And Long Occupation Depression.
Israel makes Palestinians extreme.
Some will lie under a flag of green.
America will not intervene.
Toward Israel, we lean.
11/20/17

The tax bill will make the rich richer.
They wanted to make the sick sicker,
But even Republicans couldn't go that far.
Anyway the middle-class is their mark,
Which gets a small, temporary tax cut.
When the rich get theirs, the budget will bust.
When Republicans again care about debt,
They will see Medicare not dismantled yet.
11/21/17

America and Israel are in bed.
Trump put the gun to the Palestinian head:
Plead guilty in an Israeli court,
Or I will kick you out of New York.
That's how Trump starts negotiations.
Jewish Americans serve as liaisons.
Palestinians are put under pressure
Even though in power they are the lesser.
11/21/17

In a future Gaza, will people reside?
In this time of siege, Israel will decide.
But Zionism is an international force.
Palestinians will be moved, of course.
Western Jordan will also be cleansed.
Maybe America will do something then.
Anywhere Jews lived long ago,
The indigenous people have to go.
11/21/17

With brutal Zionistic insanity,
Jews deny Palestinians humanity.
They over-killed the Gaza Strip,
And hold it in a Zionist grip.
The inhabitants of Gaza live in a prison.
Their in and out is Israel's decision.
Gazans could have beach front resorts,
But they are denied air and sea ports.
11/23/17

The Palestinians committed self-genocide,
When they did not sufficiently hide
From the tank shells we were sending,
Which they knew were life ending.
11/24/17

Workers are not worthy of the rich's respect.
Wage increases are hard to detect.
Tax cuts mostly help the top,
Which throws the middle class a sop.
Republicans want to end Social Security.
Trump voters will accept this certainly.
11/24/17

Better a thousand Palestinian mothers cry,
Than that one Jewish child die.
We bid Palestinians rebuild all they can.
But rebuilding materials are banned.
In a hospital the wounded seek balm;
Twenty-four medical facilities we bombed.
We sustain the siege
Though you don't agree.
11/13/17
*Inspired by The 51 Day War by Max Blumenthal

Impose on Israel the terms of peace.
Let the closing document have teeth.
Like loss of free trade
Until the "settlements" fade.
And loss of money from the USA,
Until the Palestinians say we're okay.
Only the two-state solution is just.
Israel needs just a little push.
11/151/7

The historic compromise has already been made.
Israel took most of the land but never paid.
At stealing land, Israel is deft.
It will seize the 20% left.
Trump has no qualms about being one-sided.
By his pious son-in-law, he is led.
Israelis must have all of this land.
Let Palestinians sink in the sand.
11/15/17
*Inspired by The 51 Day War by Max Blumenthal

Here is the far right's confession:
Nitwityahoo is not to make concessions.
Negotiations with Israel are a con.
It wants Palestinians dead or gone.
11/15/17

Israel needs a peace plan dictated to it.
If we don't spell it out, Israel won't do it.
The peace deal must be imposed.
Treat Israel like a deceitful foe.
Israel's interests are not ours
To break away we have the power.
11/17/17

Sunday, November 12, 2017
Poetry Group Four Hundred Thirtieth Posting 11/12/17

Palestinian lives were quashed.
The world stood by and watched.
Twenty-two hundred Palestinians died
Nowhere in Gaza to hide.
Five hundred of those were children
Caught up in Israeli killing.
As long as Israel is enabled,
It won't come to the table.
11/6/17

Scorched bodies piled up in the streets.
Neighborhoods lost many heartbeats.
This was The 51 Day War,
Noteworthy because of its gore.
Civilians were bombarded from the border.
Nitwityahoo says he gave no order.
But the civilian killing kept on.
Israelis want them dead or gone.
11/6/17
**Inspired by The 51 Day War by Max Blumenthal*

President Trump is dastardly.
He denies the coming catastrophe;
As sea levels rise,
Trump shuts his eyes.
This climate change mess
Is bad for business.
But Trump says ignore it.
There's nothing else for it.
11/8/17

Sunday, November 5, 2017
Poetry Group Four Hundred Twenty-Ninth Posting 11/5/17

Look at the direction our country's heading in.
More fascists and racists are settling in.
Nitwityahoo is a transformative leader.
He has been Israel's land feeder.
The West enables Nitwityahoo
To act on his fascist view.
America is his enabler
We are Likud laborers.
10/30/17

Jews of the world, awake!
The soul of Israel is at stake.
American and Israeli Jews
Are breaking into two.
Jerusalem's ultra-Orthodox Sire
Called Reform Jews Holocaust deniers.
Americans should tell Israelis what to do.
Without America, Israel would be through.
10/31/17

This is the most illiberal government in Israel ever.
Under Nitwityahoo, peace will arrive never.
For partisanship, he is the worst.
He does not put the common good first.
He vilifies the mainstream news,
And defames Israeli Reform Jews.
He accuses the left of treason,
For no good reason.
11/1/17

Sunday, October 29, 2017
Poetry Group Four Hundred Twenty-Eighth Posting 10/29/17

After their decades of exasperation,
Feel Palestinians' aspirations.
They want a homeland on their own land,
The world should give them a hand.
They owned all the land once
Since before the invention of guns.
They ask for a fifth of what they had.
The Israeli response has been bad.
10/23/17

A mother and child were among the dead.
When the shell broke through, they lay in bed.
In a flash their bodies broke into pieces.
That doesn't mean the bombardment ceases.
In fact, their house was hit again
By the same crew of artillery men,
Who never know the people they are killing,
Not caring if they're women and children.
10/23/17

They bombed civilians with intensity,
And without military necessity.
Journalists were constantly targeted,
To silence their baleful harkening.
The West cared little about these reporters,
And the targeted destruction of their quarters.
Israel killed people on a large scale.
It's easy to follow the killing trail.
10/24/17
Inspired by The 51 Day War by Max Blumenthal

Israel used 5,000 pound GBU bunker buster missiles.
On their way to destruction, they whistle.
Israel was saving them for underground facilities.
In case Iran got nuclear capabilities.
America keeps the GBU's coming.
Israel's not buying but bumming.
10/24/17

Their plan is a giveaway to the rich.
Convincing the base is a cinch.
By giving the rich money they don't need,
Republicans follow their party's creed:
Enrich the rich above all else.
Only the rich deserve government help.
Republicans want racial purity,
And an end to Social Security.
10/25/17

Dump your mining debris in the streams.
Why should the environment be clean?
Overturn the Clean Power Plan.
Clean power plants ban.
Enact huge tax cuts for the wealthy.
Take health insurance from the unhealthy.
Burn protections for workers and consumers.
The president's populism is but a rumor.
10/26/17

Israel silenced the media outlets.
Journalists couldn't do a thing about it.
Israel impeded the flow of facts.
Journalists and their offices were attacked.
American media was rare over there.
The folks back home didn't know or care.
And that's the way Israel wants it to be.
American Jews heartily agree.
10/26/17
*Inspired by The 51 Day War by Max Blumenthal

Israelis harass Gaza fishing crews.
To Americans, this would be news.
In wakes made by Israeli ships,
Fishing boats nearly flip.
Israelis cut the fishing nets.
Sometimes Palestinians get wet.
Like when the Israelis kidnap them.
Americans don't know this happens.
The suspect swims to the Israeli ship
To prison he gets a one way trip.
10/26/17

Sunday, October 22, 2017
Poetry Group Four Hundred Twenty-Seventh Posting 10/22/17

Racism, greed, and brutality
Describe Zionism validly.
It is tugging on the leash
To devour land and peace.
If it swallows the West Bank,
The world will have America to thank:
We fed and protected the Beast,
Which cares about America the least.
10/16/17

Soon we will fight another war for Israel.
The families of the dead will be miserable.
But this is what Trump wants America to do:
Abandon all else; follow Nitwityahoo.
Israel's aims will be our aims.
Our history will be shamed.
Iran has always abided by the pact.
But that won't save it from attack.
10/17/17

The world should not stand by and watch,
As Israel runs out the clock.
The world should force Israel to create
A viable Palestinian state.
Terrorists have a righteous cry:
Israel made Palestine die!
How can Israel resist that truth?
Keep Palestinians out of the news.
10/18/17

It is fine that Jews want to unite.
But why unite behind Israel's far right?
Those parties are not concerned
With America's interests in the world.
The West requires a Palestine
To give the Muslim world a sign,
That we love justice just like they do.
Palestine will make that true.
10/20/17

Sunday, October 15, 2017
Poetry Group Four Hundred Twenty-Sixth Posting 10/15/17

Merely eliminating tax deductions
Won't make up for these reductions.
From 39.6 percent to 35.
The Treasury will be deprived.
Trump will eliminate the estate tax,
Something good for Goldman Sachs.
Corporate taxes will be deeply cut.
The door to lower debt will shut.
10/9/17

The peace process has been frozen.
Will we ever have closure?
There's a stronger Israeli stench
As the Occupation becomes more entrenched.
The "settlements" have spread.
Peace is not close yet.
10/9/17

Their soldiers target our civilians.
To kill them we are more than willing.
The soldiers like to fight from a distance.
We thrust in their faces the Resistance.
10/12/17

New sanctions Congress will reveal.
Trump wants out of the Iran deal.
The rest of the world will think us mad.
Iran complied with the agreement we had.
But Trump has Israel in his heart.
He wants to help it kick Iran apart.
America's standing will plummet,
Our allies flummoxed.
10/12/17

Israelis are bad, but they don't care,
As long as they don't have to share.
Dollars flow from an eternal spring.
Zionism too America brings.
We enable the ethnic cleansing,
Which Americans are not sensing
Because Palestinians are banned from TV.
Americans are not allowed to see.
10/15/17

Sunday, October 8, 2017
Poetry Group Four Hundred Twenty-Fifth Posting 10/8/17

Some players kneel during the National Anthem,
Which sends Trump into a Twitter tantrum:
Get on your feet when you hear that song.
Anything else is just plain wrong.
But, Mr. President, these protestors are right:
For racial justice they fight.
Cops shoot too many black men.
Expect protests again and again.
10/2/17

Zionists clamor for a war to end war,
When Palestinians will be no more.
Nitwityahoo holds them back
By going on the attack.
But he must kill and take slowly
Not thinking of Israel's aims only.
Uncle Sam would probably object
If Israel the West Bank annexed.
10/2/17

Israeli bombing results were grim:
Rubble littered with human limbs.
Beit Hanoun was destroyed in an hour.
Israelis have remote killing power.
Seared limbs and torsos
Make Israel's point moreso:
Get off the land or die.
Don't expect us to cry.
10/3/17

Hamas and Fatah will reconcile
They are no longer in denial.
I knew there'd be Palestinian unity.
Chalk that up to my perspicuity.
The world will respect them more
And end Israel's incessant war.
American media keeps them out of sight,
But the Palestinians are right.
10/3/17

The Gun Lobby wants you to forget
The latest mass gun death.
Buy yourself a shotgun.
Have a little fun.
If everyone was armed
No one would be harmed.
10/3/17

He who parted the Red Sea fears not the rising seas.
He is not touched by death or disease.
Flood is not unknown to God.
Man beseeching it is odd.
Noah cries, Move to higher ground!
My ark cannot be found.
10/4/17

Las Vegas type violence is no longer exceptional.
Only Democrats find it unacceptable.
Republicans talk about anything else,
Like their tax plan that smells.
Democrats want gun control laws
But the NRA is boss.
This will happen again,
Not a matter of if but when.
10/4/17

Sunday, October 1, 2017
Poetry Group Four Hundred Twenty-Fourth Posting 10/1/17

Lies are coming back to bite the liars.
Republicans are climate change deniers.
They promised a better health care law,
But Graham Cassidy has many flaws.
They say tax cuts pay for themselves.
But they really mean something else.
Republicans are trapped by their lies.
To enrich the rich the party tries.
9/25/17

Israel uses a cruel ammunition,
Which frustrates all physicians:
Dense Inert Metal Explosives (DIME)
Kill the victims in three day's time.
Israel also used Giant Vipers,
Powerful minefield wipers.
It used them against residential neighborhoods.
Israeli soldiers thought they were doing good.
9/25/17
Inspired by The 51 Day War by Max Blumenthal

We will inflict damage to such an extent,
That Palestinians will know what we meant.
So much punishment will we mete out
They will know what we're all about.
We want Palestinians dead or gone.
To achieve this we drop bombs.
And keep them from U.S. TV.
Americans will never see.
9/26/17

Sunday, September 24, 2017
Poetry Group Four Hundred Twenty-Third Posting 9/24/17

Better to give than to receive.
Lie, and what a web we weave.
There's happiness in giving,
But not so in fibbing.
Banish mendacity.
Give even tacitly.
9/17/17

Happiness is a potent reward.
Give to another sayeth the Lord.
Generosity is good for you.
Return the West Bank Israel should do.
Giving causes changes in the brain.
It makes you feel less pain.
Israel, give back what is not yours.
Avoid a future of terrorists and wars.
9/18/17

Trump said a deal was a possibility.
The Palestinians would come willingly.
Israel would have preconditions:
Don't stop the "settlement" mission.
Israel needs a firm deadline,
By which to create Palestine.
If Israel does not comply.
Its economy would die.
9/19/17

Jewish law calls for extermination of foes.
Israel gave Gaza a bad bloody nose.
Rape the terrorists' sisters and mothers,
Even as we kill their husbands and brothers.
Kill Arab children to prevent the next generation.
The war gave fascists more veneration.
9/19/17
Inspired by The 51 Day War by Max Blumenthal

Tax cuts that add to the deficit are bad.
Much to the national debt they add.
Republicans want $1.5 trillion in new debt,
Because the rich don't have enough money yet.
9/20/17

Anti-Zionism is not anti-Semitism.
Ronald Lauder is anti-Westernism.
Palestinians he never mentions
Nor Occupation tensions.
Hatred of Israel is not irrational.
Zionism is international.
It's bad for our country,
Which is Israel's donkey.
9/20/17
Inspired by WJC ad in NYT 9/20/17

We protect folks with conditions preexisting,
So Graham and Cassidy keep insisting.
But millions will be uninsured.
From Trumpcare the compassionate demure.
Republican legislators are cruel.
Trump voters are tools.
9/22/17

Sunday, September 17, 2017
Poetry Group Four Hundred Twenty-Second Posting 9/17/17

The SOP of the GOP
Is climate change not to see.
They deny science while attacking scientists.
Republicans are also fervent Zionists.
Evidence is not properly assessed.
Their idea of truth is jest.
They call all Palestinians terrorists.
Add that to their error list.
9/11/17

Palestinians are denied self-determination.
Ethnic cleansing might cause extermination.
Israel committed politicide.
Palestine Palestinians are denied.
Israelis want forcible segregation,
And Palestinian degradation.
Israel quells internal dissent.
The few liberals lament.
9/11/17
*Inspired by The 51 Day War by Max Blumenthal

They do not live on the high end,
But Israel sends them stipends.
They don't serve in the Defense forces.
Torah studies are their courses.
Others must bear their burden
To keep Israel's security certain.
The mean ultra Orthodox
Play politics like a fox.
9/13/17

Outspoken science deniers
Live in South Carolina.
To them vaccines
Should not be seen.
And the Theory of Evolution
Won't start any revolutions.
They do not care that sea levels rise.
Some salvation God will devise.
9/13/17

Sunday, September 10, 2017
Poetry Group Four Hundred Twenty-First Posting 9/10/17

The soldiers tied a man to a tree
And shot him in the knees.
When an ambulance came,
To the driver they did the same.
They gave another man a flashlight,
And said turn it on 10 paces into night.
When the man complied,
The soldiers fired.
9/3/17

Israel's bad and we shouldn't support it.
In fact, the thing to do is abort it.
If we severed ties, a new Israel would arise,
One that would give Palestinians their prize.
Boycotting worked once before
Against the racist Boors.
Boycotting will work again.
It's just a matter of when.
9/3/17

The Israeli shelling was not ceasing.
We saw people flying into pieces.
Israelis don't follow international rules.
They bombed hospitals and UN schools.
They killed people who tried to escape.
They kept up a steady kill rate.
Black Friday was like nothing we had seen.
At no point did America intervene.
9/6/17
*Inspired by The 51 Day War by Max Blumenthal

Even the children were enemies deserving to die.
With all forms of weaponry Israelis tried.
Militant Jewish Nationalist elements
With the war grew more relevant.
Nothing cries out with such insistence
Like a cooler filled with dead infants.
9/6/17
*Inspired by The 51 Day War by Max Blumenthal

Israel destroys an entire community.
No Palestinian gets immunity.
Partial ethnic cleansing is one of the tools
Israelis like to use.
Other tools are destruction and murder.
Israel wants the "settlers" to go further.
Self-determination is also denied
Though Palestinians have tried.
9/6/17

Israel's enemies became more adept,
Something Israel can't accept.
But Israel's enemies are legion,
Both in and outside the region.
Maybe if Israel had once been kind,
Fewer enemies it would find.
Palestinians deserve a homeland
Situated on their own land.
8/30/17

Trump stands up for whites who put brown people down.
Convicted Arpaio is freedom bound.
He arrested Latinos, legally or otherwise.
He will do no jail time before he dies.
8/30/17

Israelis bulldozed the Arab's citrus grove.
Then they exterminated his eighty goats.
The irrigation wells were next to go.
Ask for mercy; Israelis say no.
They incinerated his five tons of wheat.
They knocked down his house for a final feat.
8/30/17
Inspired by The 51 Day War by Max Blumenthal

Over Earth grows a carbon black pall.
Global warming makes heavy rainfall.
Warmer weather heats the seas.
Carbon is the source of Earth's disease.
Sea levels rise before our very eyes.
Carbon abatement would be wise.
But we live in an unscientific age,
Where Donald Trump is considered sage.
8/31/17

The majority of those killed had nothing to do with the fight.
Nonetheless the bombers kept them in sight.
Israel made the Palestinians suffer.
The U.S. provided cover.
6/31/17

Trump wants to repeal
The Iran nuclear deal.
He claims there's a violation.
Iran faces annihilation
For upholding its end of the bargain.
Trump doesn't want justice, far from.
The United States will be alone
With Israel in the war zone.
9/1/17

Deferred Action for Childhood Arrivals
Ran into something tribal.
Nativists don't want immigrants here.
Trump makes racists cheer.
The Dreamers program goes out with the floods
Welcoming immigrants was.
9/1/17

Something you will never see
Is Palestinians on TV.
Americans will never know
That Palestinians suffer so.
The Holocaust we know well.
That's a tale Americans can tell.
But they don't know about Israeli war crimes
Like murdering Palestinians many times.
9/1/17

Sunday, August 27, 2017
Poetry Group Four Hundred Nineteenth Posting 8/27/17

Air strikes on homes were permitted.
With ruins the land was littered.
US-made howitzers were well situated.
Shujiaya was quickly obliterated.
Residential buildings were attacked.
The casualty statistics are facts.
8/20/17
Inspired by The 51 Day War by Max Blumenthal

Tax cuts will serve the rich and corporations.
The poor are American Dream aberrations.
They thought Trump would be their savior.
Now they're put off by his behavior
Except for the racist ones,
Who worship their guns.
8/21/17

Myself only is what I care about.
Presidential precedents I flout.
There were bad people on both sides.
Only on one side, a woman died.
There were fine people amongst
The white supremacist bunch.
And all of them voted for me.
They like what they hear and see.
8/21/17

America is strapped to Israel's hip.
A six-shooter with an excellent grip.
America is Israel's shield,
Against any UN deals.
Uncle Sam is Israel's Dutch Uncle.
Every year he gives a bundle:
Israel's slave
Is the home of the brave.
8/22/17

Investors would be protected by the Fiduciary Rule
But brokers went to the non-Fiduciary school.
They don't like putting the clients' interests first.
The financial industry is the worst.
Trump and Cohn are on Wall Street's side
To hurt investors they eagerly try.
Excessive fees lower retirement accounts.
But no more Fiduciary Rule, Trump shouts.
8/23/17

The commander called for death to infidels.
Soon the Gazan border towns fell.
Khuza'a suffered the most
The Army still boasts
About the hosts of Palestinian dead
Most of them painted red.
8/23/17
Inspired by The 51 Day War by Max Blumenthal

First the Israelis cut down their citrus and olive trees.
Palestinians ask, can we replant them please?
Palestinians tried to harvest their land;
Israeli snipers shot them in the hands.
Apocalyptic messianism drives the men.
They are always ready to kill again.
8/23/17

Falwell lauded Trump's Charlottesville statement:
Evangelicals think Trump the greatest.
Alumni returned diplomas to Liberty U.
They are Christians true.
Evangelicals don't blame Trump for his transgressions.
After each sin there's always a fresh one.
8/24/17

Trump hates journalistic scrutiny.
It brings out his lunacy.
He calls journalists dishonest.
Our president is not modest.
If only he hated Nazis as much
As he hates reporters and such.
He will scream at the fake news.
When it uncovers his Russia ruse.
8/24/17

Republicans are on a wasteful spending spree.
How big will the wealthy's tax cuts be?
Republicans will leave a mountain of debt.
The rich don't have enough money yet.
Borrow from China to give the rich more money.
A Republican doesn't think that's funny.
8/25/17

Sunday, August 20, 2017
Poetry Group Four Hundred Eighteenth Posting 8/20/17

It was an act of domestic terror, said Sessions.
Trump was slow to learn that lesson,
Because terrorists come in brown or black.
Terrorism white supremacists lack.
Or so President Trump thought.
In racism he was caught.
Finally he admitted that white racists are bad.
This made his supporters sad.
8/15/17

Hong Kong Chinese fear the loss of freedom.
They don't like the way Communists treat them.
The party puts pressure on the courts,
Which condemn innocents of all sorts,
Like Law, Chow, and Wong
Of whom the people are fond.
Communists will put them in jail
And hope the Umbrella Movement fails.
8/15/17

The soldiers did not care where the shells were falling.
Civilian losses were appalling.
258 artillery pieces took part
In tearing Shujaiya apart.
Any images of the Palestinian dead
Did not make it into the soldiers' heads.
They had no empathy for the children.
Their job was anonymous killing.
8/15/17
Inspired by The 51 Day War
By Max Blumenthal

What will happen to villages from which we are fired upon?
All those villages will be gone.
What about the people who live there?
Most will require a hearse or urgent care.
But why are we killing Gazans today?
That's for Nitwityahoo to say.
8/15/17

They were good Republicans out there.
With their Nazi salutes in the air.
Israel has white supremacists too.
Where stood a Palestinian, now stands a Jew.
Because Palestinians are inferior
And belong in Israel's exterior.
Gazans are so brown
Israel puts them down.
8/18/17

Sunday, August 13, 2017
Poetry Group Four Hundred Seventeenth Posting 8/13/17

We purge names from voter rolls.
Polling places are moved or closed.
Voter ID cards are hard to get.
Minorities are no longer a threat.
Even if some get through,
And cast a vote or two,
They will not really count.
Gerrymandering voids them out.
8/6/17

Palestinians are perpetually aggrieved.
They are no longer deceived.
Israel wants land, not peace.
It wants a Palestinian state the least.
America enables Israel's dream,
To steal while no one intervenes.
8/7/17

Nitwityahoo denies any wrongdoing,
But investigations are brewing.
His is the most right wing government ever.
It will give Palestinians land never.
At the top are corruption and rot.
He'll be reelected not.
8/9/17

Israel removed the metal detectors
In the Aqsa Mosque sector,
But not in time
To prevent losses on both sides.
Israelis can't leave that mosque alone.
They want it in an exclusion zone.
8/9/17

The US has more nuclear arms than you do.
We are going to fire off one or two,
If you don't stop your warmongering.
Your begging for war is a quandary.
Because you don't have the means to win
America will do you in.
8/10/17

Sing on in single file.
The tune is climate denial.
Resist the scientific conspiracy.
President Trump is cheering thee.
Uncertainty excuses doing nothing.
Al Gore is bluffing.
8/11/17

Sunday, August 6, 2017
Poetry Group Four Hundred Sixteenth Posting 8/6/17

Magma burned through fossil fuels.
Carbon dioxide long ruled.
Then came The Great Dying,
When life on Earth was frying.
We produce more carbon than at the End Permian.
In a few centuries, life will be terminal.
7/30/17
Inspired by "When Life On Earth Nearly Vanished"
By Peter Brannen NYT Sunday Review 7/30/17

Israel wants death and theft
And Palestinians bereft.
America enables Israel
To make Palestinians miserable.
This is worse than the Japanese internment.
Palestinians don't get the same discernment.
7/30/17

President Trump will crush under his heel
The functioning Iran nuclear deal.
Right wing ideologues want war.
Israel wants war even more.
Iran trusted the United States.
To Zionism we pledge our faith.
Our word to Muslims doesn't count.
War with Iran is coming about.
8/2/17

When a man is wounded on the ground,
Don't pump in another round.
Let the medics take him.
Doctors won't forsake him.
Use only necessary force.
From inhumanity divorce.
8/2/17

Kushner, the Mideast novice,
Pisses on the peace process.
He says there may be no solution,
And that he's not guilty of collusion.
But Mueller will determine that.
I hope he indicts this rich brat.
The solution is to force Israel to act.
It is to make Palestine a fact.
8/4/17

Walk the blue-collar, billionaire line.
Go on, you are doing fine.
Tell them that tax cuts for the rich
Will flip the economic switch,
And there will be millions of jobs!
One side the other robs.
7/21/17

Can a sitting president be indicted?
If so, President Trump would fight it.
Inquisitor Starr said presidents can,
Whether woman or man.
7/22/17

Incursions into West Bank cities should cease.
Israelis want war not peace.
Aqsa metal detectors must be removed.
It's so obvious what Israelis should do.
7/24/17

There is no temple on the Temple Mount.
Judaism is not what the Mount's about.
The revered Aqsa Mosque is there.
The Noble Sanctuary is where.
Jordan, not Israel, is custodian of the shrine.
If Jews stayed away, things would be fine.
7/25/17

The Israeli army of avengers
Goes around and renders
Live Palestinians dead.
So history says.
Militant Zionism is again on the rise.
About Palestinians Zionists lie.
Resistance is a Palestinian right.
They are the underdogs in this fight.
7/26/17

Negotiations with Israel are fruitless.
Israel's promises are useless.
Their intentions are clear:
Palestinians out of here.
Israel never bargains in good faith.
The maps have changed.
How long must Palestinians wait
For a Palestinian state?
7/26/17

Israel disrupted Aqsa's harmony
By trying to assert Israel's sovereignty.
What do you think the detectors were for?
For Israel to take a little more.
Jordan should control the holy site,
Which is worth a fight.
7/26/17

The right are in mass hallucination,
Thinking Trump a welcome innovation.
They see no evidence of collusion.
They are comfortable in their delusion.
But Trump was eager to deal
With subversive Russians for real.
Still the right sees a different drama.
One somehow incriminating Obama.
Oh, right wing, release him to the universe!
Obama has nothing to do with your curse.
7/16/17
Next to last line by Joy Reid of MSNBC

The Palestinians were not well regarded.
From their land they were parted.
They are an occupied people today.
What they did wrong they can't say.
America enables their oppressor,
Which makes America lesser.
We are on the wrong side.
From Israel divide.
7/18/17

Atone, Israel, atone,
Or be left alone.
Israel strangles Palestinians slowly.
It will strangle them wholly.
I'm betting Europe will react.
With a boycott divestment attack.
If it's not greed, what is it?
If it's not greed, then give it.
7/18/17

Seize their land and expel them.
Round some up and kill them.
This is what Zionism means.
Leave the land ethnically clean.
America helps us in this task.
It gives us whatever we ask.
We usually ask for more weapons.
The amount spent should not be mentioned.
7/19/17

Republicans can't deal with Republicans.
Donald bows to them like a supplicant.
They are glad they don't have to vote,
Because the public would take note.
Trump likes Medicare but hates Medicaid.
Republicans want Medicaid to fade.
They couldn't vote for Trumpcare.
The people had a Trumpscare.
7/19/17

That summer Israel killed Gazan civilians.
Thousands died including hundreds of children.
Israeli soldiers fired heavy shells
That made thousands of homes hells.
They had no empathy with the people they were killing.
The artillery men are always willing.
7/20/17

I don't like interests that conflict with mine.
I expect Mr. Mueller to be half blind.
My personal finances are out of bounds.
In the end I expect to be crowned.
Sessions' recusal was a stab in the back.
For hiring wrong people, I have a knack.
If there's a crime and Mueller retrieves it,
Only the fake news will believe it.
7/21/17

Palestinians are demographic threats.
They haven't outnumbered Jews yet.
But that day is fast approaching.
Israel is almost done encroaching.
Israel will be an apartheid state.
Half the population victims of hate.
No vote for the indigenous.
And other differences.
7/21/17

When they are not set up by consensus,
Metal detectors feel like somebody else's.
The coming violence cannot be estimated.
Their beloved Aqsa has been desecrated.
Shin Bet advised the metal detectors be removed.
But Palestinians are to suffer not be soothed.
7/22/17

Sunday, July 16, 2017
Poetry Group Four Hundred Thirteenth Posting 7/16/17

Men do not value women in Ghor.
Honor killing is what women are for.
"I won't swear on the Quran, but I didn't do it.
She got raped, and she will rue it."
The killers act with complete impunity.
Males enjoy misogynist unity.
7/9/16

The rich do not pour tax cut money into the economy.
They save it, already having a large quantity.
Give a tax cut to the poor and they spend it.
Tax cuts for the rich should be ended.
Trump should cut taxes on the working poor.
The rich's taxes he should ignore.
7/9/17

Menstruating women are impure.
They bring bad luck for sure.
So they are kept in rough sheds.
That's what their religion says.
Some of them die of snakebite.
Illiteracy contributes to their plight.
Teenage girls do not object.
They are part of the sect.
7/10/17

Healthcare, if you don't want it, don't buy it.
You can't come to the hospital, don't try it.
Trump will give doctors new orders.
Don't treat uninsured disorders.
The uninsured had a chance to buy.
They didn't, so now they die.
7/10/17

Trump asked, what are they trying to hide?
My demand for records states won't abide.
But why are you hiding your tax returns?
Fair play, Donald, you should learn.
My tax returns are under audit.
I thought everybody bought it.
No, and we don't believe your Russia lies.
Putin will have a 2018 surprise.
7/10/17

We have mass shooting after mass shooting.
For the gun lobby, Republicans are rooting.
They think the answer to the problem is more guns.
They are the dangerous ones.
7/10/17

To annex the West Bank, Israel is inclined.
Israel would like annexation just fine.
Palestinians would suffer under apartheid.
The world will not hide its eyes.
Israel will be despised
And not so blithe.
Boycotts will be applied,
By nations worldwide.
7/13/17

There's a tax cut coming, so the bill will pass.
It will take money from the lower class,
And give that money to the very top,
In hopes that they will go out and shop.
Taking from the poor and giving to the rich,
For Republicans has always been a cinch,
Because their Christianity is only for church.
Compassion has been purged.
7/13/17

Women pray in a separate, smaller place,
Because the Orthodox have to save face.
They run the holiest site in the Jewish faith.
They'd like to make it void of a female face.
They control conversions and marriage.
Their old ideas don't vary.
7/13/17

Ben-Gurion wanted only eighty percent,
So eighty percent of Palestine went.
The Jews created a viable state.
But nineteen years they'd have to wait,
To take the other twenty percent.
This is not what Ben-Gurion meant.
7/14/17

Sunday, July 9, 2017
Poetry Group Four Hundred Twelfth Posting 7/9/17

Thought processes are liberated for the manic,
Who solve problems in a crisis without panic.
Depressed leaders see reality more clearly,
And they empathize more than merely.
The world's in tumult, when mentally-ill leaders function best.
How soon till that law is put to the test?
When the crisis is large and circumstances bad,
You can feel safe in the hands of the mad.
7/4/17
Inspired by A First-Rate Madness by Nassir Ghaemi

Modi visited Nitwityahoo,
But didn't visit Abbass too.
Thus India shows her hand:
The Palestinians get no land.
India normalizes Israel.
And shuns Palestinians miserable.
7/5/17

Sharing the land was not viable.
The Palestinians were undesirable.
So the expulsion had to occur.
Was it humane? No, sir.
Israeli soldiers intruded.
Palestinians were moved.
Boys and men were shot,
On Israel's history a blot.
7/7/17

When attacking a village, use your bayonet.
Unarmed villagers are easy to get.
Fire your rifle too
But run a few through.
Remember, we can't kill them all.
To Jordan they will walk or crawl.
7/7/17

Sunday, July 2, 2017
Poetry Group Four Hundred Eleventh Posting 7/2/17

Israelis expelled half the people within a year,
By fomenting violence and fear.
Few of the people made it back.
The Israelis changed the map.
The world does not remember this,
But I am still pissed.
All my Palestinian brothers and sisters
Are brave resistors.
6/26/17

After the June war, Israelis were not timid.
They expanded Jerusalem's city limits.
Over twenty Palestinian villages were absorbed.
Israeli soldiers kicked in the doors.
6/26/17

Orthodox Jews control Israel's religious life.
Tight rules at holy sites cause strife.
Men and women must be severed,
Not allowed to pray together.
Non-Orthodox rituals cannot be performed.
Try it, and the religious police swarm.
6/26/17

The new threat is not believing the old threat.
Here is what President Trump said:
Hacking, Russian hacking? Proof is lacking.
(But I don't have intel agencies' backing.)
The President's opinion is a fact.
Opinions I do not lack.
Go ask Vladimir Putin.
Me he's not refuting.
And he's a very good leader.
He is a protester beater.
6/26/17

To finance tax cuts for the wealthy,
Millions will be less healthy.
Poor children and nursing home patients
Will be treated like vagrants.
Thousands of people will die
Because Healthcare was denied.
At the expense of millions who'll get sicker,
The rich will get richer.
6/28/17

Palestinians aspire to nationhood.
They'd have a nation if they could.
But the invaders won't allow that.
The Occupation is a trap,
Where Palestinians will stay,
Until they are whisked away.
6/28/17

Reduce the Palestinian population.
Massacres will help that operation.
They will keep the people moving.
The Palestinians are losing.
Get the Palestinians off the land.
Massacres will lend a hand.
Shoot a few and kick the rest.
What you do never confess.
6/28/17

Poor people don't have much,
The clothes on their backs and such.
The little money they do have
Isn't worth a grab.
But rip off millions of the poor
And your profits will soar.
Stealing from the poor must happen en masse.
That's the way it has been done in the past.
6/29/17

At 4:47 a.m. he was not somnolent.
He drove his Dodge Dart into a monument.
He was reestablishing the establishment clause.
He thought the 10 commandments were against the law.
No other beliefs were carved in the granite.
Still Michael Reed was a little manic.
6/29/17

Cut healthcare for the poor,
So that the rich can have more.
Their aftertax income would rise two percent.
That's what the uninsured would send.
Thousands will die preventable deaths.
Lackies of the rich vote yes.
6/30/17

www.ingramcontent.com/pod-product-compliance
Lightning Source LLC
Chambersburg PA
CBHW071527030726
47598CB00001B/22